what some are saying about
THE MEASURE OF CHRIST'S LOVE

This book elevated my quality of life by freeing me from years of religiously imposed guilt. I feel light, as though a burden has been lifted. The teachings introduced me to our non-judgmental God, and the knowing He only holds love. Catherine, and Vera do an incredible job of unraveling difficult concepts and opening minds, but careful never to impose beliefs upon the reader.

—Joan E. Spring, is a friend from Connecticut

Catherine Julian Dove is truly an enlightened messenger for Jesus, Mother Mary, and other ascended masters. *The Measure of Christ's Love* is a beautiful book filled with truth and love. Do you want to know more about the time Jesus spent on earth or to hear from Mother Mary on the value of prayer?

Do you want to better understand Jesus in all his different roles, and awaken the Christ within? Do you want valuable tools to assist you on your path to ascension? Then this is the book for you. It continues to contribute to my spiritual growth in a way no other book has. You won't be disappointed!

—Mrs. Dalglish, friend and student from Texas

The Measure of
CHRIST'S LOVE

In His own words Jesus reveals the mysteries of His
teachings and clarifies major misinterpretations

The Measure of
CHRIST'S LOVE

Catherine Julian Dove
with *Vera Lauren*
Editor, Compiler, and Contributor

TATE PUBLISHING *& Enterprises*

Published by Tate Publishing & Enterprises, LLC
127 E. Trade Center Terrace | Mustang, Oklahoma 73064 USA
1.888.361.9473 | www.tatepublishing.com

Tate Publishing is committed to excellence in the publishing industry. The company reflects the philosophy established by the founders, based on Psalm 68:11,
"The Lord gave the word and great was the company of those who published it."

Interior design by Stephanie Woloszyn

Published in the United States of America

ISBN: 978-1-61566-994-3
Religion / Spirituality
11.10.14

Dedication

God, Jesus, and Mother Mary,
thank you for awakening our souls.

Acknowledgment
BY JESUS THE CHRIST

I, Jesus the Christ, have found pleasure in bringing forth and expanding my work upon this world. It is with a heart-filled gratefulness to my messenger, Catherine Julian Dove, for allowing me to speak through her, and to several key disciples instrumental in the release of this book, and my teachings through the Christ Matrix.® First, I would like to thank John Acker, Catherine's husband, for his many years of service to our work. We thank John for leaving his comfortable place and opening his home for meetings, supporting and protecting our messenger, and having the courage to step onto the path of enlightenment.

Next, I thank our writer and editor, Vera Lauren, for the depth of her commitment and the many contributions toward my work, and sharing the freshness of her ideas to compile, organize, and edit my teachings given to my messenger, and spearheading this project through to its completion. Vera had a vision for the book that began as a collection of teachings given to my messenger, but were also taken from various classes, lectures, and workshops—pearls of wisdom I desired to have completed into a manuscript. Vera's knowledge and expertise are invaluable. We recognize that this was a labor of immense love and devotion toward our Lord. We are exceptionally grateful to Vera and her husband, Walt Niestemski, for having a complete image of our work and prioritizing this book in their lives, as well as additional work we are preparing to release. Their skills, dedication to service, and strength of character are honored in the regions of light and by me, the Christ.

This work has been a healing process for many who became involved with our work from its inception through our messenger. Another person we would like to mention is Martha Lopez-Durkin, who, while not involved with this book, has spent many years in the co-creation of the Christ Matrix® organization. Martha devoted years of service to Christ, Mother Mary, and the ascended masters working through our messenger. Martha spent a considerable amount of time contemplating how to present a book such as this one and preparing our teachings, which are delivered through classes, study groups, and workshops. She also held a vision for the development of books and study materials. We thank Martha, who is held in my embrace and shared the inception and the creation of the Christ Matrix® and its work.

Mother Mary and I express our gratitude and appreciation for the support of our messenger and the artwork given to the Christ Matrix® by our beloved sister and friend Suzie Addicks. In the time we have worked with Suzie, she has been the demonstration of someone who walks the talk and is a keeper of the flame. We also thank Lisa Ford Longbotham for her devotion to our messenger and offering some suggestions for this book. We also give mention to the core group members for having the driving force and the desire to understand the teaching of the higher light. Several of these light workers devoted their time in working on the various facets of my work presented in workshops, recordings, and classes. I have gifted all those who have been involved with the development of my work through my messenger. All have shown tremendous courage from the onset of our appearing to and working through our messenger.

In gratitude and respect for the courage you each hold, I am Jesus the Christ.

Acknowledgment
BY CATHERINE JULIAN DOVE

It is with an open heart that I express my thanks to Mother Mary for appearing to me, personally training me, and taking me on a sacred journey that led to the work I am presently doing with her and with her son, the Christ. I am grateful to Christ for allowing me to represent his teachings to the world, and for the blessing of working with him, and the flow of knowledge he continues to share with me. His gift has been a journey of limitless love, growth, and understanding, and I now feel close to both him and Mother Mary. I thank Saint Francis and Saint Michael the Archangel for always being by my side and the many saints and ascended masters who appeared to me, spoke to me, taught me things of a spiritual nature about myself. I thank them for helping me understand I have to be willing to establish light on this world, and contribute to the growth through knowledge. For those who know me well this would not have been a calling I would have chosen for myself. I am also grateful for their many gifts to my family members, living, and deceased.

I acknowledge all the special souls Christ and Mother Mary bring into my life. I remember when Mother Mary told me what she hoped to accomplish through me, I replied, "How can I do all that?" Her answer was, "You don't have to worry. I have many of my helpers on earth." One of these helpers is my husband, John Acker, whom I appreciate and thank and am told carries the bloodline of the holy family. He spent many years supporting my search for spiritual understandings, which was a deep desire of mine. John also supported the Christ Matrix® as I began my public work with a group of core members in San Antonio and Fort Worth, Texas. Most of them still remain with me today, and I am blessed to call them my close friends. Among them, is my dear sister friend Martha Lopez-Durkin who, along with me, began the Christ Matrix® as an organization. We created our first website when, in a moment of clarity, Martha decided we should share Mother Mary's messages with the masses. It was Martha's idea to create a school, which she now runs named, "Returning to the Oneness," and later a newsletter, "The Still Small Voice." For many years Martha was the driving force behind the development and editing of the teachings I was receiving for my classes and workshops.

Over the years, I tried to begin a book with Jesus, but kept putting it on the back burner. Jesus could not wait any longer. I then received another incredible gift when Jesus directed me to contact a long time dear friend, and my spiritual sister Vera Lauren. Vera had recently moved back to the mainland from Hawaii and easily re-entered my life full time to spearhead Christ's vision for his book. I actually met Vera when I began my spiritual journey in the early 1980s in California. I am blessed to call Vera Lauren my close sister friend, and spiritual partner, and to have the opportunity to continue our spiritual journey together. With heartfelt gratitude, I thank my sister, Vera, for demonstrating true friendship and returning to my life to compile, edit, and contribute her spiritual wisdom and writing skills to transform deep concepts to comprehensible language, motivating this book in to creation. Vera's determination, compassion, and commitment to this project made it easy and joyful, which sums up the driving, passionate person she truly is. She moved the project forward and made this book a reality. Vera kept me on track, would not allow me to stop working, and held a vision for Jesus' book. I say this because I am not a person who desires to be in the forefront, and I am very grateful to have such strong women in my life. This is why I believe Jesus brings such powerful and dynamic individuals into my life, as he knows it is the only way his work through me will go public. Vera's husband, Walt Niestemski, has also been an incredible help to this project with his tremendous computer knowledge, and I am grateful for his support, input, and the amount of time he has put into the book.

I thank Suzie Addicks for her desire to see the work of the Christ Matrix® expand, and she contributed artwork as well as her time and energy for many projects. I also thank my dear friend Lisa Ford Longbotham for her support and friendship. And last but not least, from my heart, I thank another sister, Sally LeSar, for all of her support, and my core members that helped begin my mission.

Acknowledgment
BY VERA LAUREN

With heartfelt gratitude, I thank our Father/Mother God, my God Presence, I Am Presence, my Higher Self, as well as all ascended masters, for these ongoing remarkable experiences. I am humbled by your constant presence, and the unique opportunities, and spiritual gifts bestowed upon my family, my animal companions, dear friends, (including those deceased), and me, throughout this work. A warm special thanks to a true gift from God, my dear husband, best friend, and a very noble, humble, and extraordinary man, Walter Niestemski. My darling, you take my breath away, and truly are the definition of unconditional love. If I ever grow up, I want to be just like you. To my soul sister Catherine, from the moment we met I felt the spiritual connection, thank you for never letting go of my hand. To my sainted mother, I am forever grateful to you for respectfully creating a non-judgmental environment, and giving me the spiritual freedom to explore all possibilities on this incredible journey. To my daughter and my grandson, Jake Tyler, I lovingly offer the wisdom in this book to expand your consciousness, providing a solid spiritual foundation, and inspiring you to find your own true paths and to a direct, personal relationship with God. I thank my niece, Brenda Firulli, and all my family, including in-laws, for their unconditional love and support. To all my animals, thank you for all your love, especially when you served as my canine handkerchiefs. Last, but not least, I send loving blessings of appreciation to all the brave souls who came before me, and stood alone facing persecution, preparing our way.

Contents

Foreword
BY VERA LAUREN

"Whether you choose to believe you existed before or not, at one point you each were more spirit than matter, and that is what you are returning to."

—Jesus the Christ

At first glance, some of the material in this book may appear religious. I assure you, the messages offered are universal and nonreligious; Jesus the Christ does not belong to any religion. The true purpose of this teaching is to anchor light to the world by bringing forth the divine intentions of Jesus' extraordinary life, and to explicate the true meaning behind his messages, and to set the record straight. We are shown how God only holds love for His creations, and does not need to forgive us because He never judges. Originally, this collaboration and labor of love was much longer; however, due to the volume and deep nature of some of the material, we decided to make this book the first in a series.

Jesus is the author, as channeled by his messenger Catherine Julian Dove. While reading, you may experience his loving presence as Jesus shares highlights of his life, and you will delight in his sense of humor when he divulges such sentiments as, "I was not as popular then as I am now." This credible, mesmerizing, and personal journey is seen through his eyes when Jesus gives unique insight in to his exemplary mystical existence as he delves in the symbology surrounding the events from his infancy to his final hours, while relating the ignominy his beloved Mother Mary and closest friends endured. He relates treasured childhood memories never revealed before, candid descriptions of his matted hair, worn clothing, and overall homeless appearance while traveling the countryside as a young man, quick to remind us there were no showers along the dusty roads back then.

Exactly how does he account for the so-called missing years? Why did he speak in parables, and what is the connecting thread sewn through the fabric of all of his messages? He talks of his inspiring time as a teacher up against unopened minds and the threat of the procurator Pilate and the Roman soldiers, then onto the last hours before his death. Jesus discusses the Sacraments, symbols, and rituals that have since become associated with specific religions, but were originally meant for everyone. Why does he say he did not die for our sins, he does not wish to be worshiped, and he never claimed to be the only Son of God? His answers will forever change your view as Biblical mysteries are unveiled in a clear, practical, non-dogmatic, and authentic format as ancient teachings are brought in to the reasoning of the modern world. The truth about reincarnation and the afterlife are discussed as are evolutionary theories, and details regarding the soul. In this book your spiritual awareness will be heightened by an invitation, a gift, if you will, to explore and access the Christ within, and be forever consciously transformed to whatever level you choose.

Later in the book, Jesus introduces guidelines for finding one's purpose, along with many self-help, conscious-raising techniques, as he strings together pearls of wisdom in to a necklace of practical suggestions and concepts. It is your choice to dive as deeply in this knowledge as you like, leaving behind the crashing waves of frustrating unanswered questions, and fear-filled limitations for the calming ocean of truth, while you navigate the waters on your voyage to awakening.

On Channeling
BY VERA LAUREN

"Our selection of messengers on earth is quite limited, for they have to hold a certain range of mastery previously developed within them." Jesus explains what occurs when teachings are brought forth in this manner:

"Divine messages can only come through someone who is able to carry the frequency of the Christ, and their hearts must be extremely pure. When we, other ascended masters, and I, speak through our oracles there is a piercing light that descends through the crown center and oversouls the physical form. It is how we utilize the voice to bring our work onto this planet. Do not feel shame for believing we have the ability to speak through messengers; this form of communication has always occurred. Many original Biblical accounts were related in this way, and in those days it was accepted as a means of communication by many, including myself. Allow the master within you to recognize the mastery within another."

The way to measure a channeled teaching or any spiritual experience is to introspect and discern how the message leaves you feeling. Anything fear-based is not from God. Spiritual teachings must always uplift you and ring of truth. Keep in mind, all channeled information is only as clear as the messenger and often shaded by their core beliefs. The Christian Bible is a perfect example of this. Jesus confirms, "Some of the apostles had intentions to make changes for what they felt was for the good of humankind and took it upon themselves to change my teachings." Unfortunately, many religions and some countries still use this methodology, becoming apoplectic toward anyone who dare disagree. As Jesus states:

> "It is a tragedy the misconstruing of my words brought about destruction, for that is not the way of love nor was it a part of the truths I embraced. You do not have a corresponding language to fully comprehend the levels of mastery it takes to clearly experience your God Presence; therefore, we use many words to give you illustrations to help support and deepen your understanding for things of a divine nature. Love, in its purest form, is the closest image and understanding most humans are able to grasp."

Introducing the Messenger

Catherine is more surprised at her role than those who know her best because she does not desire the spotlight, preferring to quietly serve God. An unaffected spiritual oracle holds a true desire to raise the consciousness and they are not motivated to do this for the credit. To bring forth ascended masters is indeed an honor, and Jesus only comes through very few in the manner he comes to Catherine, and not in every time period. Ms. Dove began her journey as a conscious messenger by first working with Mother Mary and Saint Theresa. Later, Mother Mary introduced her to Lord Jesus, and in 1989 her spiritual journey was heightened with visualizations from them both. Mother Mary and Lord Jesus also introduced Catherine to the Ancient of Days, Lord Melchizedek, Lord Buddha, Lord Kuthumi, who is an incarnation of Saint Francis, and many other ascended masters, and archangels who spoke to Catherine. Over the years, Catherine trained with the masters, and Christ asked her to share their messages of love and expanded teachings with the world through books, classes, and private sessions, requesting Vera Lauren, "whose soul," he said, "is as light as a feather," carry on this work. The messages are hopeful, practical, inspirational, and often profound. Under the guidance of Christ, Mother Mary, and other ascended masters, and in order to fulfill the expanding mission, Catherine set up this Website http://www. Christmatrix.com, where CDs, books, and DVDs are available. It is both Catherine and Vera's desire that as many people as possible have the opportunity to improve their practice and comprehension of becoming a Christ on earth, and fully understand this path is being given as part of a divine journey each soul will someday take.

"May your path lead you to your own heart's desire and an increased awareness of your true soul identity."

—Catherine Julian Dove

The Measure of Christ's Love

An Invitation

Greetings, I am Jesus the Christ, and I honor each one who comes before me now. Long have I waited to embrace you with the truths this book brings forth, and welcome you to an understanding of my work. I am also known by other names, such as Savior, the Redeemer, Celestial or Cosmic Christ, Beloved, Lord, Father, and the Good Shepherd. As Jesus, I chose to come as an example of the love embodied in our Creator, and I brought the illustrious energy of the Christ to the world. I walked among the people, and ministered to them. I spoke of the deep love our Creator has for everyone, but not all my words were recorded, and many of my teachings were tampered with; I have much more to say about this throughout this book.

Many have lost the meaning of their lives, and forgotten God is ever present in the world of form. My messages are meant to inspire people to explore a one on one relationship with God, as this is the experience you are all intended to have with our Creator. I remain aligned with churches developing disciples of Christ, and to those who seek me outside of *any* institution. It is the work I continue, and many on earth assist me with this endeavor. As I stated, the sum total of my messages was not properly recorded, and for that reason, I continue to develop disciples who clarify misinterpretations of my original messages as well as contribute additional teachings that I intended to give to humankind. Not only I, but other higher masters are able to develop their students sufficiently enough to reveal truths absent from this planet for a period of time. I work with many of these divine beings, and we stand side by side, as there is no segregation in the heavenly realms. You may know some of the divine beings as the saints, sages, avatars or if you prefer the term ascended masters, who have also embodied on earth at various times. Before going on, I must point out that there is no rank in heaven either, and the status given me has incorrectly placed me in a position to be worshiped. *It is important this message be known. To ensure my point is remembered, over and over, throughout this teaching I state how I never asked or desired to be worshiped, nor did I ask to be held in a position above you. This idea was created after my death. I am much more popular now than I was during my life as Jesus. Being equal to one you consider has surpassed you is a frightening concept for many, and one not fully embraced by everyone incarnating on earth at this time; yet this is the reality.* In truth, not even God requests to be worshiped. Our Creator's only desire is for you to love yourself, because when you love self, you love Him. Please understand the message I conveyed is God is a part of each one of us, for we are of one expression. For some, it is as if you love your body, and hate your finger. Our Creator is not the ring on the finger that can be removed; He is part of the complete essence of who you are. Your love toward me is the utmost gift I receive, but I am truly honored when I am allowed to step forward as the elder brother guiding your way. I am also going to drive another point home: I do not belong to any sect or religion. As Jesus Christ, I did not wish to be split apart, and this just adds to the vibratory patterns of beliefs I do not stand for.

I call to the hearts of many, but not everyone replies, and not all who do respond understand my true messages. They continue to fall to their knees, worship me, and place me above them. As I reign in glory, I hold the position of the Christ concept for everyone, and I am a *symbol* of all that is within you. The title *Christ* should *not* be seen as belonging to any particular religion or sect because all of you are intended to become Christs. To be a Christ means to hold a higher pattern of light, and operate within a level of spirit, and light, which is a stepping-stone to returning all who work in these patterns to the Godhead. This is why the Christ is the way, and the light. I experience tears of happiness as each soul enters attunement with their own Christ self. I pour tremendous joy, and mercy onto all who come before me, and honor what I represent. Truly, there is no one among us who is lesser or better in the eyes of our Creator.

Consider this work to be a sacred teaching, and we will explore many hidden truths because the ancient mysteries have not been properly recorded or widely available for quite some time; thus preventing humankind from understanding the Will of our Creator. However, with all teachings there is a surface meaning given to the masses to help them deal with their everyday lives. I suggest opening your hearts, and removing judgment from your minds as you read the pages of this book. To deepen your understanding of my messages try to experience peace within, then savor the words, and ask me to assist you in the interpretation. Commune with God or me, ask for direction, and put in to practice the suggestions offered to initiate this process of self-discovery. Humankind has the freedom, and the right to discover its one on one relationship with our Creator. Although, without deep reflection on scriptures, this teaching or on any of the doctrines written by scribes, you will not open to the depth of wisdom experienced by spiritual adepts. *My messages have been simple until now, and within these pages it is my gift to bestow upon you their true interpretations, and to reveal hidden mysteries.*

The Journey

Jesus' Life and Mission

The journey to the cross did not begin with my birth nor did it end with my death. The desire of the Godhead is to return to Its people a loving, and compassionate Father, which was to be conveyed in the messages I brought. God chose Israel as the backdrop for the work He would conduct on the planet to become known as the God of love, because of the many promises made to His prophets of old. In the time of Jeremiah, rational thinking was not the norm. God knew it was necessary to bring forth a messenger who held the Christ energies the masses would come to honor and respect, and to undo Jeremiah's teachings of an angry, punishing God. A call went out from the elders into the heavens for a highly developed master to take embodiment on earth to complete this mission, and what some of the residents of this planet would perceive as a sacrificial life. In the higher heavens where I existed this would be considered a very short span of time; yet the accomplishment of such an assignment would benefit an enormous spectrum of souls, assisting them in uniting under the kingdom of Christ. To me it was an opportunity for enormous service, and since I was prepared, I volunteered, and was chosen for that lifetime. Brothers and sisters from those realms of Christ have visited numerous worlds on many occasions, including earth. Therefore, I was especially grateful to be chosen to light the world that appeared dense, and impoverished.

The Immaculate Concept was the pattern of light I held. I also held the energies of divine love in masculine form, and chose to be the demonstration of God's flame of love. As Christ, I am as brilliant as the brightest star in an evening sky. The spirit that dwelled within me was very uplifting, and nurturing toward others. The ego left me at a very young age, and my relationship with God was awakened; thus I felt free, and did not experience the limitations people often dwell in. While I walked in human form, I was in constant communication with our Creator concerning my mission. I aspired to understand the meaning behind life and suffering, and made calls to my divine nature that showed me the truth.

The system of beliefs I stepped into were very rigid; however, much time has passed since I walked on your planet, and the opinions of today are tempered, and in most regions people are more educated. Yet, I still see suffering in the eyes of many. God is ever present, God is love, and that love will always remain. People need to learn that it is not the color of one's skin or his faith that is the enemy, it is judgment. In other words, it is the consciousness held toward another that releases a frequency as a wave pattern into the ethers, and is shared by group consciousness, be it of love, bigotry, hatred or anger. When you speak down to another my message is neither valued nor understood, and you dishonor everyone, including our Creator, and yourself. Look in your brothers' and sisters' eyes and see my face, and then you will understand the Will of our Creator. My message has always been, and is one of immense love, and mercy. The concepts, feelings, and thoughts held by people either assists earth in creating well being and healings for all or contributes to the expansion of the illusion of separation. My desire for people is to work out their differences in a manner that brings balance, and respect to all parties.

A relationship that takes place in the spiritual heart is when the human soul, and the divine soul merge. It is a marriage, and this is where true power resides, not when force is imposed over another. Beautiful is the song of the soul; it is the whisper in the inner Mind of our Creator. Satisfaction can only be experienced within the understanding of knowing the Will of our Creator, and opening to His wisdom. This is where people gain spiritual understanding, and self-worth. Much of the world population that calls out to me feel imprisoned in one way or another. They believe they are suffocating in emptiness, but I never felt imprisoned in life. I experienced myself as being expansive, and part of the spirit residing within all creation.

I taught those who would hear my words that the Christ mind and wisdom need to be the indwelling spirit within, then the soul will soar to enormous heights. In this coming era more of you will have the opportunity to look upon my face, because all who ask are given the chance to come to the bosom of my light, to know the Will of God, and know you are loved by our Creator and me. My beloveds, to be created in the image of God is a beautiful gift, and it is what I represent for each of you.

Highlights from My Life

My family moved to Egypt following my birth, and we returned to our homeland after Herod's death. I was a fair child with light eyes, which was unusual for those from our region. I learned to walk when I was nine months old, and by the age of six a number of events were already occurring in my life; like the time my mother recalls seeing me speaking with a large angel she knew as Gabriel. I remember feeling majestic, even though I was a small child, and then discovering I could create. I would pick any small object and turn it in to something else, for example, I would transform a rock in to a feather. I also started to heal small living things. I was able to communicate with adults, and understand conversations beyond my years. By the age of seven, I became more aware of my special abilities, but with the mind of a child, I grew frustrated with my gifts, not yet understanding that I would become a beacon of hope. It was in these early years, I developed a continuing interest in studying languages, and easily learned them from those on caravans passing through our village.

As a young boy, I could see the veiled worlds, and worked with those who had passed on. I could call souls out of the Bardo, which is the deep sleep some find themselves in after death. I experienced what many understand as mysticism held in the secret teachings of the Hebrews, but it is not in mainstream Christian religions. I learned about spirituality from my parents, Mary and Joseph, who were part of an underground secret society that had roots in the Essene teachings, and they embraced these philosophies that were pure and very close to the truth for the times. (*Vera's comment:* What Jesus means is necessary discoveries to fully grasp deep concepts, such as understanding energy, were unknown then.) My mother and father were educated in the spiritual laws, and obedient to them. The Essenes brought through a higher doctrine, and it expanded on the beliefs of Moses and David.

My mother had training and education, which was rare for women then, and she lived many of her younger days in a temple. What is not in the scriptures is that my father, Joseph, was an experienced technician of the higher light. In other words, he was a conductor of light and very open to receiving it, and able to work in unison with his Christ Oversoul, which is the Mantle of the Christ. His mind expanded beyond the principles being taught during that era. (For more information on the Oversoul, please refer to the chapter, The Divine Blueprint and the Oversoul, page 187.) Another fact not written in the scriptures is the long talks I had with my father, and as I became older I spent my evenings studying with him. In those days, educating the male children in the spiritual laws was extremely important, and I based a great deal of my later teachings on works I learned through my father from the wisdom of the Essenes. I also studied with John the Baptist and of course with my mother. We were all in attunement with the energies of the Holy Spirit.

In my early years, my parents taught me to hold light in my body without limitation. They trained me to go within, and to hold a state of mind called concentration or what is understood as meditation. As a child, I did not have the worries of an adult. Still, it was difficult to train my mind not to think about playing with the other children or get distracted when they would tease me by name calling. In those early years, I developed communication with my own God Presence, and I walked in the sense of my Presence, and my own knowledge that I was divine. I spoke to our Divine Father and Mother, and they spoke back to me. (For more information on the Presence, please refer to the chapter, Templates of Creation, page 88.)

We had a family farm and lived in a farming community where people grew most of what they ate or sold food to others. The area was surrounded by gardens where I found solitude, and enjoyed listening to the birds sing. I was taught to work the land, and this was when I learned to communicate with the Elementals, who are the guardians of the animal, and vegetation kingdoms on earth. In my youth, I also worked in a vineyard.

I was the eldest son; therefore, many opportunities were given to me, and I had an obligation to contribute more to the family. Although my father was a carpenter, he also worked with stone, which was common in those days. We had a family business too, and my father had to frequently travel away from home. Often, he would be gone for a few days or even weeks at a time. Since my father wanted me to experience more cultures than that of a small village, as I matured, I was given opportunities to take trips with him. When my siblings grew older, and could take on more of my responsibilities, I traveled with him for longer periods of time.

While I enjoyed tending the fields on our farm, working with my hands in the shop, and traveling with my father, I saw the ships in the harbor, and longed to experience journeys abroad, and I knew my life was being orchestrated to learn from many scholars. I prayed for guidance, and received it. I was told by the angels that as part of my spiritual heritage, I was heir to the throne of David, and that rang true in my heart. The Celestial Christ became the voice I communicated with in my younger days, and seeded my consciousness, and embraced me while I was in prayer. As a youth, I had several mentors, one of which was Balthazar of Arabia who visited my family and me many times. In the scriptures, he was not identified as one of the three Kings in relation to the young Jesus, and it is not until much later Balthazar is mentioned as one of those wise men. (Other incarnations of Balthazar include: Pythagoras the Greek philosopher, Saint Francis, Kuthumi of Kasmir, and now he is an ascended master and the master of wisdom.)

After my father died, I was awakened to deeper service. This is when Balthazar returned, and asked my mother if she would allow him to be my guardian. I was still having a hard time with the limitations being placed on my gifts and controversy abound concerning the miracles I performed. With money provided to her by this noble man, and with the help of my siblings, and our extended family, my mother allowed me to leave, and continue my studies in other lands. Our farm was very productive; therefore, I knew my family would be taken care of in my absence. Still, my mother had difficulty with my leaving again because we had grown closer. My mother was a woman purified in her heart and deeds, and even then she held the light of a saint. She never said an unkind word toward anyone. Knowing she was taken care of, I departed at approximately sixteen years of age.

This is how the door opened for my travel to many other lands, and for my decision to study their ancient teachings with their spiritual leaders. I had sought to learn more of the deep truths of the east, and desired to travel there as well, and spend time in eastern monasteries. These are the so-called *missing years,* the years at home and abroad when I was studying to become a scholar.

I spent a portion of my youth traveling in ancient Egypt, India, and in what is considered to be Nepal. Throughout these regions, I studied under many masters who spoke to me about a multitude of topics, and they focused on love, and kindness. The teachings were somewhat different from my homeland. I internalized what I was learning, and turned inward. In a sense, I held onto many of the traditions understood as coming from the Orient. The languages I learned allowed me to communicate my teachings to different cultures; I considered myself an educator. I held a prism of light, and could see the future. I understood the minds of the people of those days, and wanted to free them. I truly did not believe I was put on earth to harm my brothers, and sisters or any creation. As I understood it, the spiritual doctrines emphasized that we are all sons and daughters of our Creator. During my training, I was also visited by a number of divine beings, and they taught me to develop wisdom, and compassion.

In those days, there were many enlightened scholars. In a sense, knowledge, for some of us, was entertainment. We would sit around campfires, and discuss the Laws of Moses, and the teachings in the various ancient texts. There were many texts we studied then that are either lost, not accessible to everyone or are not commonly read today. If you knew me then you would have thought me to be a dedicated scholar or even a nerd. Hungry for knowledge and instruction, it was not unusual to find me surrounded by ancient scrolls, which developed within me the desire to become a spiritual leader. This is why I left my homeland to travel, because the skills within me needed to be nurtured, and developed. I could see and cast out demons. I had soul recognition with those I met, and knew if they were intended to work with me. I performed various healings, and many miracles including raising the dead, and I could still the waters. I was also a respected seer with the ability to see the future, and the past for individuals, and globally. The Son of God, who is Christ, shined upon me. This is why I was the son of man; yet the Son of God. I held both currents, and this is what is intended for all souls to eventually achieve.

As a young man, I knew what it was like to experience anger and frustration, but chose to overcome it. I moved around quite a bit during that time, but I was able to stay centered in myself because I chose deep contemplation. I bore my soul before our Creator. In doing so, I was taught divine love, and how to surrender to the Will of God. I knew my life was given to me for a reason. I made mistakes, just as you make mistakes, but I learned from them, and eventually performed better.

The more I evolved the greater the light I held, and the deeper my understandings grew, strengthening my will. I always saw myself as one with our Creator. I was able to make a large contribution to earth because of my training, and staying connected to my I Am Presence or God awareness; therefore, I awakened to the level of an avatar or a Son of God, a Christ, who felt love, and compassion for each person. (For more information on the I Am Presence, please refer to the chapter, Templates of Creation, page 88 and the glossary.)

I knew my mission was to alter the frequency of the majority, and I stepped upon the world in ignorance. This may astonish you, but like you, I had to draw in my Divine Blueprint. I was well aware of this, and was able to access it at a young age because I chose parents who were spiritually developed, and assisted me in awakening. Early in life, I was shown service to God, and service to life is the path that brings forth the Divine Blueprint, and this is why I teach that we are all called to serve. Still, I had to master many of the issues, and daily struggles of human life all of you deal with.

I took time out of each day to commune with God, and my Christ Oversoul, which is the Christ within me. At night, I lifted my eyes to the heavens, and spoke to our Creator. I wept plenty of tears on earth, but those are not the footsteps I would have you follow. The tears that fell from my eyes should not fall from your eyes.

My personality was soft, and I had a happy upbeat temperament, and laughed often. I was taller than most of my race and as an adult my eyes were hazel with a gray hue, and my hair was somewhat wavy. I was a man who cared immensely for the condition of the world, and the Word of God, and I also looked at my stay on earth as an opportunity to learn about the many cultures I visited. My followers and I traveled from town to town, and we did not have access to showers or baths; consequently, we were always dusty, and our hair was matted, we were quite the sight. My mind scanned various planes of consciousness, and I continued to perform miraculous acts. I brought with me the Seal of Abraham, which is a passage of light, and an activation of a level of initiation, and the release of the Holy Spirit, and I returned the Office of the Christ to earth. John the Baptist, many other masters, and I, all taught, "Ye are the sons and daughters of the Most High God." (For more on the Seal of Abraham, please refer to the chapter, Vehicles for Spiritual Awakening, page 200, and see the glossary for an explanation of the Office of the Christ.)

When I was traveling abroad, I did not see my mother very often, and she was pleased when I finally returned home to start my mission, but not prepared for the pain it would bring to her life. As I grew in to a man, I found myself surrounded by hatred. As I walked the streets, I continued to come under heavy attack, and ridicule by the elders who believed in their religious foundations they were passing to their congregations, and my teachings brought fear to many of them. They did not understand my ways or my words, I taught my disciples under the stars, and not at the temples. Even without a structure around it, I made any place I stood a house of God. In those days, I was among pioneer thinkers, and that did not go well with the clergy, and their followers. There were those who spat upon my supporters and me as we walked through the streets. Yet, here we are in a new day, and my followers, those who say they love me, not all, but some, have anchored down, and harnessed themselves to limiting belief systems and judgments. As a result, they are having difficulty expanding their love, and understanding to all who dwell on this planet. This was not the message I left behind. I welcomed all to my midst, and spoke to anyone who longed to hear the truth of the heavenly worlds. I did not show prejudice toward women, and this also created problems because back then women were not elevated to the level of men, as they should always be.

I walked earth as an ascended master, able to elevate myself above the masses. It was such an honor to visit earth in the magnitude of a holy Christ being. To many I was seen as a saint or an avatar, and my will could determine the outcome of my spoken word. Layers upon layers of information would need to be unraveled to understand the rituals we performed, and the words I chose. I deliberately spoke in parables; so my messages would lead to a contemplative state. I did not want to deal with their minds when their hearts were filled with bitterness, and envy over the possessions of others. Again, I must emphasize my teachings were not completely or correctly recorded, and most of them have been misinterpreted, and rearranged. In the first century the scribes of the day began to go back, and write what was handed down, but by that time it was too late as a good deal was misunderstood or verses were changed. It was never my objective my legacy become a limitation. I, the Christ, am like a bright star shining light on all who come before me. I do not choose one over another because of inadequacies some see in others. Whether someone was sick, poor, a rabbi or a priest, I regarded each one as a spiritual seeker, and a beloved child of God.

I did not claim to be the only son of our Creator. I stood apart from the crowds in deeds and actions; so much so they looked to me as a father. Through deeper understanding in working with the Universal Mind, I was in attunement with a range of heavenly hosts. Many understand this as the energies of the Holy Spirit, which flowed through me like lightning, enabling me to heal.

Understand, I had decisions to make when I stood in front of the Romans, and there were various reasons why they sought to remove me from the planet. Know I always had the option of allowing it to play out as it did or leave that country. I had the freedom of choice, just as you have the freedom of choice. I could have *revealed myself* to them or escaped the cross, but I chose to allow my capture to occur. I believed by being martyred in that way would cause a shift to higher consciousness. I saw a world religion would develop around my death, ending the cycle on the planet at that time, and for some it did, but there is a new expansion now. It is a time when the Holy Spirit is descending once again to raise those who have the "oil in their lanterns," and are ready, not to take up the cross of the Christ, but to take on the consciousness of the Christ, and move into the Christ Oversoul.

Many try to mirror me, and I long to give my disciples wings to fly, but it takes courage to walk on earth as a spiritual leader. Your belief in what I stand for assists me in continuing my messages of peace, and love to this planet.

Days before My Crucifixion

As I already alluded to, in modern times there are more educated people, and many are even-tempered, but in my day the belief system was unyielding. As a young man, I found myself surrounded by anger. Some Roman soldiers and those who stood by old beliefs would yell vulgarities at me; however, there were some kind soldiers, and before my arrest they invited me to their homes to perform healings, and to receive my blessings because they recognized the quiet power I held within. When I was first arrested there were times the soldiers allowed several of my disciples, especially the women, to accompany me. They were not treating me cruelly then, for many believed I would withdraw my statements, and apologize to those in power who were offended by my teachings. The harshness came a few days later when it was clear I would not retract my statements, but they continued to put pressure on me. When that did not work they began to search for my disciples. Many loyal to me, and to their faith in a God revealing Himself to them through my teachings, were hunted down, stoned, ridiculed, judged, and persecuted.

The Final Days

Often, I am asked about the last days of my life, and the following recap will give you a glimpse of what it was really like. When those in power realized I was not going to give in, water was withheld from me. The physical body was unable to endure the beatings I received, and the body could have died during my time in the prison cell. As I said, if I desired I was able to escape because I had the ability to dematerialize or pay the soldiers to leave the cell unlocked, but the heavenly hierarchy overseeing this project and I chose not to take that path. You see, it was important to the Hebrew teachings to have my life end as prophesied in the ancient text.

While imprisoned, I felt safe within the bosom of God because I was an awakened son, and they could not break my spirit. During that period, I left my body many times, and dwelled in the higher heavens, communicating with ascended prophets who gave me guidance, and protection. Also, I sang hymns to God that brought forth a light substance that sustained me on every level, physically, mentally, and spiritually, giving me renewed energy and love. Outside the prison the women of my order, including my mother and Mary Magdalene, would wail and cry, causing the soldiers to send them away. What really offended the Romans is, I would not fight back, and in a sense, this is also what some of my followers hoped I would do. The Romans made a spectacle of my imprisonment, parading me through the streets to disgrace me, and used me as an example to discourage others from seeking the truth. I walked as a Christ, and as I explained, I could have released myself from bondage; however, I knew my suffering would soon be over, and I would not respond to being ridiculed. By that time, many who followed me were angry, and perceived me to be weak, and turned away as well.

The heavy cross was only painful to the flesh, and when they impaled me it physically hurt, but not my spirit, by then I was no longer bound by earth's frequencies. What was agonizing for me is the shame my mother, and those closest to me endured. Again, nearly all of them were shunned, stoned, and beaten, but that was not their karma. They chose to remain with me during that painful exhibition. Also, a good number of people came looking for, what they perceived should be, a demonstration of God's power.

My suffering in those days is not what I desire for you to hold in your heart. There was a passion within me that knew and understood the works of God. I allowed myself to be consumed within this relationship with our Creator; *there is only one reason, one way to live, and that is to live in God.* It is what I came to express to humankind. Many work very hard on earth; yet there are few who experience the true measure of love God desires all of you to experience.

Most of you have or will encounter those that need everyone to conform to their beliefs, to their power, and to their will, and this is why I am sharing this message in this way. Individuals must be allowed to freely explore God, and this can most satisfyingly be accomplished through merging with the Holy Spirit. *God speaks to those who are "chosen," and you become chosen when you allow the higher light to merge with you, and permit the Presence of God to fill you.* Few experience being chosen because they block the inflow of love, and light from our Creator. Some souls have an opportunity in this lifetime to know God, to know their I Am Presence, and to deepen their spiritual path. Whether or not this creates an opportunity for ascension is weighed within the level of light held inside their soul. Those of you who aspire to this, who answer the call, are shown a brighter path.

Too often people think receiving spiritual gifts is the path to ascension, and God gives numerous gifts of enlightenment, but what they are missing is the true union I experienced with the Holy Spirit. *Much of what earth's hierarchy contends with is an irrational understanding of God.* Sometimes people are not receiving their spiritual gifts or abilities because they have not yet developed the true understanding of their spiritual light, and their place within it. Many are not fully healed; they hold anger, and resentment on several levels, and this causes energy blocks. An unfortunate consequence is that my complete message about unconditional love will not be understood, and I am passionate about my disciples comprehending this in all its nuances.

Judas

The one called Judas did not remain with us to the end because he could not maintain his light or the coding of his higher light bodies. His mind continued to follow frequencies of resistance to my teachings. While on several levels he believed there was an imbalance among the people, he still did not unfold the deeper message, and incorporate it within his own mind and heart. There was an energy Judas held that was selfish; he did not enjoy sharing me with others. He was one among the group who did not approve of women receiving the same level of teachings as the male disciples, and he had many other issues that took him away from the center of knowing Christ. Subsequently, he fell away from those who were occupying a higher level of light than he was able to hold.

Judas was also lied to by those who told him they only wanted to question me, and in the weeks before my arrest he was approached to be a spy within our camp. Before he became divided within himself, Judas did receive several warnings from his I Am Presence that he was beginning to stray from the path, but during those moments when he made his decision he did not realize it caused him to relinquish his own soul.

Judas was chosen to be a disciple because he was passionate about my work, but on many levels he could not settle in to the higher image of himself. His life is a lesson in limitation, where the soul was only able to inhabit the heart, and the consciousness to a limited degree. Judas could not fully merge with his divine nature or soul's essence. The true image of self as an ascended master is somewhat challenging to understand, and it has to do with the ascending consciousness as it begins to merge with the Divine Blueprint. (I explore this deeper in other chapters and in a future book.) *For some people, the ego creates a division through a sense of self-righteousness where they feel justified in finding fault with others.* If they do not have the ability to rise above the circumstances they will continue to play out the role of the victim. The brotherhood and sisterhood of Christ work in accordance with the Universal Laws, and the Doctrines of Peace.

Judas held a considerable amount of wisdom, and it was always my hope he would master his lower nature. In that life, Judas earned a small degree of mastery, but he was unable to tap the full current of his light codes available during my stay on earth, and I would say he came up short. I stood by him in the etheric realms when he took his life in shame, for he did not understand the meaning behind his actions, which were based in fear. After that event, he reincarnated many more times on earth. Allow his life to be a lesson, and remember there are continuing tests upon your paths of how much love a person can elevate themselves to master.

The Last Hours before My Death

I had drawn my last breath during a beating several weeks before my actual death, when the Oversoul walked into the body. This means that in the last hours I walked the earth as my living I Am Presence. In other words, I already had become the Christ, and my consciousness soared upward. I physically left because I was ready to release the body, and my transition was a joyful experience for my spirit. My life as Jesus must never be misinterpreted to cause you to feel guilty or take on any responsibility for my death. Nails were driven in me because I chose to be martyred. I left earth as a king of humankind, and I reign within the higher spheres with the wisdom I gained from that incarnation.

As I stated earlier, the whole crucifixion experience was deemed necessary to fulfill the prophecy, and only the body experienced pain and suffering, not my spirit. The angels supported my limbs, and the weight of the cross, and my heart stopped at the moment this grand design was accomplished. In heaven, I was exulted, and as I rose there were marvelous sounds of ecstatic joy for my ascension. I moved very quickly into my light body, and this is how I remained with my earth-bound disciples for years, coming and going as needed, and appearing to many. I am still present within the frequency known as the Holy Spirit, which descends to you through the Higher Self.

My life on earth gave rise to the rebirth of a higher consciousness, to an awakening, and to the renewal of the Christ mind, entering this plane. I was pleased that I uplifted a wealth of people to higher consciousness, which was my purpose, the reason I came to this world. Yet, my last duties as Jesus drew more tears from my eyes, for I knew, even with all those I had uplifted, there were still a myriad of souls whose ears were closed to me and to my messages, and that the renewal and the awakening were met with resistance. You see my beloveds, many who say they love me; still do not know me. They isolate themselves, and put words in my mouth. The illusion that is reinforced is a belief system in support of duality and fear, and has the figure of Christ above you, not beside you where it belongs. This is a huge hindrance on the hearts, and spiritual progress of most Christians.

Truly, I took strength from the cross experience, and I was not in fear. I wish to see humankind walk fearlessly. Easter week, including Good Friday, is when you acknowledge my walk to the cross, and now I am giving you a new symbolic vision. Instead of relating the walk to my crucifixion with fear and pain, think of it as a walk I made to be with our Father in heaven, where we were gloriously joined together, and I was reunited with that sonship. It seemed like it was only for a moment when I descended from my seat of power in my heavenly kingdom to come to earth, and when reawakened I very quickly merged back with that heavenly threshold I occupy. My birth and death became your inheritance, the riches of a loving God.

Lessons from My Murder

Although it was my choice to go through with the crucifixion, it was still a murder conjured up by those levels of the priesthood out to silence me because they did not want the lower classes to be empowered. This misuse of power is still going on today, and has created quite a negative karmic pattern on humankind, destroying much of the light flowing through tributaries from the higher heavens to earth. To combat this distortion choose to be the reflection of our Creator, our Source. This is how individual knowledge will once again free each of you. Then more will do God's bidding armed with the light, and not the sword. *The mind of the human can never be free until it allows the light of God to amplify it, and this is how human souls move through corridors of love, and gain understanding.*

Currently, some religions are experiencing a transitional period for souls still requiring a form of worship for comprehension of the greater truths. This evolution is often misunderstood, and congregations end up worshiping me as the Christ *outside* of them in the form of the man Jesus; instead, of completely igniting the Christ consciousness that is meant to dwell *inside* of them. My beloveds, the Christ representation and the descent of the Holy Spirit are the rebirth, the awakening, and the resurrection, and together we rebuild the tributaries of light intended to become your future self. As the Christ light contributes to your energy you will experience situations with more patience, clarity, and wisdom.

John the Baptist

John's Role

I am John the Baptist communicating this message. For such a long time I heralded the coming of a new regime, a new system of thought, and new energies that would come to earth. I waited to be a part of this movement that has now begun developing the souls of my brothers and sisters within their hearts and minds, and how wonderful was the day when I heard the angels announcing the time for awakening is upon us.

I was a man of deep reflection, and still hold the memories of that lifetime. During my life with Jesus; indeed, I stood in the muck of the river for hours upon hours, but I was in the ecstasy of the Holy Spirit, anointing and baptizing my brothers and sisters to assure they would be ready for the light of the Christ to awaken within them. God often told me He would send forth the Redeemer, and I was to baptize all to prepare the way. I did this with enormous enthusiasm and love, thrusting forward in my work. Crowds saw me standing on the shores or in the river twirling my hands, and they thought I was speaking to myself. Some believed I was a madman, but I was truly in love with our Creator, and filled with an incredible amount of joy communing with Him, and Christ. I was also a healer, but I was not an educated man, and because of this I was not able to affect the number of people I wanted to.

When I first saw Jesus on the shore he was taking off his sandals, and then I witnessed him walking toward me. I was overcome
with happiness, for all around him was a golden light of wisdom,
and childhood memories flooded my mind of when we played
together. I blissfully remember baptizing Jesus, and my hands coming upon his forehead as I lifted him out of the water. Then a Dove
descended over him, and spoke to me and to the crowds. The ela-
tion I felt in that moment is a joyfulness I wish upon all of you. I
knew Jesus was the Messiah come to release the light of the Christos to the world. I did not see that I would stay on earth very long
after Jesus was baptized, and I knew my work upon the planet was
coming to a close.

My time in prison was not difficult because I had angels all
around me. I knew that many of the people who freely walked in
the halls outside my cell were the true prisoners. They locked up my
body, but I was free to drink of the love, and light of God. This is
what true freedom is. It does not matter what they do to the body
as long as the heart and the mind are free to experience the inesti-
mable love, wisdom, and understanding of the Mind of God. Enter
communion with Christ and with God, and release yourselves. Do
not be a prisoner of the outer realms. Life is a mirror reflecting what
you hold to be true within self. Sometimes it is easy to get caught
in the energy or the dynamics of another; instead of creating love
within self, for self, and around self.

Jesus is the Redeemer because he released immeasurable light
and wisdom onto earth, and in each individual. He walks with
a staff as the Good Shepherd to remind followers of his role as
guardian of your world. He speaks with a soft tone in his voice, and
with deep understanding. He believes in each and every one, and
he loves you to the depths of his being. His arms are open wide.
If you allow the energies of the Christ to awaken within, you will
expand with great measure, and notice your thoughts, and feelings
becoming balanced as you gain spiritual wisdom over life. This is
the mastery we understood in my day, and Jesus was unparalleled;
there were quite a few wise teachers who knew and understood the

scriptures, but Jesus walked with an intensely deep understanding. He was a prayerful man. He raised his head toward God, and he was not afraid to share his gifts with all who desired to hear him speak. Jesus brought forth the concept that God chose to love His creations through mercy. He taught not to fear God, but to know God's love is immeasurable. These were not the teachings we had in those days; instead, we were taught to fear God, and mercy only came through big sacrifices.

The majorities still hold deep judgments toward other belief systems, and this is the most difficult negative energy to transcend because it blocks the light from entering you. The seed of awakening needs to be birthed, not only within the heart, but also within the mind. Those desiring to know Christ must enter, and maintain an energy grid of unconditional love. Being able to hold the Christ attunement is, and has always been, intended to be your deliverance.

The flame within me, which is my love for God, burns brightly, and my energy remains with earth through the stories that share the experiences of my life. This knowledge is passed on in the form of a blessing for all to receive. I still watch over the earth, and with the energy of John the Baptist, I continue to bring the baptism of the Holy Spirit.

Jesus' Commentary on John the Baptist

A number of dogmas created revisions surrounding the symbology of John the Baptist's work, and the true meaning became shrouded in mystery. John fully comprehended the deeper truth that the meaning of life was to integrate parts of self still scattered, and allow the wholeness, and the healing to take place. He knew in this manner that the shaft of light that guides and protects the disciple, the spiritual seeker, fully clothes them in the light. This transpires on various levels, and it is also referred to as *the rapture.* During his work on earth, John prepared souls to receive love in the form of the Lord, and it was given to them.

On that glorious day when I was baptized the *Seal of Abraham* was released, and the down pouring of the Holy Spirit descended upon me. The Seal of Abraham is the uniting of the Higher Self's light now available to initiates on earth. It is living energy that supports a path of awareness to true soul identity. I was asked to gift this Seal to those who desired to learn from me. This is the deliverance and qualified my energies as the Redeemer.

Many thought John the Baptist was crazy when he stood on the land, and in the water speaking to heavenly beings from the invisible realms. I cannot emphasize enough that this form of communication—channeling—still occurs today as it has since the beginning of time, and it is how eminent teachings, including the original Bibles, have always been received. God's messengers have always walked the earth, capable of moving back and forth from realm to realm, and we continue to use these divine souls to communicate messages. Until now, the majority have not been informed of this truth. Some will be chastised for their belief in receiving my teachings outside of what they believe to be the norm, but do not allow this to reduce the flame within self. Nor should anyone feel shame for believing God, other masters, and I, have the ability to speak through messengers. In a sense, this is John the Baptist's message.

Many Titles, Many Roles

The Good Shepherd

As the Good Shepherd, I reign over the kingdom of earth. I came as an example and taught my followers to draw strength from me. I was not a man of the sword or of violence of any kind. I came as a healer, not as a mass murderer, and my armor was of peace. I do not speak these words to bring forth guilt, but to right a wrong. I consider all who breathe to be my brothers and sisters. I do not discriminate one from another, and fully embrace everyone who calls out to me. I know each soul as an individual spark, and we all are connected as a whole, extending out from the heart of our Creator. The truth of my words is within each individual soul.

Unfortunately, most of my original messages are no longer available. The dialect we spoke in my life conveyed, in some cases, a different message from current meanings. Again, a belief in one divine son is never what I chose to leave behind. I presented the teaching of the Mantle of the Christ to be equally shared by all the sons and daughters of God. In those days, the term for me would have been prophet or master. I walked earth for a short time, and was able to affect the consciousness because I turned inward, and learned to resonate with my God Presence. I entered a vast light I called the Holy Spirit or God in action, and was drawn upward. Never did I set myself above others, although the multitudes believed I was chosen. I only appeared to stand above the people of my day because of my higher consciousness; I held the light and memories of my expanded self or God Presence.

Those in the earthly seats of power do not fully embrace or understand my teachings, and because of that there is a significant amount of people suffering from ignorance. War is never the answer. Murdering the innocent is not demonstrating faith in my words or in my teachings. Many embodied now are also ready to embrace the hidden truths, and master higher teachings. I am committed to remaining with earth, and continuing my work with all who now aspire to be my disciples, the spiritual seekers, because the shepherd never leaves his flock unguarded.

Vera's comment: You will notice Jesus interchanges the terms disciple, spiritual seeker, devotee, and student. They are one in the same; however, once spiritual seekers reach the stages of becoming an avatar they are fully committed and raised to a level of discipleship. He also uses the term initiate and this is explained indepth in the chapter with the same title. What is important to remember is each term holds a different vibration.

Savior

The Savior is not necessarily an outer being. It is the mind and the heart in attunement with the Oversoul of your own Christ body of light, your own Christ mind, your own Christ heart or sacred heart. The levels within the Christ orders move you into the Oversoul. You, as a spiritual seeker, develop a burning desire that grows very bright causing you to enter the Mantle of the Christ. In a sense, this is the true Savior.

My title and responsibilities as Savior hold the same pattern as the title Redeemer. The concept of Savior came about because of the effects of the Lucifer and Satan rebellion, which involved much

more than two beings. It is important to say here Lucifer and Satan
were eradicated from this universe long ago, and I will speak more
about this in other chapters. Before that time, there was no need for
a savior or a redeemer as all existed in bliss, as do I. As Christ the
Redeemer, I am able to assist you by dissolving karmic patterns. For
this reason, I am allowed to take upon myself the meaning behind
the word savior.

Being a Savior does not mean I take responsibility for the sins
or all the negative karma of the world; that idea was born of ignorance and misunderstandings. Some sects teach a philosophy that
states their members need only to accept Jesus as their living Savior. This is also incorrect. In truth, what my being a Savior really
means is individuals take on their own Divine Blueprint, which is
them learning to hold a pattern of Christhood.(For more information on the Divine Blueprint, please refer to the chapter, The Divine
Blueprint and the Oversoul, page 187.) Accepting me is not enough
to open the gateways to heaven, for each soul is responsible for its
own intentions, actions, and merit toward others. Some believe their
business dealings are somehow separate from their spiritual life, and
this is a grave mistake not to recognize that the business arena is also
where souls are tested. It is all under one umbrella, and asking me
to be their Savior does not exonerate them from acts of compassion.
The boss, who unjustly fires an employee, then sits in church pro-
claiming he accepts me as his Savior, cannot burn the candle from
both ends. Everyone must live a balanced business and personal life.
Otherwise, upon their death they will secure a date to appear before
the Lords of Karma to review their actions, and reflect on how their
choices affected the lives of those they caused to suffer. *Believing to
be relieved of personal responsibility one need only accept Jesus as their
Lord or older brother is immature, and not what I taught.*

All souls are part of a colossal drama, a tremendous experience; yet the majority of paths to God are filled with dogma and
limitation. For many, this is why having a Savior has been necessary
because the soul's development in the matter realms is uneducated.
Many masters, like me, came to earth with doctrines to create a

belief system that is still part of most religious doctrines currently in power; however, as the clergy and ministries developed they became too powerful, and lost the purity of the original divine messages. As a result, the individual role and the responsibility to the spiritual path, for most sects, became lost.

The honor given to each divine creation needs to be the new revelation born again within the minds and hearts of each person desiring to be part of the brotherhood and sisterhood of Christ. God continually calls to His sons and daughters on this planet. We, who dwell in heaven, suggest that if you are a true spiritual seeker, go within and open your mind and heart, and listen for *the call* specifically directed to you. All of creation, including the Elemental Kingdoms, responds to the will of a Christ being. This is why it is important to embrace the concept that all are chosen, but few answer the call. Responding to the call is empowering. You will find the Savior you seek outside is given to each creation willing to come to the center of self, and develop the soul qualities to open to the Higher Mind. Allow that indwelling spirit, that divine Presence from the higher spheres, to take on the vestiges of the human body. This is what occurred during previous Golden Ages, and at that time the divine design was not as fully entrenched in dense bodies like the ones you are currently experiencing. Whether you choose to believe you existed before or not, at one point you each were more spirit than matter, and that is what you are returning to. In other words, the divine soul gives life force to the human soul, and when it ceases to, that is what death from your planet is. Upon death, most of you will have the opportunity to once again experience more light if you choose to evolve back through a process of causation to a more heavenly light-filled garment known as the Oversoul.

Each person is a product of their own thinking and feeling world, and this is the reason certain circumstances occur. Inside everyone is the prism of light that is sealed over and it holds the higher memories and higher consciousness. It is the doorway to the Christ Oversoul I am speaking about in this book. It is the Diamond Mind, the mind of the Christ, the mind of the Christos, but it is buried under a massive amount of debris. For some it will take unwavering faith to discover that this is what awaits them. The time has come for everyone to take that inner journey to unmask the truth within; decide what parts of self are going to dissolve to the earth that were born of earth, that were not born of spirit, not born of the divine nature. What I held within is not any different from what each of you has the ability to discover within self.

The Redeemer

Great is the light I come forth from as the Christ and as the Redeemer. The teachings of the Christian faith have placed their followers beneath me, and out of deep love and yearning to release them, I remain as the Redeemer. In truth, no one needs redemption; however, you do need an elder pointing the way, and I will speak more of this in the following section.

There are vast misunderstandings of my work among many religious orders. Everyone is a part of the being you call the Christ. Not the personality of the man known as Jesus, but the Oversoul of Christ; the grid of protection that, if allowed, will elevate those who are prepared into that Celestial being you are all intended to share consciousness with. This is, in fact, what makes each person a son or daughter of the Most High God. A belief in one's own accountability is what is missing from nearly all religions. Each individual is accountable for their own behavior, thoughts, feelings, actions, and intentions. This is their redemption. No rewards or gifts are waiting for anyone who kills or harms another, even if it is done in the name of someone society deems to be a saint or a high being. I tell you truthfully, the majority of religions are not born of the higher heavens. They were created by fallen angels and others who experienced the fall of humankind; this is often referred to as the time of Adam and Eve. Stop the wars and face the truth that there is only one God and He loves all, every creation. That message was my mission when I was Jesus. As a Redeemer, I stand beside those

I counsel, speaking the truth, and directing their path. It does not mean I take away your soul's lessons, for you each have the gift of freewill from our Creator.

My beloveds, the sound of the Christ vibration moves like a wave of light through souls developing this frequency within, and because their hearts are ready and open, it does not extinguish. Not everyone chooses to carry the light of Christ inside, but if you ask this of me I will amplify and guide these sound currents through your heart, which diminishes the effect of the ego, and the Christ light will penetrate the many layers of imbalance held in the human consciousness. Some may even experience the vibratory patterns of my voice. It is time to pierce the veil and allow the Christ energies to fill your hearts, and minds, and guide your every action. Ask me to assist in opening that shaft of light. As the Redeemer, I also regulate the flow of life to humankind. If you can accept it, I will place a portion of my light in your minds and hearts. This is the light and the knowledge of the Christos St. Paul extensively wrote about. St. Paul's work dealt with his relationship, not only with me as Lord Jesus the Christ, but also with his own Christhood and I Am Presence developing within.

The Will of God needs to be invoked, never in a punishing way, but in the concept of oneness as your rightful fulfillment and inheritance. As Christ the Redeemer, I elevate those who are ready for this advancement and this is how I gather souls unto myself that will someday dwell in the higher heavens with me. I am also available to all who love me, and continue to teach them to choose the Christ light for their own ascension or resurrection. I came to earth as the Redeemer to create a bridge and the awakening. I did not come to shoulder the blame for anyone's creations.

Redemption

Some may be wondering if indeed your soul was created to be divine and you need not be redeemed for sins, then why would you need a redeemer or even redemption? It is a great question, and in modern days I can now bring forth a more indepth teaching on this subject. One way of understanding this topic is that I am beginning to till the grounds for a new harvest to make sure the weeds are no longer in the field. Similarly, I am doing this so what flows through your life, your actions, and your words, are the blessings of the Holy Spirit. Individually and as a whole, develop an understanding of redemption as the knowledge I brought forth. As you move into this pattern of light, I teach how to hold gratitude and appreciation for the opportunity to experience yourself as an individualized spark of the divine, as a part of God. The repeating patterns of negative cycles many experience created the need for a being such as me to embody, and assist in giving humankind the opportunity for redemption, and for demonstrating God is Love. The soul's light, in all of its divine glory, is created in perfection. Redemption is a temporary state of consciousness. That is until each person trusts that the divine momentum of light that raised the man Jesus to become the Christ, also exists within humankind, and has the ability to raise every soul to become Christs or at least lift them to a higher position in the light.

My sacred heart is filled with love for all and holds the diagram of the heart of God, and its frequency is unconditional love. For this reason, I am able to give dispensations for negative karmic imbalances, and forgiving is part of redemption. During the process of redemption, I teach you to unmask the truth about yourself, and how to qualify the light of God that is entering you. I speak words of truth to your inner mind and heart. I stream light and love in the form of joy to spiritual seekers the world over. As the Christ and your Redeemer, I am allowed to become the memory pattern that unites you with our Creator. You enter a relationship of deep love with me, but it is not physical love that exists between a man and a woman; it is spiritual love. I hold a vast body of light, and as I come closer what flows through me to each of you is the frequency of the Holy Spirit.

Salvation

I became your Redeemer because you were in need of deliverance, but salvation truly rests in the actions of each human being. As a people, it is unfortunate you have been taught to place your salvation in another. Consequently, many have not learned or are not even aware that they must complete the circuit to God for themselves. As a result, most humans are spiritually misaligned, making it even more difficult to gain authority over self, and this has impacted society as a whole. *Waiting for another whose name they think they can never measure up to, and then expecting him to be your salvation has prevented many from developing their own relationship with God, and committing to deepening their understanding of the kingdom of heaven.* Rather than thinking of me as your salvation, I prefer the image of your protector, as one committed to attuning to his own God Presence and our Creator. Walking in my shadow with your head hung down should not be anyone's destiny. Your mistakes, your accomplishments, and your ability to move into the light and retain light, are all contributing factors to your salvation because we are each rulers of our own fate.

I came as others have come, to remind you not to depart from your own Christ nature. Learn to make choices that bring greater harmony, balance, and unconditional love. The records show, I passed many tests, and came to earth with the Divine Blueprint to become a Christ, and be oversouled by a magnificent light from my I Am Presence emanating from my own God spark, which brought knowledge of my divinity to me. I had faith I could deepen my relationship with my own personal Christhood. In this life, many of you also have the opportunity to decide if you are ready to be raised into that piercing light, and I will not turn anyone away who truly desires to take this upon them. To commune with those in the higher heavens is a magnificent gift, but emphasis must be placed on your intentions to ask for and receive the Christ Oversoul or the Mantle of the Christ, if this is your desire. *What those who dwell on earth are unaware of is the fact that there are races of beings from other planetary systems that are all Christs.*

At these stages of awakening, there are many gifts the Holy Spirit brings to assist humankind in becoming who they are intended to be within the heart of their I Am Presence. During this time, I have chosen to strengthen those who follow my teachings by merging the higher light with them, and assisting them in learning to match the frequencies held within their own magnificent light bodies. In this sense you could say I am their salvation; however, holy is your name also. I look forward to the day when more souls will embrace and trust that their I Am Presence and I Am Flame, which is the heart of their I Am Presence, also resides in the Trinity energies. *The majority are still accustomed to singling me out as the only son of God. Unfortunately, this is the real cross placed upon the Christians.*

As you learn to come in balance within the threefold flame, the flame of the Christ, also called the God spark, it expands and attunes you to the Trinities. Many will not trust that these words come from Christ, but if you ask, I will assist you with recognizing God has also chosen each of you as His beloved. It is through the Divine Blueprint the image of the Christ is reflected through you. (For more information on the threefold flame please see the chapter entitled, Templates of Creation, page 84. You can also refer to the glossary.)

God selected a certain few to visit earth, and become spiritual leaders. This is how I prefer to be remembered, not as taking away anyone's divine inheritance. No one has heard it enough times how very much our Creator loves you and you are each intended to develop a close relationship with God. I challenge all of you to walk in silence for several weeks communing with our Creator, and regard yourselves as worthy as I am. By doing so, you will realize you truly are the sons and daughters I am speaking of.

My role then and now is to bring dispensations of a magnificent light, and to teach seekers how to receive this light that becomes a crown of glory. It is your salvation too, because all abide as one in the heart of creation.

Unraveling Selected Biblical Teachings

The Doctrines of the Bible

The doctrines in the original Bible can be best understood if you ask for Christ, and your God Presence to come into your heart, because initially written within the scriptures were hidden meanings. Ask to be raised in the light to uncover these secrets, and then you too will be the chalice filled with the light and wisdom. I believe the intentions behind creating the Bible were good, although it is somewhat strict in its form, and left out a good deal of my true teachings, and their meanings. The overall problem is this has limited the mass consciousness from opening and developing. Instead, it created a momentum to worship me as God, and not as the Christed example of the ascended master I am. The New Testament teaches to worship Jesus as the only son of God, and hinged me as being the only way you can succeed. As I say over and over throughout this book, I did not ever intend for this to occur. It is what happens when group consciousness is instructed by teachers that have placed themselves above others, and believe they are not to be questioned.

When reading the Bible or any spiritual teaching, open your heart and allow its real messages to resonate to the truth within you, and do not make your beliefs the law for others. Everyone is a disciple of the Office of the Christ, not just the one person known as Jesus. I,

Jesus, guide many souls, surrounding and teaching them to expand their love, forgive others, and have patience, and I will continue in this relationship for as long as I am needed. This brings me back to the subject of redeemer. The divine soul, governed by your God Presence, truly understands it does not experience the need for a redeemer in the higher realms or heavens. It is only your un-awakened mind that does not fully know how to breathe the breath of life from its God Source. *It is very disturbing many are still involved in teachings reinforcing the belief everyone is born of sin, and live sinful lives; therefore, in need a confessor to punish them.* This is the reason they think they require a redeemer to "save them." Actually, this is why I prefer the concept of the Good Shepherd, as it is closer to my role. I am in service to those who call upon me, and I hold the frequencies of the Father's energy of divine love and mercy for all who are awakening. I call to many hearts, but like you, I also serve the Great Architect and Designer of all creation. I wish to remind you again that in my life as Jesus, I retained the memories for my Divine Blueprint, and this placed me in a higher consciousness to better serve God and humankind; however, even in those times there were many others who spoke the truth, as I did, that were from the higher heavens.

The Chosen Ones:
What it means to be in Favor with the Lord

Around the earth is a band of energy, which is an astral field, and this is where many thoughts and emotions reside. You are uplifted while learning to harmonize and utilize light rays expressing the qualities of God coming from the higher dimensions or from the countless bands of light emanating from the Godhead. This is because, in those moments, you allowed the accumulated extra light into your bodies, minds and hearts, and experienced your divine selves and its reality. I explained earlier, becoming the chosen ones is when you, as spiritual seekers, permit the higher light to merge and allow the Presence of God to fill you like a chalice. To be chosen is also understood as, "being in favor with the Lord." For example, in the Bible it references, "to a virgin pledged to be married to a man named Joseph, a descendant of David. The virgin's name was Mary. The angel went to her and said, Greetings, you who are highly favored! The Lord is with you." (Luke 1:27–28). What it was thought to mean was a particular person was chosen, when in reality they were just in tune with the higher Will, and with cords of light descending to earth from our Divine Source. In truth, each person is chosen, but not everyone chooses to answer the call. Will you? Will you rise to the occasion? Will you hold the staff, be the Christ, be the Shepherd, and show others to the light? This is the service I chose to walk in. Prepare yourselves and I, the Christ, the bestower of all good, will return for you. I come swiftly and pull unto me all who are prepared through the action of the Holy Spirit, and all you need to do is listen for my soft voice. I love each one of you, and my love is eternal.

What I Really Meant When I Said, "To Turn the Other Cheek"

When I gave the teaching to "turn the other cheek," as referenced in the Bible, "But I tell you, do not resist an evil person. If someone strikes you on the right cheek, turn to him the other also" (Matthew 5:39). What I meant was *not* to hold destructive patterns. Never put yourself in such a situation, unless you choose to be ridiculed or mistreated. Many people are easily offended by the words and actions of others; therefore, comprehending the Universal Mind of our Creator will greatly assist your understanding there are no victims, just those who have not yet released victim consciousness. Every person has a light inside that is a beacon of hope to create change. Discern what associations to be involved with, those that raise you consciously or those that put you down. Life really is a succession of choices, and some bring too much sorrow and hardship.

I came to earth with a powerful dispensation, and columns of light descended with me. Like each of you, I had to let go of negative thoughts and emotions because the memories of persecution, and the criticism I underwent could have been even more difficult had I chosen to hold on to those frequencies. Do you understand what I am teaching? Life, existence, is a ball of energy that is held at the magnetic core of earth. Humans also have a magnetic core allowing certain tributaries of light and darkness to be absorbed into the aura and stabilize there. In other words, your experiences are actually energy corresponding to a magnetic alignment with similar thoughts and feelings. You must not allow darkness to be absorbed. You are to release those currents to be transmuted in the violet and blue flame of the Godhead, just as I did.

The Prodigal Son

The prodigal son goes out with a substantial measure from his father's kingdom, but because he does not have true wisdom he is caught up in the material world. There he fell for the short-lived pleasures that play to the ego, and foolishly lost his inheritance. Forlorn, he went back penniless, and feeling beneath a servant in his father's home. Out of love and mercy his father raised him back to the stature of his son. He was treated without punishment, and rewarded for learning a lesson.

The story is not to give a lesson in being miserly, but the ego tends to take the spiritually innocent to a place the spirit does not wish to be. A vast number of people can relate to this because they live beyond their means. They do not use the wise judgments they were taught on the spiritual planes, which is to balance their finances by taking a portion for charity, another to save for a rainy day, and a percentage to live within their means. It is the same guidance given throughout the ages. The world runs in cycles, but the lack of balance is what brings about famine, and all other disharmonies. It is important to keep an open mind so love, in its many forms of abundance and prosperity, flows through every life in accordance with the Will of God to deepen the understanding of all spiritual truths. This is the mercy and charity that is your inheritance.

A Glimpse at the Godhead

Aspects of God

There is truly only one God we were all birthed from. *Every single person came forth as part of the Immaculate Concept, just as I was birthed during that same process.* Every soul evolved in the higher heavens for a very long time. Some beings, such as the archangels, were creations of God that never left those higher dwelling places; these are the heavenly worlds of the offspring of the Godhead. Some chose to experience the outer dimensions where those on earth currently reside in a matter body, which is just a small part of the being you were created from still existing within the heavenly worlds; however, the larger portion of every human is located in the divine realms. These teachings may be disturbing for those not understanding they are part of a greater whole, and actually have an eternal self.

As we explore the nature of the divine, and to help integrate the teachings I am now giving, I must emphasize everyone is capable of moving into the Divine Mind and the Divine Heart of our Creator. As stated, as Jesus, I believed in past and in future lives, and most souls come to planet earth for many lifetimes. During my life as Jesus, I was aware of my past lives, and also recalled my previous experiences beyond earth. I knew why I was chosen to take on the life of your teacher in many forms, such as the Savior, Good Shepherd, Redeemer, and Lord. I developed my consciousness through a series of incarnations, and moved it through a holy gate of light. When I stepped out of the sepulcher, I was totally immersed within my own divine identity.

The story of Jesus is, in fact, the story of each one of you. It is the developing consciousness through the gateways of the Higher Mind, the Christ mind, the Oversoul, and then the God Mind. Excerpts within the scriptures speak of the divinity within self, and of God's immense love for His creations, and they assist the offspring of God to attune to their divine nature. The parables were given to open that seed consciousness of remembrance; so everyone will know themselves as the sons and daughters of the Most High God.

The Divine Mind, the Mind of God

The Divine Mind of God is everyone's inheritance. It is where God speaks individually to each He has created, and He did not create you apart from Jesus, Buddha, Krishna or the saints. All were created to drink from the Fount of Light.

When entering the Divine Mind of God you learn to step aside, which is part of the process of surrender. Many think they must gain favor in the eyes of our Creator to receive a blessing; however, this is not the teaching I gave to my disciples. Each and every one is favored by our Creator. The misunderstanding of this concept has brought about much bloodshed and tears. Open your hearts to receive the truth of my teachings, and allow me to be the guide on a path that will bring about a deeper appreciation of what was taught in the ancient mystery schools. It is a noble intention to hold a goal to understand the mind of Christ, and eventually the Mind of God, because developing an understanding of the Divine Mind is what it means to have God's favor. Once on a path of initiation, permission is granted for your council of master teachers to release spiritual truths to your hearts and minds; however, it must be stated you will be taught within the parameters you have set up for yourselves. (*Catherine's comment:* Christ is saying you will not be forced off your path, religious or otherwise. Christ can still expand your knowledge of the mysteries without asking you to leave your chosen faith or path.)

Within the core of each individual is a divine nature ready to unfold. Outer circumstances are temporary. Yet, many place most of their attention there; rather, than on their inner spiritual life. The comments you make, and the thoughts you hold are what I am referring to. Many struggle with honesty within self and trying to be upright. Learn to constantly monitor yourself. I cannot overstress how important it is for you to realize you are solely accountable for every detail of your life, every intention, thought, and action. It is why I taught: even as a man thinks he creates and is accountable for that creation. It is imperative you understand this. As referenced in the Bible, "For as he thinks within himself, so he is; or for as he puts on a feast, so he is" (Proverbs 23:7a).

Being conscious of your intentions is what honestly matters. People take on karma not only by carrying out the deed, but also by thinking, and dwelling on the intention of causing harm. *This teaching is paramount because each one of these actions releases a negative current that disrupts a light stream coming onto the earth.* Strive to purify your heart and mind to hold all creation in balance. The Holy Spirit only listens to people's hearts and their intentions, not what they are saying, and this is done without judgment; however, when a person speaks against themself or another, the vibration from the words affects the balance and structure on the planet. That is why negative karmic patterns are an action against the Holy Spirit and the Divine Mind. All of life is interconnected, and people are responsible for the disruptions they contribute to the patterns of consciousness developing on earth. Destructive thoughts and emotions disturb the cohesiveness, and block light from dissolving damaging energies. Venomous ideas, deeds, and intentions, are energy frequencies causing anger, and hatred to feed upon itself; they are then picked-up and used by those with criminal minds. This also adds to the fear, anger, and imbalances, held by the majority of the human race. Do not allow these currents to freely flow through you or you will continue to hold thoughts of the illusion of separation. If you have or had these issues, put them aside and begin anew with this teaching. Do not chastise yourself for not having the knowledge to live a better life; most of us make better choices when we know better.

The Nature of Things

The following information is rarely given because it is not tangible enough for the human capacity to relate to. Understanding ones divine nature takes the mastering of many evolutions of reawakening the spiritual mind and spiritual heart. My intentions are to give a short overview of the Great Stillness and Its immensity, and invite those interested to the grand mystery intended to reveal Itself to each returning spark, as it did for me. As Jesus, I developed and eventually held the mind of an avatar, and was able to relate to the memories I held of divine regions. My beloveds, it is possible for you to experience the true essence of God. Many desire to experience our Creator through me, Jesus the Christ, but I am the Son radiating from the Father. This is why I speak as the Celestial Christ.

Throughout the God realms is where eternity is, and it is quite pure. In the center of the omniverse there is a resounding Silence that spins called the Nucleus, the Great Silence or the Great Stillness. All of creation exists within rings expanding out from the Great Silence; the rings have also been understood as the Breath of Creation. The Great Silence, of course, is where those who have maintained their original Divine Blueprint also place their origins.

The door opened within the Great Silence, and the Great Stillness expressed Itself through an orb of radiating light. It was thought vibration, but souls had not yet been created. Its thoughts moved into a spiral around Itself, and manifested temples It utilized as instruments to occupy in outer regions from Its Nucleus. As God's Mind moved into another frequency the Great Stillness became the Holy Spirit, and the experiencing mechanism was Its offspring. The diamond pattern had begun. The establishment of the Godhead came in to being and now contributes to your understanding of the Trinity. The three work in harmony, and they assist in balancing the Great Silence. We are all called to return to this Diamond Mind, and this is how I emerged as my true being. The Trinity flame is how you enter the spiral and make the return ascent; you enter an attunement with the Trinity flame by developing Christ consciousness and that becomes the open door.

There is a Magnificent Being, represented as the Voice of the Eternal Father, which those in heaven have come to know. He is the All Abiding Light. He is the Father. Held within Him is the Son. His Spoken Word is the voice, heart, and memory as represented in the Holy Spirit. This Divine Being is commonly identified as of the masculine. It is only by lowering the consciousness that the mind held the idea of masculine and feminine as individualized sparks of consciousness departing from heavenly realms. Labels such as masculine and feminine became acceptable terms because the human part of soul, through many experiences, held a preference toward one. It is best if it is thought of as a blending of the two, and then the deeper truth of God as co-creation will be revealed. For the human, God is both masculine and feminine; God is limitless. As humans evolve they will discover that in eternity God is neither a man nor a woman; rather, it is a heart desiring to expand Its understanding of Its creative nature, and all are part of Its vastness.

The meaning behind *becoming saved* has been misunderstood on earth. Being saved refers to returning to the full complement of energies called the Christ, which is part of everyone's divine nature. This gives every soul entrance back into the higher spirals that began creation. *All who enter these regions are there by their own merits, and not by the merits of the man I was.* Once again, each human being is fully accountable for their behavior, actions, and deeds, and required to raise the light within and be as I was; the demonstration of that light. My role has always been, and still is, to assist and guide humankind in this process.

Earth's radiations are coming through an attunement with Alpha and Omega, an ancient sun system. Alpha and Omega hold a magnetic grid for your galaxy, but it is not God; rather, His creation. Darwin was not accurate in his theories of the human race. The human consciousness developed along an intentional diagram. The story of creation is the forming of individualized experiences sojourning through denser spheres of reality. Your heightened intelligence is still whole, and housed in a prism of pure light. Even now it remains in the higher heavens being expressed through your Higher Self, your I Am Presence, and even your God Presence.

The solar system, including earth, is located within a distant spiral from the Great Silence in an outer universe and ring. Both earth and the solar system have been tampered with by fallen hierarchies, and many system lords or co-creators. This fact contributes to reasons why life is demanding for the human race, and why suffering is present. As humankind departs from a structure of beliefs given to them from parallel creations that divided you, one from another, some will turn their hearts toward the Abiding Light, and they will be taught to become a beacon of light, and unite under one loving God of Peace. Once accustom to what this feels like they will usher in a Golden Ray, the light of Christ consciousness, which will bring the planet and its inhabitants to a higher constellation than earth is currently occupying. The doctrines taught on the planet were given to humankind during stages so small gains could be made in developing spiritual consciousness. This advanced some cultures in attaining spiritual growth, and opened the door of mercy.

The Holy Spirit

The Holy Spirit is neither masculine nor feminine; however, sometimes the masculine is used when discussing the Holy Spirit, although it comes from the Womb of Creation. The Holy Spirit is an energy alignment, more accurately it is the Spoken Word of our Creator. The Holy Spirit is also the *thrust* forward or the action of God, the Word made manifest. It is the grand comforter God sent forth as an expansion of Itself to the forms of consciousness birthed in to being to accompany them on their journey. The Holy Spirit is part of the Mind of God, and reacts in the world of form, but not as a being. When you encounter its softness some minds will perceive it as masculine, and others may feel it to be feminine. I recommend you apply no gender to this divine release from the Godhead because your words for defining the Holy Spirit would create a limitation of it, for it is an all-consuming light. In many instances, this symbol of the Dove joins with those in deep prayer and meditation. The Holy Spirit assists you in receiving the blessings of our Creator, and it is the spark of life. This is why when you are not partaking of it you feel as if you are closed off from the eternal self, which is light. The Holy Spirit also contains a memory all its own, and can be understood as part of the Love of God. It is the experiencing aspect of God, and it is part of all life, it is a structure of life.

In the regions of heaven where I reside the soul is not detached from the Holy Spirit. In the beginning, the Holy Spirit establishes a home within the developing human soul, and for many it is like a friend who occasionally visits. Few, in their experience of this vast light, have recognized it as being a part of their own Higher Presence. Nonetheless, that is the teaching I left behind. I began to recognize these frequencies at a young age, which is why I was more comfortable than most now having this experience, and when I spoke it was the energy of the Holy Spirit flowing from me. It is part of the higher spheres, and part of a level of consciousness I enjoyed.

For those working hard the Holy Spirit will remain with them, as it did with me. My beloveds, it was always God's plan that the Holy Spirit remain with all of you when you departed from the higher states of consciousness on this journey. Whoever allows the Holy Spirit to remain with them will be filled with joy and face less hardships; however, once again I say you must pass through the Christ energy grid to reconnect with the Holy Spirit for your ascension or as some call it, resurrection. Working with the Holy

Spirit will enable you to unlock some of the mysteries of this universe. This occurs because as the Holy Spirit descends there is a flutter of light from the level of the soul encompassing the mind with clarity. This is what is intended to take place during times of silence, deep prayer, and meditation; these are all different states of consciousness, and periods of stillness each developing soul will eventually enter. Within the stillness is a current of light, of energy, a frequency, that is the call to awaken. It is what some mothers feel when the spirit of their unborn child enters their womb. This is how you are intended to "hear" the Holy Spirit sounding the call to awaken. This garment of light has been known throughout the ages by different sects and religions, and it is actually a part of the Universal Mind. The Holy Spirit descends as the Dove and connects to the spiritual heart center, not the physical heart. In Eastern philosophies it is understood as the sacred fire of the Kundalini needing to rise and connect to the higher energies entering the physical crown, which is the Holy Spirit. This creates activation in the lower chakras, and they proceed to open and hold additional light, bringing balance to the mind and emotions. (The Kundalini is energy located at the base of the spine.)

The Holy Spirit is also the energy within the Seal of Abraham, and within the balance of the threefold flame. It continues to levitate you into a spiral of energy to an awakened state of consciousness, which holds thoughts present in the high heavens that are the higher regions and realities. The Holy Spirit opens a tabernacle within and ignites the fire of the light bodies and the threefold flame, allowing them to expand. Your light or crystalline essence known as divine love will continue to expand the prisms of light held within the threefold flame. This expansion of light creates a corresponding resonance opening a tributary of light and passage for the anchoring of the I Am Flame, the heart of your I Am Presence. These bodies of light are the mechanisms used by the I Am Presence and the Holy Spirit. You, as spirit, hold many dormant columns of light frequencies or tonal sound currents not yet attached to the physical, emotional or mental bodies. (See more on mental bodies in glossary.) The anchoring of these columns is the work of the I Am Presence and the Holy Spirit. None of you can obtain this initiation without learning to love your neighbor.

Earth's small solar system has innumerable gateways for those longing to know God, and experience the gift of the Holy Spirit. A developed threefold flame is the gateway to my home, an illustrious city of light.

Templates of Creation

The Trinity and the Trinity Energies

I n my sermons, I continuously said humankind was part of the Trinity, and not disconnected from a loving God. I spun that message throughout my lessons, but personalities, controlled by a range of fear held in their ego, could not fully comprehend the multiple levels of my teachings. Even today, a good number of folks do not understand the meaning of the Trinity we are all a part of, and it should be understood as all of creation. The Trinity is the Plural Nature of God, and makes up the Godhead, and it is a governing force created by the Godhead to be the hierarchy of the worlds of creation. It is this governing action that is part of the Universal Mind, and the Holy Spirit is the driving force of the action of God within the Trinity. It is divine in nature because it has remained in its purest form. The Trinities are also the elders before the Throne of Creation.

The energies of the Trinity are found in the threefold flame and connected within the heart, and entered through the cosmic fire. Dormant within each human DNA system is a replica of the Trinity body called the I Am Flame that belongs to the I Am Presence, and adjusts to the energy system through a series of initiations. This is the blueprint of your divine nature. When you are taught through discipline, such as in meditation techniques, to still the lower aspects that are part of the earthly experience, then you learn to dwell in a consciousness beyond the evolutions of the third dimension. As the structure of the DNA awakens in you, just like Adam and Eve, you will have the ability to work through your Tree of Life, and return to the memory cell you originated from without obstacles on your path; not only as a Christ being, but truly as a member of this high and holy family. It is the story of the prodigal child returning home, and not knowing the majesty it came from. (For more information on Adam and Eve and the Tree of Life please refer to the chapter, The Hidden Meaning of the Story of Genesis, page 137.)

There is a delicate vibration or an outer manifestation that descends on the planet understood as the feminine energies of creation. Remember, concepts in higher regions are less masculine and feminine than on earth. Even at the levels of the Divine Monad the pulsations of light are of our Creator. (The Divine Monad is the spark of God within each person, and is a collection of experiences of an all-pervading consciousness. For more information please refer to the chapter, Templates of Creation, page 85.) The Trinity holds the Father, Mother, Son, and Daughter aspects of the Godhead. The Father represents the masculine energy; the life-giving force nurtured by the Mother. Through the Mother aspect and the many rings of light in the Womb of Creation, we are all called to being. The Christ is both male and female, part of the Trinity, part of a flower, and the bud that is each one of you.

There is not one aspect within the Trinity more important than the other. This is somewhat misunderstood by the human mind, for the heavenly hosts that brought forth life are also experiencing that same action. God is the Creator and the Creation. God has many faces, and those in human form are certainly part of this experience. Although, for a time, the level of their consciousness, thoughts, and emotions, are the only parts of them appearing to be outside those rings of higher light. When more people become conscious beings, and by conscious I mean holding unconditional love and tributaries of light, they are awakened to higher levels of service to humankind, and will work closely with their higher light codes coming from their I Am Presence. This is why the I Am Presence is also termed the God Seed.

There are many wondrous spiritual gifts I truly long to return to my brothers and sisters residing on earth. Through an open heart, working together, loving life and humankind, we will traverse the world. You will come to know what it means to have an opportunity to stand in the halls of the Holy of Holies, and to know and love God, the Creator of all light. I will share with you the peace within my heart, and the deep love I experience from our Creator; it is a gift I wish all to receive. I encourage everyone interested in awakening to take time everyday to develop interaction with the energies of the Trinity. Those who do will stay in communication with these energies through a developed consciousness. Returning to the Trinity attunement is the true meaning of the word resurrection, and the energy of the resurrection is programmed in the remaining DNA you receive during deep preparation for ascension. More correctly, I am calling those who are ready into the resurrection flame.

Catherine's anecdote: In some instances, Christ uses the term Father/Mother God. Christ knows certain groups feel comfortable with the balance of this energy, and on many levels of co-creation there is a balance of the two; however, the following is an experience I had with Christ that may clarify the use of the masculine and feminine in relation to God.

I stood with Christ looking out onto a massive spinning vortex of white light. He told me it was a more advanced universe than earth where he existed prior to coming to this planet, and where he now resides. I heard myself asking, "Are all universes masculine in nature?" He replied, "Yes, because as the energy left the Nucleus, the Great Silence, the masculine energy had the strongest thrust forward, and actually created the universes." While thinking about this experience I could relate his story to a super hero coming to earth from another universe to help the inhabitants of a spiritually deprived planet. No wonder Jesus the Christ was not understood.

The Threefold Flame

In the higher heavens you will experience a sweet smell, and hear a voice that speaks from a vast Majestic Light, which is our Creator. This experience also manifests through many ascended masters as we assist in stepping down this frequency to allow souls to attune with their divine image, and with the flame residing in the Heart of God. Within each developing soul there is a threefold flame. It is the flame of the Christ, that spark of life, residing in each person's light bodies, and burns within the secret chamber of their spiritual heart center. One can best come to know themselves through a concentrated desire to work with their threefold flame. It is where the spiritual seeker meets the master and is taught to understand the nature of God and creation. The threefold flame is made of three intertwining plumes of sacred fire. The center plume is golden yellow representing God's wisdom. To one side is a pink plume signifying God's love, and the other side is a blue plume signifying God's power. The balance of this triple plume is also held in the pattern of the fleur-de-lis.

When you first work with the threefold flame you enter a cycle of love and this causes many to feel as if they are reborn. The flame teaches you how to hold vibrations that are an energy signature from your divine nature. It is then some souls have the opportunity to expand into the Christ mind, which is a concept I love teaching to all who call upon me. The Christ mind is cultivated in those who have a well developed threefold flame, and the chambers of this flame are expanded through prayer and contemplation of your divinity.

Divine Monad

Starting at the higher heavens a long time ago, some chose to depart from what many understand to be the Divine Monad. They went forth with our Creator's blessings into myriads of worlds and expressions. Consequently, some experienced more and more distance from the light, and there was a spinning action that created their descent into the matter realms. As part of the ascension many of those souls are now spiraling upward through columns of light, and for most, but not all, this becomes a joyful expression of self. I wish to show those interested the many wonders and realms beyond earth where the words *lack and limitation* do not abide. In these realms are souls, actually they are your brothers and sisters, experiencing existence in a higher position from within their Monad. This means they hold more light, and most are not as dense as humans.

A Monad is sometimes symbolized as a staircase leading upward. A simple explanation of the Divine Monad is how consciousness began the illusion of its separation from an All Abiding Light. Your Monad is above the crown chakra, which is located at the top of your head. When you advance spiritually it connects to a ray of energy-filtering light to the spiritual heart center. It is also a timing mechanism given to you ages ago, and the sound of its alarm is your call to awaken; subsequently, when it goes off it causes you to search for answers. When people are not seeking to understand their divine nature some feel unhappy, and experience bouts of emptiness and depression coming from their memories. Most will strive to raise their consciousness, and as they progress in reconnecting to their spirit they will not succumb as easily to the lower suggestions rampant on this planet. I have already clarified Lucifer and Satan no longer reside here; yet many sects still mistakenly identify lower frequencies with those beings.

Your Divine Monad, your eternal self, opens you up to the Will of God and your divine purpose; to the part of self that knows the path to joy and happiness. Seeking is necessary since it is the awakening, and it is truly part of the soul experiencing the stirring within, hearing its Divine Monad calling. Meditate on this aspect of self because this is how your God Presence will enrich your life; however, to achieve this you must first develop respect for self, and a love of life. This step will not only do you good, but it will also help the evolving Elemental Kingdoms you co-exist with. Each person's divine soul knows the truth behind the details of every action they have ever taken. As the divine light expands within self it will become the inner teacher, the inner master, which will point out parts of your life in need of balance, and show you where higher patterns of light can be gained. While on this subject it is important to mention that to reach your Divine Monad you travel through many Monads that are all part of this wonderful body of light. The Divine Monad holds the higher, purer parts of self, and always experiences being part of divine love in motion in multiple spheres, operating simultaneously throughout the numerous worlds, galaxies and universes; God created omniverses and earth is in one of the smaller outer galaxies.

Self-hatred has darkened this planet, and victory cannot be gained with many still holding these currents. Malice in any form is a conductor of a negative flow of light, just as the opposite is true. When negativity is present it is difficult harnessing the light coming from the higher realms through the mind and body. The out-picturing of life's experiences will seem negative and unjust, but you orchestrate this; however, by learning self-mastery gains in control are made the world over. Your actions regulate the light coming to you and experiences are shaped according to those levels. The negative results are from an insufficient amount of *qualified light* entering your eight mental bodies holding layers of your memories, creating an unfavorable reality. (For more information please refer to the section, Mental and Memory Bodies, Lower and Higher Bodies, and the Causal body, page 90.) Simply put, qualified light is pure, positive energy we receive from our God Presence through our I Am Presence that supports the soul's continued growth; however, qualified light is actually particles of light received from your Presence. Search for books and meditations holding the patterns of light that teach how to stabilize the frequencies you intend to hold, that you long to be a part of. Catherine and Vera are examples of this as they are assisting me in planting seeds of greater awareness as you read my words.

Allow the stirrings of the soul to expand in to the brilliant star all of you are intended to become. A determined spiritual seeker will experience a breakthrough in consciousness, an expansion of light, and the columns of light will flow through the tones of your I Am Presence, and of who it is you are within the Mind of God.

Did you know the stars in the heavens are allowed to be visible to those on earth as a reminder of the enormity of God's Mind? They are also a reminder of the possibilities within your reach. I spoke of the beauty before us, but everyday beauty escapes most people because they are held prisoners in the concepts that still exist on earth. Many minds need to release themselves in to the greater light. Ask for the Celestial Christ to remain with you. Try not to criticize yourself or others, and learn to appreciate the heavenly stars, and everyday beauty all around.

All who are reading my words must decide if they are willing to embark upon a new chapter of their existence as part of co-creation if they wish to enter the spiral of light that comes to them from the Divine Monad.

The God Presence: Addressing Your Higher Self, Christ Self, and I Am Presence

All of you have been with your God Presence since God said the words spoken in Genesis, "Let there be light, and there was light." (Genesis 1:3) A soul's God Presence is a massive being of immeasurable light and joy and a reflection of the prism of the Light of God. At the level of the God Presence the soul is still connected to Source and abides as a sound current within God. To add to its individualized expression the God Presence created some of the I Am Presences, which further divided, and consciousness traveled through a Divine Monad into more individualized Monads. *This is the amazing story of you.* Consciousness emerged as an individualized flame experiencing Itself spiraling out, but it still maintained its original code and the Divine Blueprint. Many encounter their God Presence in their lifetimes, but deny it. At one time or another most people will feel a stirring within, when they know God or a higher power is communicating with them in some form. Some listen, but others do not. Many today are telepathic because they still carry part of the Divine Blueprint from a previous expression that allowed that door to remain open.

The physiology of the human with its thoughts, reasoning powers, and emotions are precious vessels of our Creator, but many do not treat their life as though it is a sacred walk with the Lord. Each of you, as an individualized spark, is intended to be the Mantle of the Christ in physical form. Be it your I Am Presence, Christ Self or Higher Self, it is quite evolved in comparison to the developing personality with an ego, and they are the exalted aspects of self. Your I Am Presence is an enormous vessel of light or being that cannot be measured or fully understood by humans, and it comes forward from realities long forgotten. It exists in present time in God consciousness and thought, and knows all God knows. This is a challenging belief for humankind, and why many turn to me, Christ Jesus, to be their Savior, for in me, and through various masters, they are able to understand the truth, and the messages coming to them, speaking to their hearts. Some religions continue to teach doctrines of unworthiness, and this has gone on far too long; consequently, their congregations cannot fully attune with those of us existing in the heavenly realms.

The I Am Presence is a step down from the frequency of the God Presence, meaning it became more individualized. Each soul is gifted with the ability to know its I Am Presence. The reason this experience does not occur for the masses is because the spiritual seeker must be patient and prepared to enter the stillness when their heart is open, as in meditation and prayer. Spiritual progress is made as the mind is stilled and free of dogmas, then the master within provides additional instructions. Many ascended masters and I are in service to each person's God Presence. This is another reason why I am allowed, based on the teachings on this planet, to step forward in the position of the Good Shepherd, the Savior, and the Redeemer, until my followers hold enough qualified light, and are able to reflect the code of the master within self.

In time, each person will realize they are kings and queens over their domains, but first they need to be taught the information that was removed from my teachings. When I lived as Jesus many were biased to my messages. Class systems existed, and those of high status did not want to hear that the prostitute and the villain were equal to them in the eyes of our Creator. Although the words I spoke resonated with some of the people, my messages did not always appeal to everyone. That was mainly because my teachings did not coincide with what they had been taught by their religious leaders and society; therefore, I was truly a lamp unto those who sought change. I heard the call, and responded to it. Even now some of you are having that same experience when the light within the heart chamber can no longer be denied.

Mental and Memory Bodies, Lower and Higher Bodies, and the Causal Body

Earth's dimension exists in one octave called the third dimension. The physical body is all that is seen, but understand there are many invisible layers to each person, plant, animal, and mineral. The human has four "invisible" lower bodies that are actually four sheaths of four distinct frequencies surrounding the soul: the physical, emotional, mental, and etheric bodies, providing vehicles for the soul in the journey through time and space. The etheric sheaths hold the highest vibration, and are the gateway to the three higher bodies: the Christ Self, causal bodies, and the I Am Presence. The causal body is made up of seven concentric spheres of light surrounding the I Am Presence. You also have eight memory bodies. They are each folded on top of one another, and appear like blue grids that your Higher Self, with my assistance, begins to clear. This allows the physical chakras to open. (Every being has a chakra system. In the physical form they are located along the spinal column; however, there are additional chakras extending beyond the matter body and in other parts of the physical body. Essentially, they are sound currents holding waves of light within the body, and they vibrate to a sound current the Christ Oversoul utilizes in the higher heavens. (Please refer to the glossary for more information on chakras.) These memory bodies are sheets of grids that completely surround the individual until a time when the human experience reaches the momentum of light called the Christ Oversoul. To reach this spiritual plateau the higher mental body opens the doorway to levels of light called the Oversoul's octaves. To varying degrees a human soul passes through the mental astral grids before incarnating on earth, and this is based on initiations from previous earthly lives or initiations that occurred between lives in other dimensions. As consciousness is lowered through the eight mental bodies a pattern of forgetfulness is ascribed. This is for the soul's protection because, in most cases, the memories from other lives held within some of these layers will cause insanity. On the returning cycle, termed ascension or resurrection, soul clears these lower grids, and then the quality of the mind energy improves greatly, and the light within the spiritual heart expands to universal light and love. (This is the work of Mother Mary, as well as others, and they assist the planet in harnessing divine love through soul levels to the levels within the human heart. We are constantly working with spiritual seekers, our disciples, and those who desire to follow in our footsteps.)

On the other hand, many embodiments hold lopsided memory bodies because the light is folded in on itself, and it is difficult for most to maintain their light. When this occurs we formulate our plan together, and create a re-polarization starting at the heart, and draw soul upward to clear its astral fields. (*Vera's comment:* This is the reason mantras work. Repeating a word or an affirmation creates a powerful energy and light builds surrounding the person, becoming a bridge of light. Prayer works in the same way.) This is truly the meaning behind Holy Communion; it is intended to be a sharing of my light with all who partake. For as long as you are focused on emulating me, and walking in my sandals, I assist you with holding the energies of your radiant body of light. The saying, *"when the spiritual seeker is ready the master appears,"* really means you need to be willing to surrender to the divine existing within, which is the master within or the Christ Self.

The Soul Call

Listen for the Knock on Your Door

In each person's life there needs to be a time to settle their debt with their brethren, because everyone has contributed to the fall of humankind. At some point everyone has had limited consciousness, and did not uphold the higher prisms of light; consequently, contributing in different degrees to racism, concepts of illusion, and improper intentions toward humankind. All of you need to think of yourselves as being called to the one true light of understanding, of oneness. Precision is in the attributes of the Higher Mind intended to be humankind's inheritance, and those who search for this receive a higher understanding of the accuracy of God's wishes.

There is a portrait of me you may be familiar with. It is the painting where I am standing at the threshold of the door and knocking, and I am asking those that are ready to allow me in. This is the image I would like each reader to remember as I make the call to all of you to become the sons and daughters you are intended to be. I am asking if you are ready to let me assist you in raising the divine flame within self, and qualifying the light around you. When I say, "around you," I mean in your spiritual heart, and in your thinking. When I knock, I am calling each individual soul to focus on your divinity, the flame given you upon your day of creation when you left the Godhead, and descended many planes of creation.

I counsel everyone who calls upon me. I am the Celestial Christ, the Oversoul of all who are able to carry the frequencies of their own Christ consciousness. Eventually every person truly needs to attune to the Christ mind in the Lord Jesus, and become the freshness, the newness of the vessels of light I held. Search your minds and hearts to find the quiet place within the secret door, therein you will find me. The Divine soul spins in accordance with the Will of our Creator, and you are raised in a vortex, and held within the light of the Holy Spirit that descends around you. I, the Celestial Christ, need to be the indwelling spirit within your minds and hearts. Creation is a reflection of the great love of the One who sent me to earth, but it is also a reflection of you. Set aside time to develop a relationship with me. Those who seek me call to me, I awaken the Christ mind within them, and they move into a prism of light. Many times the archangels also assist with this endeavor, and a significant shift is experienced.

Some wear a medal with my image, and when it is blessed it carries the sound frequency from my sacred heart. Most do not recognize their own divine nature, and unnecessarily take their medals to clergymen for blessings, but if you ask, I will bless these medals through you. In our walks together the awakened soul realizes they become the living energy of the medal radiating light, one to another. I am giving this information to assist in the understanding that not everyone, but for many, the journey begins with Jesus the Christ. As human souls awaken, and become self-realized, there is awareness that they are also part of the great out-picturing of God in action lifting many souls to heaven.

From this teaching you now realize our Creator does not work *only* through Christ Jesus or a masculine form. The Christ is a frequency in harmony with all parts of itself. It is neither masculine nor feminine, but holds those frequencies of balance. Male and female are equal, and all have permission to represent God. Mother Mary is actively working with the planet, but many have not recognized the work of the divine feminine as also being an equal part of the work of the Godhead. The streams of light of the divine feminine need to be held in balance, and this energy is now becoming more powerful on earth in order to stabilize the frequencies of the Oversouls.

Many are waiting for me, the physical man, to return to earth, but I already return through the hearts I am permitted to rise into the Christ light. This is how I return as the bridegroom, by oversouling those ready with the energies of the Christ. If this is your will, prepare for this union that is *the call* I have been speaking about, which is also the call to freedom. God is all things, and the nature of self is divine. Again I tell you, all of creation sprang forth from divine origins, just as I, Jesus, sprang forth from the same divine origins. You pale in comparison to the light of your God Presence that is truly who you are. Most religions teach that people can never be this light, but this was not my message. I came as an example of the future of humankind, when souls will ascend back to their divine light.

The majority of you traveled in and out of earth's patterns many times, and became masters in the reincarnation process. I delight in this advancement; however, this prevents you from experiencing the higher heavens. As a result, most human beings have lost the ability to know their true nature, and to remember the Will of God is they remain in communion with Him. Your hearts need to stay open to the constant flow of light and love from your I Am Presence, to the lower vessel understood as the current personality. It is easy to over identify with the physical form and relationships, remaining tethered to group consciousness. Far too many people seal the door preventing them from hearing the God spark speaking, while continuing to question the purpose for being. It is why I, Jesus, asked to be chosen to come to this planet as an advanced soul having developed within higher constellations. I was able to love and respect myself enough to be of service to humankind, but this scenario has occurred often on this planet. There have been even more advanced souls that prepared themselves during previous root races or in other systems, and then volunteered to come to earth to assist humankind in developing. *A big obstacle for earth's residents is the tendency to imagine us, the visiting masters, as God, wherein our true mission is to show everyone who they are intended to be.*

Begin the Journey with Christ

The journey can begin right now. I am calling, but will you answer? To walk down this path surrender to the qualified light, and emanations of God I amplify from Creator to creation. As the flow of light is experienced, a sense of renewal occurs in this higher, purer light, and you are shown parts of your life that do not honor you or bring heightened joy, and where change in these areas will be beneficial. This path should not be looked at as a path of sacrifice, but one of ecstasy. Each time anyone partakes of the gift of union with me we create a sacrament together; however, physically eating a communion host is unnecessary. I am merely describing the process behind our relationship.

This is a pathway of forgiveness. Humankind needs to learn to forgive others, and face the truth within, as I have demonstrated. That was what I meant when I gave the parable about the splinter in your brother's eye. Almost everyone is very adept at judging others, but not even reasonable when it comes to taking a truthful look at yourselves.

The journey with Christ is based on teachings that develop the mind and heart in a pattern of oneness. I introduced my disciples to a method of prayer where each person went directly to God, no middleman, and encouraged them to trust in that relationship. I did not set in motion the division that exists today, even amid religious sects. I sent my disciples as my instruments to console and guide the people, not to take away their individual rights. *Presently on earth, there are spiritually advanced consciousness initiates studying with high level masters, while working closely with Christ and God. Seek guidance from them for they are genuine examples of humankind's future, and what all of you should aspire to emulate.*

The uncertainty on earth would disappear in a moment if everyone thoroughly understood my words and lived them. Putting Christ as the central figure of the Holy Wars was misguided, and contradictory to my teachings. Those involved thought they were emulating valor, but of course this is not true. *I never spoke of using a weapon. Violence is not part of the teachings I gave then or now.* If you sought to walk in my sandals there would not be wars or discrimination, and no one would turn against another. All of you would look in the face of your neighbor, coworker, even your enemy, and see me, for this is the teaching I brought forth; however, I honor each path because every person is given the gift of freewill as part of Cosmic Law, and I do not interfere in the choices of another or their belief system. As intelligent beings you have the opportunity to discuss your viewpoints and make decisions, hopefully in a peaceful manner.

Yes, the robes I wore as Jesus were torn and ragged, and I walked among those in grave despair, but my outer appearance did not matter. I come now as I did then, to those whose hearts are conditioned to receive my tones of love and my vibrations of light. If you ask me to be your teacher, I will treat you as my friend, but together we will take a candid look at what keeps you beneath my level of consciousness. I draw very close to the brilliant Light of Creation, for the Will of God emanates clearly with divine purpose for all of creation. The rose cannot be anything other than what it was created to be; it cannot be the tulip just because it desires that form. You are each created as I was created, to be an emanation of immeasurable love. That *is* the Will of our Creator, but this is also a choice for those residing in parts of creation with freewill, such as earth.

I witness many tears on your path, and this certainly *is not* the Will of our Creator. The memory patterns were altered to keep earth's residents from the true knowledge of who they are because, due to the fall, the flame within the heart was reduced.

Each soul has a purpose, and direction. Take an honest look at your lives, and see if there is room for growth. Make a choice in this lifetime to light the fire within, to respond to the call, to open that doorway of service to humankind, and to love of self. Still waters are within each creation, and they carry a momentum of light, which cascades through the heart. It is there you merge with self, with the person you are within the Heart and the Mind of our Creator. In this book, I explain that when given permission, I oversoul human souls by merging with their light, raising their vibration, and creating a greater light. In the early stages, I also raise the vibration, but this only occurs temporarily when I am close or until you are able to remain within this magnificent rebirth. It is a gift I give, and a way for me to share my essence, and create a protective filter for my followers. This is accomplished by learning to completely ground light through you; thus creating a shift to the positive side. (Please see glossary for more information on grounding cords.)

If you refrain from judgments, cursing, negative thinking, screaming, yelling, jealousy, resentment, and holding on to all forms of anger and violence, you will be able to hold a higher, lighter vibration. All adepts must consider taking personal responsibility by focusing on raising their intentions, and improving the flow of love until it is consistently unconditional or it is not love. An over dramatization takes place in the minds of many who are now in embodiment, and sometimes they really enjoy and revel in the dramatics. It is not the proper use of the Will of God, and often creates frightening experiences for them in their outer manifestations. It also causes continual suffering for everyone on this plane, and these are the cords that bind souls to the cycle of rebirth. I teach how to keep your footing in balance and harmony, to develop inner knowing, and gain wisdom. Please do not feel guilty, we, the ascended masters, also came forth in our past lives with a great deal of drama.

The wars will continue as long as humankind dwells in fear, and is consumed with envy for the riches of other's land. Domination needs to end for humankind to experience an understanding of the higher heavens. The idea of God is accepted by all religions, but what is not yet understood is the concept of a just and loving God that isn't revengeful or hateful toward Its creation. There is only one God, and as I already explained, He has many, many names. Even those that believe in one God do not always understand the one path and the One Mind. There has always been and continues to be different forms of worship, and they all need to be honored and respected by everyone. Contemplate the vastness of this Eternal Being in prayer and meditation. God will eventually reveal Himself to the mind and heart of Its creations and some souls will be allowed access to memories once held of dwelling in the paradise kingdoms of greater light; this is what I experienced and shared in my teachings. Fear is your oppressor and causes limitations. The gates of heaven are open for those who have a strong enough spirit and craving to enter, and my intention is to come to enfold and love all who call out to me.

I am heralding a message of love and peace as I have for the last two thousand years. The reason I do not appear to the multitudes on earth is because they do not create a space for me within their hearts; subsequently, I remain veiled from their sight. I am not saying this is true for all people, but the majority of souls have lost the ability to hear me. Even those who frequently attend Mass or spiritual services do not open up to the light, mostly out of fear of judgment, but I do not deal them a heavy hand. I love and cherish all souls, and guide them back to our Creator. Hearing the Voice of God, as I did in my life as Jesus, was a blessing I honored, respected, and cherished above all. *Countless souls lay down their lives through acts of violence in the name of God or Christ, believing it is a way to demonstrate their love, but in truth they contribute to the misfortune and destruction of this planet.* Their level of understanding of our Creator comes only from the ego mind, and shafts of light do not surround them. This weighs heavy on my heart, for it is not the counsel I left behind. That is another reason why the eight mental bodies that are connected to the physical body must be cleared of latent memories and darkness. As I walked the planet as Jesus, there was plenty of bickering among those who were close to me, for even they did not fully encompass the Divine Mind I dwelled in.

Perhaps among those reading or listening to my words now, I will find the fruits of my labor that will dwell in the exalted spirit of their Christ Oversoul. You, as spiritual seekers, need to experience the freshness of my spirit, and together we will turn the pages of a new life, and a new love in spirit. I will take you by the hand and walk with you, not whom I choose, but those desiring to be chosen, and I will groom each one of you. We will work in tandem, and through the energies of the Holy Spirit we will return to you the consciousness, and demeanor of a peaceful heart; a heart that recognizes truth and honors all living beings.

In every individual there is a beautiful tabernacle, and within it is the threefold flame, but for some the flame is very small. Call upon this vast light within self, and ask that it develop and grow. Then the flame will become very bright, and you will truly understand the meaning of life, and connectedness to all living things. You will live as a just and honorable being because making time to work with God, with Christ, is what you seriously need to take upon yourself in this lifetime. I commend those who pray deeply, and see them move within a higher frequency experiencing the energies of the Holy Spirit descending upon them. In those moments, they share a blessing with the Christ, and this is also what it means to share communion with me.

The Heart of God is a heart that loves Its creations; Its children. God does not devour them and does not ask for sacrifices; rather, He pours out mercy and love. It is my desire for you to trust your relationship with God through the workings of the Divine Mind. God exists as an Abiding Presence within each and every creation. Emanations of God come through a doorway called the Holy of Holies. The night skies are cycles existing within an omniverse, and are alive with evolving cultures. The majorities of these cultures are more advanced than earth, and hold loving thoughts toward humankind. For such a long time they watched over the planet, and some visited earth, but not many have come in recent times.

There is a design to this universe. Do not be preoccupied with doubt, and do use your higher spiritual intelligence to reason out your circumstances. Know I am close. Know the veil is temporary until you gather a profusion of light. When this occurs, the understanding I had while embodied as Jesus will bless your life, and you will be of service to our Creator and me. A magnificent soul initiation is taking place for many now; yet most of you come before me still holding judgments, and this really needs to end if you hope to experience the energies of the rapture. Until such time, more souls need to hold the illustrious light of the Holy Spirit for that grid to open. Each soul is intended to be the spiritual seeker, and must decide if they will permit me or another ascended being to take their hand, and guide them to a path of love beyond measure, incalculable joy, and mercy.

Resurrecting the Christ Within

Christ beckons you to be Open to Unfamiliar Possibilities

Some of you have reached deep within, and are contemplating that there may be a spiritual existence superior to the one you are currently experiencing. There certainly is! When you, as a spiritual seeker, consciously move into my kingdom you realize you are not servants of Jesus the Christ; rather, initiates of the Body of Christ preparing to receive the mind of Christ. This places you in the position of discipleship. As the Christ Oversoul, the individualized focus of the God spark embodies all on this path. In truth, if you are a serious spiritual seeker, all your intentions should be focused on becoming a disciple of this Holy Order of the Body of Christ. Not in worshiping me as Jesus the Christ, but as joining me in its frequency. This is what I meant in the Bible when I spoke the words:

> "I tell you the truth it is hard for a rich man to enter the kingdom of heaven. Again I tell you, it is easier for a camel to go through the eye of a needle than for a rich man to enter the kingdom of God" (Matthew 19:23–24).

I came to teach the hidden mysteries of how to complete the path to your own Christed Oversoul and Christed mind. It is what I taught my disciples while I was on the planet as Jesus, and what I still teach in my sanctuary. Many secret meanings are in my teachings, and to understand them takes an open heart, and a willingness to work with me. Excessive materialism is consuming, turn away and take upon you the staff of the Good Shepherd, as I have done. It is the Celestial Christ Emmanuel, I, as the man Jesus merged with, and he is the one holding the Mantle of the Christ for all beings. This is why *I am the way and the light* to the pattern of energy known as the Christos, the Diamond Mind, and to the purity of the Spoken Word that brought consciousness in the form of flesh. It is for this reason I come forth to make humankind whole once again.

Be patient, it takes time to raise the holy fire within. My staff is charged with an enormous light, and I never use it to control anyone, only to guide souls. I truly honor each individual choice, for I understand there is a lesson in the outcome the soul desires to experience. I speak of the divine nature that dwells within all beings, and in each breath there is a resonance of the Trinity energies. It is a light flowing through me, Jesus, as well as through every individual, because we are all a part of it. I shepherd you until you are able to hold your own light. Within the chalice of my heart is also the bread of life, and everyone who partakes of this gift is brought to my home. In truth, I bring onto me all who love me and ask me to be their teacher. Many will follow me, their way-shower, to the columns of light that lead to the heavenly worlds.

Commit to a daily exercise of noting where your thoughts and emotions wander. Create a fixed point of consciousness that eventually will become the still point within self, where I will be experienced. True spiritual seekers of wisdom will discover that serving two masters will not work because you cannot serve the lower thought forms, the thresholds of the poor of heart, and still be a part of the higher consciousness. As you become comfortable with monitoring your intentions behind every action you will notice an increased desire to make more conscious behavioral changes, especially when handling everyday situations. If called upon, I will respond and be that guidepost. I knock often on the door of the hearts and minds of all who call to me; yet there are times when I answer, and those professing they love me, hold judgments and block my way. To be totally free you need to be born anew, and this newness will create a freedom within. One way to experience a rebirth of thoughts and emotions is by working with spirit descending through the Star of David. The star raises the energy frequency around the human aura field and the physical body, and the frequency rises because it opens additional chakras that are not part of the ego personality. Then you will stand as I did and say, "As I am above, so I am below."

Each of you consciously accepted uncertainty as a tradeoff for the experience of coming to earth. This is why there is much indecision, and frustration regarding the outcome of situations, and the birthing process causes humans to forget they are all multifaceted. Flashes of wisdom do occur, and there are times when the human spirit soars to impressive heights, and you seem to know truth within self, but these are momentary awakenings. The reason for this is human consciousness is not developed enough to hold the transfer of higher thought forms, which is the state I continually dwell in. I am the living master of unconditional love, love divine, and respect for all evolving consciousness.

I taught a doctrine of never causing harm to another; yet there are wars, hatred, and division between people, and often in my name. That was not my message or the message of any ascended master communicating with earth from the regions of the highest heaven. Begin now to recognize there are divisive teachings given to humankind throughout its evolutions. The sub-planes, astral planes, and various regions between heaven, and earth, are populated by many levels of beings, overlords, even demigods. They are not fully carrying the light of their own God awareness, which regrettably played a role in releasing doctrines of faith to earth through their dark messengers. Unfortunately, what is not understood is even in these regions there are hierarchies of teachers, angels, and others posing as beings of knowledge many confuse with teachers sent by God. Their doctrines are mixed, and while some hold certain truths, they are largely lacking in the message of divine and universal love for all creation. Connecting to these lower realms also created distortions in certain religions. If teachings divide humankind, promote fear, empower one sex over another, and do not show respect toward human or animal life, know they are not a teaching from the gateway I speak from. God never condones war nor does He hate or show favor to His creations. If you believe God is saying anything other than to love one another, you are following a false teaching, and not receiving the information from those who dwell in the regions of paradise. I came to earth to set in motion the awareness that God is a loving and forgiving Father, and not a Being that scorns His creations. Sadly, what a good many do not realize is when they follow these lesser doctrines they descend to the level of the being that created these principles of limitation, and after death they may even be convinced it is heaven, but it is not. In other words, those partaking in that behavior will end up in an astral world or a lesser realm. There they will be with their tribe sharing beliefs under the ruler ship of the being that created that doctrine, but they will not gain entrance to the true heavens, the regions of paradise, by following such a path. Some regions have set up their own idea of a trinity, but they are not the Trinity of the Immaculate Concept. Hatred, anger, and killing those who do not share your beliefs are not gateways to heaven. In many cases, these misguided souls eventually return to earth with the same belief or gender of those they oppressed, for this is karmic law. (*Vera's comment:* For example, if a person is prejudice toward a race, religion, gender or displays fanatical patriotism, they could reincarnate to experience what it feels like to be disgraced. Consider another case, an insensitive, pretentious, wealthy, and greedy individual might return born in poverty.)

Each human being has a divine soul desiring their personality to eventually come home to a greater awareness of its divine nature; to an expanded consciousness where I have prepared a place for them. The Oversoul I ascended to is where I am guiding those who choose to follow, and it is where I wait for each soul to return to; however, not all will arrive there after this lifetime. Again, it is a choice and all certainly may enter the path of enlightenment now by asking to develop their spiritual understanding. When in harmony with all of creation your spirit will feel as if it is soaring, and you may identify this as the spirit of me, Jesus or as the Love of God within you; it is the Higher Presence awakening the spiritual path within the seeker who is developing a sense of divine purpose. Each person is a gift from our Creator expressing God's love onto the world. How God creates or expresses love through each creation may not necessarily be the same, but there must be respect for one another, and that alone will turn the tides on this world.

I now introduce the concept that an intention needs to be held to make a significant inner discovery to evolve the currents of light, sound, and energy, pouring forth through your crystal cord, which is a membrane of light from your I Am Presence created in the image and likeness of the Divine Mind. This crystal cord connects the human soul to the unseen regions of the world of the divine soul, and it is what keeps the physical body alive. Its energy pours down from the I Am Presence through many regions to supply the body with life. As you evolve, the crystal cord extends beyond the astral and mental planes into higher regions made available to the evolving human soul from the I Am Presence. As the light progresses an awakening occurs on many levels, and the human personality develops some of its divine characteristics. Your consciousness expands and you experience greater wisdom and gifts from spirit. *It is important to mention if you are tied to a limited belief your advances will only grow to the level you are comfortable with.* This means if a spiritual leader or a spiritual seeker believes in the teachings of an ancient doctrine and will not release those tenants, they will only penetrate wisdom to a certain degree, for they are still limited in their ability to see all of creation as one living energy from one loving God. To receive additional light from the heavens you must develop proper intentions, and be willing to embrace all doctrines of truth. As you understand the consequences of intentions on your lives, and the lives of your loved ones, you realize when you are aligned with spirit you receive more of God's radiance through the crystal cord descending from your I Am Presence.

When I walked the earth as Jesus many were preoccupied with outer disturbances; therefore, unable to understand my messages. This is the reason I sometimes spoke in parables, but the times are different now. The messengers I work through today are more spiritually developed and hold higher initiations. They can bring through profoundly clear comprehension and explanations of the words I spoke as Jesus the Christ, but do not be distracted by those calling themselves the earthly fathers. Some are extremely serious about taking on that title, but not all are worthy of becoming shepherds of my flock. To be a slave or controlled by anyone is not the pattern you were created to uphold, now dwell within and reflect upon this. Each day and in every moment call upon the blessings of the Holy Spirit to walk with you, to guide your path, to assist you in knowing God. In knowing our Creator you begin the journey to your placement in the heavens.

Everyone exists for an eternity, and it is one of the reasons our Creator patiently waits for those developing far from the heavens. The seed of awakening sprouts when soul decides to embrace it, but I will never step in to control anyone. As a divine being I am, in a sense, an arm of God, and I allow those weary on the path to rest within my arms. It is a service I gladly give, and I truly honor each traveler on their path. I am proud of spiritual seekers and those who desire to know me now, and understand what I represent. I have the ability to be with everyone who turns toward me, and be their counsel, their guide, and to help them understand that the greater part of Christ also exists within them. Every one of you is given the power of knowing the Christ within, and this is accomplished by severing acts that disrupt the light of the divine soul yearning to dwell within humankind. The majority is more familiar with following energies that bring destruction, despair, and illness; rather, than unmasking the gifts of joy God has bestowed upon our souls.

The Office of the Christ

Most of earth's religions teach that it is only a few others and I who are allowed to reign in heaven, and this belief system has created an albatross around the neck of their followers. In truth, there are a vast number of divine beings in the universe. I was chosen to be earth's representative to the Office of the Christ, which is part of the Trinity energies, and responsible for assisting souls in receiving their Divine Blueprint; so they too will eventually make their heavenly ascension. This office is intended to become filled with new members as many rise into the Christ light all were created to embody.

In becoming the Christ a soul initiation is experienced that slowly raises the light, and the divine consciousness given at the time of your Immaculate Conception. An enormous misunderstanding of this Divine Law has altered the mental activity and the love most experience. The love the Christ has for you, his brethren, is without judgment, and it is not marred in any way by your past deeds. I represent the resurrection of the light of God within the soul, and it begins at a cellular level when the human soul first awakens; this is called a rebirth. During this process, all my past and present disciples, and you, as spiritual seekers, experience enormous joy in knowing you too are divine, and you will learn to respect all of life, including yourselves. Many divine beings, even beyond the Christ, also need to be recognized, but not worshiped, for like me they are also guardians of earth.

The Christ Mind & Self-Realization

The Christ mind is a pristine garment of light or strands of light depicted as a white robe, and it is a reflection of the human soul's God Presence created with the seed thought form of the Word of God brought to manifest in the outer kingdoms. Over many incarnations or even over a period of years, your quest to grow spiritually will ground more of these strands of light, which are energy strands of higher consciousness toward self-realization. They will allow you to remain attuned to a consciousness far beyond earth, and your intentions will carry you a considerable distance when preparing to enter the Christ mind. Until humankind is ready to hold these strands of light for themselves, I will continue to come in the role of a guide, a teacher, the Good Shepherd, the Savior, and the Redeemer. Acknowledging my many roles meant to assist humans in becoming Christed is misused by religions, not by me or my original teachings, to mistakenly place me above humankind.

There are many steps to spiritually awakening, but you first enter self-realization where you become aware you are part of a Higher Self. This step is called a soul initiation, when the spiritually advancing adept is taught to dwell in its divine soul body that now surrounds them. During this stage of the soul initiation you, the spiritual seeker, are now the initiate and spiritually advanced compared to most human beings. At this level you will experience many appearances and visitations from the heavenly realms, and you are able to communicate, often by carrying on two-way conversations, with those in the higher levels of the heavens. You are preparing to become the master by working closely under the tutorship of one or several ascended masters like myself, and further demonstrating the process I came to teach; however, there are many steps you must take before you are self-realized and from self-realization to God-realization.

Attuning to the Christ Mind

My beloveds, the mind of Christ is truly clear and without judgment, and leads to the Mind of God. This is because Christ holds the eternal flame given to him by our Creator, and I pass this flame onto you. Spring is the time of renewal and rebirth of the planet, but it is also a spiritual reminder of what is occurring within each individual. Everyone has the option to open up to this God flame located within the higher light bodies, and invite the light of the flame from our Creator into the lower vessel, into the mind preoccupied with daily activities.

I abode in the light of God, and sought to share this with anyone who would listen. The Christ mind is a powerful initiation and a gift I imagined sharing. I continue to offer this opportunity to everyone, because when you are able to work at this level of awareness it is a gift of enlightenment from the Higher Mind. When this is achieved there is a shift within self, an attunement, and part of this is unconditional love. Now the personality has the choice to develop qualities, such as the ability not to anger quickly, to have more patience with others, to experience greater possibilities, to use discernment more often, and to hold higher states of consciousness, enabling you to step aside and to simply love. Then opportunities become even more expanded; within the mind and heart you are taught to work in a frequency of gratitude through stages of light expanding within and around the physical body. Some of you may even laugh and experience joy more frequently. Not all of creation abides in lower consciousness waiting to be uplifted, and you need only to look at the petals of a flower unfolding or the beauty of a butterfly to realize this. It is what I meant when I told my disciples that the flowers and the birds do not struggle because they are in a constant state of receiving God's bounty of love. What blocks human beings from maintaining these expressions are levels of fear and improper attunement with the Source of light.

Discipleship and the Christ Mind

The Christ mind and those who walk in the footsteps of the ascended masters are pure and without judgment. It takes time to develop the ability and focus to access such a mind, and I love to assist those who ask this of me so the Will of our Creator will be experienced by more. This is the meaning of true discipleship. It is the understanding of a covenant between you and me, and you and our Creator.

Some of you get tangled in a net of confusion and experience group consciousness, and consequently mass karma. This happens because the magnetic core held within self is not properly attuned, and it magnetizes you to mis-qualified light. As a result, you leave yourself wide open for misfortune. This is often seen when generations pass down hatred toward others, and then racism emerges, and cast systems are formed. Learn to transcend this by holding the energies of love and gratitude in your heart, and that will alter the magnetic frequency within this core. Soon you may feel lighter and a sense of freedom, having been released from a tribal belief and dogma. Continually holding these gratitude energies within the heart will energize the core; thus making it easier to experience unconditional love toward all creations. From within the depths of self evaluate the current conditions of your life. One way to accomplish this is to focus on the attributes of our Creator, such as love, peace, joy, and abundance. This practice creates a ring of light around the heart center, and you enter a vortex of peaceful stillness, and it is this peace I spoke of. When you fill yourself with the energies of love and appreciation you have a new outlook toward life and there is a positive shift. This process ends the cycle of rebirth in spheres like earth where planetary systems are still evolving through discord. When I said I was preparing a place for you in my Father's Kingdom, it was in reference to what many today call *cosmic ascension,* and I spoke those words to comfort.

"Do not let your hearts be troubled. Trust in God, trust also in me. In my Father's house are many rooms; if it were not so, I would have told you. I am going there to prepare a place for you. And if I go and prepare a place for you, I will come back and take you to be with me that you also may be where I am. You know the way to the place where I am going."

John 14:1–4 (NIV)

Becoming Christs

I am the way-shower illuminating a path through kindness and opportunity. I represent the Divine Blueprint you, my brothers and sisters, also hold. In this world there are many souls unaware of the knowledge of their true divine nature. Most of you are not accustomed to thinking or believing it is intended for you to evolve in to my nature to being the out-picturing of the Christ-man or the Christ-woman. Christ is a pattern of light, and indeed many divine Christed beings have appeared and still appear on earth today. Every day I invite all of you to consider becoming Christs, and if you ask, I am happy to deliver light and love to those choosing to be with me; in fact these are reflections of your divine being. I do this with divine mercy; I do this in service to our Creator; I do this in love, in divine love, and in unconditional love; for true love is without conditions. Hold these thoughts and develop that expectation. Acceptance of your own divine nature will cause you, the seeker, to show more love and respect for yourselves and others. Give me your consent to deepen your understanding of your divine self, and you will develop new levels of wisdom and truth about divine realities, and how you are a part of it.

I can actually stand next to you, close to your invisible sheaths of energy surrounding the physical body; these sheaths are called the auric energy field. During this process of spiritual growth I bring you through a doorway into the grid of the Christ. Many of you have dark masses in your auric field; therefore, the first step is to stabilize more light around you creating a brighter and stronger aura that builds a filter of protection from undesirable tones held in group consciousness. What will assist anyone interested in learning how light enhances your experience is to understand that thought forms hold magnetic energy and always attract like energy. All energy, be it dark, gray or light, is attracted to a like vibration and energetically fills the mind, emotions, and auric field, and will magnetize to a resonating frequency because it seeks out a match.

It helps to have a strong will to begin to rearrange your thought patterns, and hold the intentions to experience more light; however, most of you will have to be firm with yourselves to stop destructive patterns as you learn to hold onto this light. Facilitate this process by recognizing these negative patterns, and consciously being aware if you continue to hold certain thought forms and emotions you will remain in an energy field polluted by their resonating tones. I focus light on those negative and densely matted energy fields surrounding the physical body, and you are all truly deserving of this gift that brings you into the energy of the Christ mind; it sets you free, and you are all intended to have it.

The circumstances on earth will change, and each person's attitude is an intricate part of this, just as I, Jesus, was an intricate part. Your name may not be in the headlines or written about in books as mine is, but as previously stated each one of you is a gift to this planet, and contributes to the consciousness. If you can understand that every infant, every single soul, incarnating on this planet is affected by every intention, thought, action, and emotion, because every spoken word carries a tone and a frequency, then you will have the greatest desire to change the world, as I did, beginning with yourselves. For example, each time you lose control you contribute to the anger and hatred a murderer feels when he contemplates or commits a heinous crime. This is what I am addressing. All of you are responsible for one another, and accountable for the conditions of the world. As you entered this incarnation you fully understood you would be contributing or diminishing to the light quotient on this planet.

I know everyone has the seed, the mustard seed of awakening, I spoke of in the Bible. Like the mustard seed you have the ability to develop in to an outstanding offspring of the Divine Mind. As you walk the earth and choose to be a divine being, answering the divine call, there is a divine contract, an acceptance on the spiritual planes that you will consciously co-create with divine love. *Whether you are consciously aware of it or not you are all co-creators. It is the experience you all came to earth to have.* Humankind co-creates with the divine energies of earth, and many bring spirit in to matter on a regular basis. It is a splendid gift to enjoy. Wherever you are in life, if you were conscious of this creative ability from birth or if you are only now awakening, your experience will be different. Teach the children that all they do contributes to the earth and humankind. They are either a part of the negative or positive flow or somewhere on the scale between. *Most of you will be shocked to learn that during your lives you are instruments of the lords of darkness, and contributing to their work, as well as being a mechanism of the Divine.* Humankind on a whole is learning to develop more stages within the ego to hold a higher consciousness. This is why my teachings are not understood to the same degree by everyone and the reason I am telling you there are multiple levels to understanding truth. Many consciously choose to put their best foot forward and continue to follow in my footsteps becoming a perpetual spiritual seeker, and in turn teaching others. Be that teacher and the amplification of light to the world, while keeping in mind my work was never intended to pit one against another. I walked with the Holy Spirit in my heart, and as the man Jesus, I was appalled by the conditions of earth. I learned to control my attitude and thoughts, and chose to go to the wellsprings within that became a furnace for the fire of God's flames that guided, directed, and spoke to me. I had unwavering faith, and this needs to be instilled in all of my followers.

If the conditions occurring in your life are in a negative flow, they are not the Will of our Creator. You have a hand in all you think, do, and speak. Once again, you must fully understand you are continually releasing vibrations from your every intention, word, and deed, drawing to you the possibility of certain conditions. You deserve to have a life free of pain and suffering, to be whole and healed. Everyone deserves to feel safe, especially when driving to and from their homes.

If the masses hold gratitude and unconditional love in their hearts the planet will rise in vibration. Then the laggard souls, who believe in hatred, fear, and disillusion, will be banned from entering earth. What is being taught in some nontraditional metaphysical communities is to once again stand together and develop a consciousness that, to some, may seem outside the mainstream. Become a beacon of light and the guardians of this blessed world. It is what I taught my disciples and those who heard my words *to be the chosen ones* who would hold the light of God in such a dark world. I am still a patriot of these teachings. I instill within my followers the love of God, and the tendency to demonstrate love.

Walk the Christed Path of an Avatar

An avatar is an ascended master or Christ returning to earth as a teacher in support of humankind. The majority look upon the lives and accomplishments of the avatars or ascended beings and saints, but do not recognize these same qualities are within them in a hidden chamber in their spiritual heart. To be *born again* in the spirit is to take upon the coat of many colors. It is an opportunity to harness the light of the I Am Presence, the God spark, to reawaken the coding within of the remembrance of a place and an experience beyond matter. It takes courage to walk the path of the Christ Self or higher consciousness. The energy I send to you is for the sole purpose of releasing you, and as many souls as possible from being bound to the earth plane, and living lives of hardship and pain. Yes, many good and kind souls exist; yet not all hearts are completely open, and most have quite a ways to go. Your spiritual gifts and abilities, as wonderful as they seem, are still in the process of development. If you are seriously considering awakening then step in to the empowerment that you are one with our Creator. This alone will awaken you and it is another reason why many turn to me as the Redeemer, the light on their path, the Way-Shower. Everyone has the opportunity to be as empowered and blessed to the height and depth I was.

Dear children, when a human soul develops in to an avatar they work within the Mind of our Creator. At this state of spiritual attainment that personality is occupied with cultivating thoughts to expand consciousness, and assist in developing soul qualities in others. An avatar's mind is crystal clear at this level, and the memories that do not serve them are no longer part of their soul records. All of their accumulated good stays with them, and is actually part of their surrounding light. I did many noble works resulting in good energy that enveloped me. As you read these words, I invite all to surrender now to a higher level of consciousness.

I encouraged my disciples then, as I do now, to develop a deeper understanding of a relationship with their Higher Self and I Am Presence, which emanates from their God Presence. Everyone has the opportunity to become omnipresent, to know future and past events, and to be counseled by divine beings. In this book, I am giving the option for many to be seeded with the gift to drink from the fount of the Host of heaven, as I did. I spent many hours in deep contemplation of my divinity. I communed not only with our Creator, but also with my God Presence. My soul was drawn upward into columns of light descending from my I Am Presence; much like what some of you are now learning to do. At this level, the human soul surrenders its ego identity, but not its uniqueness. Soul takes on the expanded dimensions of its divine soul, and sees its earth life as having a higher purpose as a teacher or as an example for others.

Often during these stages of learning to become an avatar, you, as the spiritual seeker, now an initiate, observe in others what appears to be the action or behavior of young children, which may cause you to want to judge them. And at times the budding master may feel pity for those still spiritually asleep, and have a real yearning to share with them the deeper meanings of life and the truths you are learning in the mystery schools; however, not everyone is ready for these teachings. Therefore, you must be patient, and never forget your behavior is the best example.

The Christos

The Order of the Christos

Happy am I to represent the image of the Beloved to earth, and to also share my essence with each individual, but understand I am part of an order called the *Christos,* and there are a large number of us. The Christos is a frequency of light that forms an energy matrix.

These are levels of consciousness the soul understands more clearly as it passes through the higher thresholds of light. In Biblical days, as in present time, there are many who are consumed by lower thoughts and emotions, such as hatred, anger, bigotry, and envy. Those individuals cannot pass immediately into the purer regions of heaven; instead, they will spend time in a mansion realm before having an opportunity to move on. These planes of reality were created to assist those embodied in the lower circuits in learning different degrees of self-mastery, which is moving the soul toward self-realization. The more qualified light a person draws from the columns of light descending toward earth the deeper their spiritual experiences will be, and the higher their spiritual attainment. I remain a contributor to the light on earth, and as part of the Celestial Christ, I am able to surround this planet with light. I have no earthly ego, and completely love each creation. I hold love in balance, and love everyone enough to respect all your choices.

To be reborn in the Christ light means the spiritual seeker becomes a chalice for the frequency of light, the Christos. As we build this relationship, I ground my energies with you through the Christos. Part of the Christos is the descending light of the Holy Spirit that also holds levels of the Divine Mind. During this process, I work with a band of light codes that are streams of energy, and for a moment you are able to touch the fire essence, which is understood as the Holy Spirit. This power source of energy has also been identified as the Miraculous Body of the Divine Mother. While everyone's I Am Presence is with us in heaven, on earth most continue to stand apart, not recognizing we all exist within this one Body of God. On the surface it may appear as though everything is okay, but humans have more to overcome than they realize. When I closely examine the level you are on, I find unrest and quite a few of you are at war within. The lower thoughts of the mind and emotions humans experience truly contribute to the illusion of separation from God. This is in combination with guilt, trampled emotions, and from fears accumulating in the lower chakras. Most religions do not teach the full spectrum of spiritual ways to get back to becoming whole again in spirit, and the understanding we are never separate from Source and exist in oneness. Religions tried to "protect" the masses from secret knowledge; so much so they eventually lost the truth. (*Vera's comment:* One example of this is some religious leaders thought a belief in reincarnation might cause followers to put off seeking God, thinking they have plenty of time to prepare in a future life.)

As you allow other ascended masters and I to assist you in completing this circuit, and contributing our light to your light will someday lead you to a deeper understanding of the mysteries, and eventually toward self-realization. In moments of communion when you are able to touch spirit you are removed from a restrictive, limiting consciousness, and experience grace, which may feel like a rush of light. Everyone will eventually recognize a standard of living, thinking, and feeling that will ignite the passion within, resulting in a yearning to know thyself; to know self is to know

God and to walk with Him. The deeper your desire to know self, the more love you will experience, and then you will embark on the path mystics and saints walk that lead them to become avatars. In this experience is a superior wealth of knowledge, and many scribes were taught in this manner. Earth languages lack the words to express the enormity of the Holy Spirit. If you crave enlightenment, and wish to gain knowledge of these topics then continue with your studies, be passionate, and you will be guided to the columns of light, and instructed there.

Marriage to the Christos

Understand beloveds, this is not a marriage between a man and a woman. Communion is a sacred gift I gave to all of you. When you receive this sacrament with the understanding of what the Holy Eucharist is you will truly attune with my frequency, and marry your Christ consciousness, and in the end we will dwell in heaven together. This is what is meant to marry the Christ. Over the centuries, the secret meaning of the sacred marriage became misinterpreted to mean a marriage between you, the precious initiate, and Jesus the Christ.

Each son and daughter of the Most High God must eventually be wed to their Holy Christ Self. If this does not occur in your present life then soul will continue the cycle of rebirth until this is accomplished. The sacred marriage of ordained clergy, nuns or you, proceeds with Christ surrounding and raising the person to their Christ Self as they hold the frequency of their Holy Christ Self, which is part of the order of the Christos, and this is who they are wedding themselves to. You do not need to be in the clergy or belong to a religion to have this experience, and occupy this octave of light. Each son and daughter of the Most High God is meant to walk in the image of the Christ, and should aspire to wed to the Christ. Holy vows are a covenant between two people, but in these cases they are vows between an individual and their own crown of glory. They are recommitting themselves to the body of light of the Christ Oversoul. The "marriage" ceremony is intended to be a miraculous time, and this is the reason the holy order vows are sacred. In ancient tradition it meant you took on the visages of your own Christhood. It is an absolutely high-level initiation in to a holy order, and I still perform these ceremonies for all my devotees who attain this level. Your Holy Christ Self holds a prism of light, and when the soul is prepared to receive it by embracing enough qualified light it descends, and marries or merges with its counterpart, not yet ascended. This action raises you into the Christ body of light. During the wedding ceremony a current is passed between the Christed Oversoul and you, as the initiate, which makes the initiate a Christed being. A circle of light is placed in your consciousness and you experience a sense of knowing deep peace, and advance in your understanding of wisdom. It is by holding an intention to become your Holy Christ Self that brings you to this level of experience. This sacrament can be meditated upon.

The chamber in *my heart* I seek to duplicate within *your heart* is an initiation depicted as a flame inside the *sacred heart of Christ*. A silver thread penetrates you from the sacred heart of Christ. This silver thread also aligns with you when making any request of me, and I become your Redeemer or your Savior, which means we are in constant counsel. You do not need to make any decisions apart from the Christ. The Christ walks beside you and all who ask, and this current of light spins a protective energy field. As you move into a union with the higher light you will find more synchronicity occurring in your life, and experience more of a diamond pattern of energy. Teams of angels will go with you, hither and fro, you will never be out of my sight. If you take to this understanding you will enter the secret chamber within self that opens the door to your own Christ nature, where I will greet you. As we work through this process I will charge you with light, and start to clear the mental activity and behaviors that do not serve you in understanding your place in the grand expression of the Godhead.

The wedding garment spoken of in the Bible is a metaphor for the marriage of the divine qualities, the embracing of the Lord's light body, which is the Christ Oversoul to the ascending human soul. As initiates receive the wedding garment they are oversouled by the energies of the Christos. Many light beings within the cosmic realms also hold vestiges of the Christ, and I, the Celestial Christ Oversoul each one of them. In this lifetime, the Christ within you can awaken in a joyful expression of itself. Some have been taught that the divine thoughts experienced during these encounters only belong to me. I assure you, your own vessel of ascension is within reach. In time, those who desire ascension will receive larger and larger emanations of light from the Oversoul. It is a bridge of light called the **A**ntakharana, and it needs to be completed.

Eastern philosophies hold the most accurate meaning of this marriage metaphor than what has been taught in the west. In early religions there were huge debates regarding this, and most of my original teachings were not included in the holy texts. The forefathers of religions did not give or intend to give the true meaning of this divine joining. Instead, they promoted saints and a belief based on blind faith. I took it upon myself to give the deeper truth and meanings to my disciples; therefore, many on the path who entered deep communion with their Oversouls experienced significantly greater independence than was the norm within the clergy. A large number of seekers have memories of me during those times, and there are many with profound wisdom in all walks of life set to accomplish magnanimous things. Please know you are all intended to receive the Mantle of the Christos, and recommit to this holy order.

Communion

The ceremony of the Holy Eucharist known as Holy Communion, the host, the wine, and the bread, does not belong to any religion. Communion is the symbolic body of God working in Christ consciousness, and raised in the energies of the Holy Spirit. I chose to leave behind the receiving of this sacrament of Communion as another reminder of our union, and as a way for the Christ to join with all of you. The ceremony allowed me to share the energies of the Celestial Christ with those who longed to partake of the body of light. The sacrament is blessed with the energies and the love of the Christ for humankind, and I suggest those desiring to stay connected to me do this in memory of our union together, as it is a reflection of a higher attunement I wish to share. The sacrament also represents the coming of the Christ within you, my devotees; so I may raise your level of consciousness. *The wine does not represent the guilt or the blood I shed. It is the gift of life that runs through each of us God has reflected in me.* The wine represents the life-force energy I gave when I descended through a physical body to walk in human form among my brothers and sisters.

Even as the wine is poured in the cup, I am blessing and raising its attunement to the frequency I hold as a divine and celestial being. Each time you eat a wafer and sip juice or wine with the intention of receiving this sacrament of Communion, it represents the body and the blood of the Office of the Christ, and you receive a part of my essence. It is a way of raising your attunement to hold the light codes I give to you, and it is how you actually benefit from this blessing. This satisfies your craving to walk with me on a journey out of the past to a new day, a new light, and be born anew in the energies of forgiveness and grace.

Limiting Thoughts Create
False Prophets and Fear

Separation from Christ Consciousness

M any people use my name without embracing the truth of what I taught. They attempt to keep alive a belief in separation from our Creator that was never a part of my teachings. As each soul descended into the density of matter the illusion of separation from the consciousness of Christ became the outer manifestation the majority still hold. It was because of these thoughts that I came forth with a mission of mercy and love from the higher heavens. A belief in separation stems from not understanding the principle of love, I brought forth. As I already told you, humankind is not separated from our Creator. It is a *sense of separation* from Christ consciousness, the Christ mind, human souls experience; rather, than an actual separation. I opened my heart and brought teachings of divine love that are part of the kingdom of God. The divine soul is quite beautiful in the corridors of light that are my true kingdoms, and exists in dimensional layers in the higher octaves each soul needs to eventually transcend. Once again to be clear, your true soul resides in a corridor of light located in the light bodies that are part of the Higher Self and the I Am Presence.

I did not come to represent a split in consciousness; yet many wars have been fought under my name. I assure you that was not the purpose of my embodiment or the reason I took the cross unto myself. I was continually chastised, and that is not the energy I will have anyone embody. I am a divine being, one who holds the Divine Mind, and sees everyone equally under an umbrella of immeasurable love, and I hold sympathy for those incarnating on earth. *Perhaps the most important teaching I gave to my disciples is to love one another as I love them, for this is the Will of our Creator.*

As people face the pressures of life it is challenging to remain in the energies of the rapture. This is because the descent into matter is extremely difficult for most, but the suffering experienced during an earthly life is a temporary state of consciousness, and for numerous causes it is not fully understood by the human mind. Many lives are shaken for the reason they do not have the degree of mastery necessary, in some situations, to bring about the desired change. Again, this is due to the misconception of a belief in separation from God, which is the belief in a false prophet. The only real truths that need dwell in your mind is God is love, you are divine, the person standing next to you is divine, and so on. My disciples respected me, and there is a big difference between holding reverence toward your teachers and worshiping them. I washed my disciple's feet to teach them humility, and to show them the path of service, which I did by not setting myself above anyone. The limiting thoughts most experience leads to the emotions of not feeling connected, which is not the Will of God. Thoughts and feelings that degrade the soul are the temptations I spoke of.

Once again, I am setting the record straight, Lucifer and Satan were already destroyed when I was in embodiment on earth, and there was no physical devil in the desert with me; the fall of man had already occurred within the levels of the lower mind. This concept is greatly misunderstood and has been used to take the power away from congregations; however, evil does exist in this realm of duality, and there are lower currents of energy, and lower astral characters wanting humans to believe they are Lucifer or Satan. Some are demonic, meaning they choose not to hold light, and these are misguided and dark beings that create havoc whenever they are called upon or unintentionally summoned by humans. A number of them are in physical form, and those that do not have bodies wander the earth plane looking for human weaknesses to prey upon. *Since I have made it clear, Satan and Lucifer are no longer in this universe, recognize most of the negativity emitted is coming from unmanaged minds and hearts held in illusion, and attracting lower creations not choosing to hold light.* These misguided souls cannot enter your columns of light, which are a filter of protection; nevertheless, dark beings still have access to the planet because earth's inhabitants are not yet united. Those who believe that their neighbors, folks in other countries, and people of another race are not a part of them are tragically misguided. You must discern the intention behind the vibration you hold, and what is coming in from lower astral planes. It is what has to be done to resist lower forms of duality still present in regions of the lower creations, such as earth. Each individual has a voice and a choice to move beyond these levels of fear, and oneness is the only way to heal this planet. It is the indwelling mind that lowers its sights below the level of the Christ mind, which consumes people in evil thoughts and deeds. *Temptation should not be blamed on anyone outside of self.* As you acknowledge the Christ within, you take on a new pattern of light, and the desire body proceeds to clear. You now realize you are accountable for all your intentions, actions, emotions, and words, including levels of stinginess, racism, and vulgarities. Each of these tributaries creates a wave pattern, a vibration of frequency, which either pulls the person away from their own Christ nature or consumes them in dark patterns. Those thinking their lives are not whole and complete will experience life that way because of feeling divided, and following a doctrine that is not part of the pervading light of the God Presence. Destructive thoughts and emotions are an imbalance that destroys the family unit, and most of you do not accurately understand the message of my life. Judgments, the illusion of separation, and the misunderstanding of my doctrines, drives a wedge between individuals as well as communities, race, and even countries.

I choose to remain as a watchtower over the development of each of my devotees, and will show them the way home. Truly, everyone is loved by all of us residing in heaven, and you must overcome thoughts and feelings that we are somehow disconnected from each other. The Christ has the ability, through the Immaculate Concept, to live within each person, and I am willing to approach anyone who calls upon me. If you choose to take this walk with me, I will teach you to master yourself, and I will greet you each day and surround you with loving energy. Be very clear about your intentions toward our work together, and know that each time you say my name or contemplate me, you set up a mind-to-mind and a heart-to-heart link between us. Like a homing pigeon you are able to locate me wherever I may be. I will not control anyone, I am only here to guide you, and honor each choice you make.

Within each developing soul is a still point where you are able to not only connect with me, but communicate with your God Presence. A shaft of light expands, and you are filled like a chalice. As I have said, it all begins as a seed within the heart, and when given permission I amplify currents of energy to those calling upon me. All of this prepares you to hold the higher garments of light, the bodies of light, and the frequencies and attributes of your God Presence. When I stand before you, I am experienced as a pulsating light, a higher being of consciousness than yourself. This feeling is somewhat misleading and I assure you it is only temporary, up to the time you too become Christed, and I ignite the flame within you that continually develops until it is burning brightly. You take on the Christ nature for the rebirth of consciousness and embark on a new path. Many experience this as the sensation of coming home, of being reborn or reawakened within the spirit of the Dove energies of the Holy Spirit; hence my title, the Good Shepherd. The Will of God is to penetrate the limited consciousness, the lower mind, the small I, and turn it in to developing tributaries of light and sound, reflecting the divine qualities of those dwelling in the higher heavens as ascended beings, as Christed beings, as lords and ladies, who occupy the heavenly realms. I counsel those who call upon me through their heart, and bring them as far as they are willing to go. Know you would not be drawn to this material if you were not seeking answers, and ready to advance in consciousness.

Spiritual energy is brought into the physical body by developing the spiritual heart, and also through the crown center chakra, which is a spinning vortex of energy that opens like a flower to receive the attributes of God. To fully benefit from this allow Christ, the Holy Spirit, and your I Am Presence to enter your heart as you focus on soul qualities and God qualities; this is the nectar of the fruit from the higher heavens, such as love, kindness, forgiveness, oneness, joy, and laughter. Concentrating on these traits will cause the mind to shift to greater patterns of light, and invisible realms may unveil. The more I am allowed to come to you without dogmatic restrictions placed on me, the more the lower thoughts and the physical chakra system will receive an even flow of light, and be able to develop this embryonic state of consciousness. On this planet, everyone is affected by the memory cells held within the subconscious mind. Working with the Christ Oversoul will correct deficiencies experienced during, what seemed like, the process of separation.

Many of you have been under the illusion of separation from our Creator in mind and soul for such an enormous length of time that even when you are in prayerful states of consciousness it is a challenge to enter the stillness, and connect with the memory patterns that unite you with the Godhead. Nonetheless, there will be a time when many of you will learn to stand side-by-side with me and take on the energies of the Christ. When that time comes, a force of light will descend in the form of the Christ to bless, assist, and encourage you to remain on the path of light and acceptance of self.

Fear Is Limitation

Many have a profusion of fears, and when in a lower state of consciousness, depressed or in a fearful state, all that is outside of you are seen as the enemy. Release those concepts of limitations because fear, in any scenario, is limitation. From ancient writings many were incorrectly taught a negative concept about judgment day. God is not angry with His creations, He does not experience time, and He does not lower His consciousness. These are reasons why I have been instructing you to enter into union with the Divine. Your subconscious memories are like turbulent waters, some are raging, and others seem to be in divine harmony. We, this includes other ascended masters, saints and me, have all spoken harshly during our embodiments, but this imbalance can be changed through divine love and understanding.

Substance abuse was created by limiting thoughts, hatred, fear, and disconnection from the I Am Presence, and the qualified light it supplies you. The planet's current conditions amplify the frequencies that continue to keep the Will of God hidden. This is why earth has such widespread poverty of the soul and the mind. A degeneration of the spiritual forces exists because the masses are not holding qualified light, and there is anger and hatred, pitting brother against brother. Decide to stand apart from group consciousness. Choose not to give the negative ego continuous control over your minds and emotions, and ask for guidance because inside every soul is the key to deeper spiritual understanding. Those who choose to follow the lower currents still available on earth will continue to experience them, and it is why they are not judged. A significant number of people wrestle with these conditions on a daily basis and struggle to receive the greater light. It is why I come forth to shepherd and guide my flock onto the higher path where you learn to sustain my energy field. As we work together we erase the memories that create disturbing thoughts, and prevent you from understanding and attuning with the Will of God. As the Good Shepherd, I will share the wisdom I learned, and we will overcome various hurdles together. One of these is the human defense mechanism that releases anger and a lack of love for self. Understanding the teachings of mercy will help balance these emotions.

The majority of humankind experiences life as a double-edged sword. Most walk earth in a polarized state of consciousness and that state becomes a cross they bear. The underlying thoughts held deep within the consciousness slow the process of elevating oneself in the light. Within these corridors you will find you will know thyself, which is your Divine Blueprint.

Life without Limitation

During my time away from earth as the Christ, I have been expanding on my understanding of my life as Jesus through many of my own higher light vessels. I lived my life then in accordance with the laws, but this could have become a hindrance had I blocked the light from coming within me because of the limitations of some of the belief systems of the day. Similarly today there is plenty of manipulation going on in most of the major religions on earth. I am not saying all are a part of it, but to one degree or another it is occurring. These currents are not the inheritance I left behind. The injustice that continues stems from the belief we are not connected as one, that you are estranged from each other, our Creator, and me. This enormous shift from the true meaning of your divine nature has been taught to the majority creating fear, lack, racism, cast systems, and limitation. The suffering of humankind is never what I asked for; yet there are many sects and religious orders established on this premise. Most egregious is that a large number of religions have made their members a prisoner of punishment, and for this reason they need to be uplifted, not in order to stroke the ego, but to embrace the reality God chose to create to enjoy. In creating life God experienced a level of satisfaction within; similar to when humans choose to conceive an offspring out of love divine. This concept is a reminder of each soul's birth in creation, form, and matter.

The masses have not been properly educated on the sheaths of light surrounding their physical bodies, although some are now beginning to understand auras, and the chakra systems. This is only part of the vast light that has the ability to overshadow you. Veils exist between earth and the heavenly regions where I ascended to. For the majority, the mental bodies connecting to emotional bodies are flooded with disturbing images that would cause concern if you were able to see them. They set in motion a current or a frequency that manifests in the outer world. It is how you create your reality, and many create it in suffering, limitation, and lack. They do this out of fear because of the religious teachings I spoke of that deceptively speak about limitation, call their congregations sinners, and strip away self-empowerment. These doctrines are not accepted in the heavenly worlds, as we are ascended bodies of light. In Truth, you are accountable for your intentions, the thoughts you hold in your mind, what comes out of your mouth, and your actions. Spiritual beings realize that where they place their focus and intention is what they will eventually live, and this alone is rewarding or a punishment. Please watch what you are focused on, and heal the emotions of not feeling connected to our Creator. Instead, concentrate on your heart holding the Christ light, and I will place my hand over your heart, develop you, and watch over you like a Good Shepherd. Do not live in resentment or fear. Outer control must come under the direction of your divine spirit, and not from another, such as your priest, minister, rabbi, monk or reverend. They are there to help point the way, but not to remove your lessons or to take away your individual walk with God or Christ. I brought forth the awakening of the Throne Energies from God to help guide those who felt empty inside and apart from our Creator. That was, perhaps, one of the most important teachings I gave, and by no means were my suggestions ever meant to strip anyone's personal power away. I strongly urge congregations come together to empower and instruct each other, and to offer mutual support.

God entrusted me with the Christians, and with others who are spiritual seekers, and no longer enjoy labeling themselves with that name or with belonging to any organized religion. Nevertheless, I work with all souls that call upon me, whether or not they belong to any religion; we are all one. I also work with numerous congregations of different faiths, and do not judge them as being limited in their comprehension of my teachings. I surround them with the energies of the Christos that will raise them. In time, all who desire will get to know their divine heritage. I come for those who call to me, whose intentions are pure, and governed by love. No matter what path a person may choose, I am always available to everyone who whispers my name, and I do receive the prayers directed to me. Keep in mind I never gave a teaching requiring anyone to be in a church or a temple to receive me, for I am with my spiritual seekers wherever they are. The chapel or temple I spoke about is not a structure outside of you; rather, it is within everyone, within your hearts, your minds, and within the patterns of love. In my absence all places of worship signify the energy of faith. *Being in faith means to know something within your heart, and to claim it as your own before you actually experience it.*

I reside within the threefold flame inside each person's heart, and I came to earth to destroy false beliefs. It is a tragedy that the misconstruing of my words brought about destruction, for that is not the way of love nor was it a part of the truth I embraced. I spoke of the possibility of greatness within each being. The Christ is a momentum of love that reigns supreme, and every soul has the right to have it dwell within. Sheer light is the realm we truly exist in across the veil, and I see the Dove above every person's crown center, and I am waiting to welcome you home when you awaken.

Through love, I instruct my followers on the art of mastery, and there is a long training process each spiritual seeker goes through. Please be patient and do not give up. I will show those who are ready an expanded universe that knows no limitations, a universe governed by divine beings that light up the sky and your hearts, and they do not choose to see you suffer. It is your choice to embody light and the qualities of numerous divine beings that have walked the earth or to take a different path.

"I am the way and the truth and the life. No one comes to the Father except through me" (John 14:6). The true meaning of those words has been lost, and the new meaning is misinterpreted. I was not speaking of me, Jesus, but of the Christos. What I meant is the energy of the Christos is the doorway to the higher worlds where we exist as the sons and daughters of the Most High God, and I am here to show the way to those who are ready. I take my work seriously, and I am with you in those moments of deep sorrow, and when you experience your utmost weaknesses. My followers are always in my arms when they allow me to hold them. Hence, come through me and I will lead my flock to our Creator. I repeat throughout this book that it was never my intention to trap or restrain those who love me in a belief system that honored one creation over another. *Don't ever forget, I was not created differently from any one of you. God did not single out the man Jesus and name him the sole heir to the throne.* This concept has brought about tremendous misery and destroyed a range of distinct kingdoms. I would not have my disciples or my students, then or now, destroy anyone in my name. Favor rests on those who learn to love and hold compassion for the world, and have come to work and share their gifts; this is what I spoke of. Every soul is a pearl of hope that can bring forth this knowledge, and each soul is deserving and worthy of God's love, and of my love. Anyone can come to me, and I will assist them in holding the greater light that is their rightful inheritance. Choose to walk in tune with my frequency and my love, and destroy the old paradigms that hold limitation. Swing the doors of your heart open, and accept all others for who they are regardless of their race, color, gender or creed. I am not saying to invite those who hold malice in their minds into your homes. While no one should be judgmental, of course have discernment for those who cause you or those close to you harm. Know and understand they also have choices to make. They can develop and consciously become the loving beings they were intended to be.

The night of darkness must end now on planet earth. Humankind needs to unite as one group, with one voice, with one God that emits a signal or a frequency of divine love. A large amount of blame is going around. Don't stay a prisoner in lower consciousness and dwell in the realms of limitation, anger, resentment, fear, lack, and blame. Forgive your debtors and those who have debts against you; so everyone can move forward. Start living life with joy. Each day is a ceremony to our Creator, and an opportunity to actively bring the Will of God forward in life.

The Hidden Meaning of the Story of Genesis

Adam and Eve in-to-view

Adam and Eve were originally at the level of their Higher Self, an awakened state of consciousness, and dwelled in a Christ-like consciousness. They represented the soul departing the higher community of light, and were not yet conscious of the role they chose to play as catalyst.

In the Biblical story, when it refers to a deep sleep it meant as they slept their light was diminished, not due to a punishment, but because of their choices. In other words, as they slept they were removed from a higher state of consciousness into the density of earth. The hidden meaning of the metaphor is that the Tree of Wisdom represented Adam and Eve's descent into matter, and as they departed from the kingdom of heaven they began to create the earthly chakra system of the human DNA that, over time, held less and less of the light. They became a part of the consciousness developing on the planet, and no longer felt they were pure in the eyes of God. Thus, the metaphor, "they were no longer clothed in the light and sought to hide." Those evolutions of Adam and Eve did feel shame, but it was because they were no longer in attunement with their purer states of consciousness. During this process they succumbed to the thoughts and emotions that existed in a denser dimension, and it started to pollute their minds. They went through a dimensional phasing, which brought them in to human form; however, at a certain level they remembered the structure of light that birthed them.

As told in the story of Genesis, Adam and Eve were counseled by their I Am Presence whom they called God, and asked if they wanted to continue experiencing a deeper understanding of the human form. At this point they were given a choice to remain in the inner octaves as the overseers or to continue their experience in the denser reality of earth, and the latter is where they chose to carry on their evolution. Understand a part of them did remain with their Presence as the Higher Self. In order to occupy the denser physical forms, like the human, they momentarily stepped out of their sheaths of light, their light bodies, which was their Divine Blueprint.

The story in the Bible evolved over many generations as it was not an automatic descent. Adam and Eve descended through a series of gateways, and their journey is the story of the Divine Monad creating many avenues of expression to experience co-creation by lowering its consciousness through the lower part of the Monad. This is usually depicted as the *serpent of temptation* that eventually lowered the mind, and mis-qualified the light that brought about a different level of consciousness. It is also important to understand that Adam and Eve did not break any laws by asking to understand those denser thresholds that are the dimensions within creation. All was in accordance with the Will of our Creator, and they went through the thresholds with wisdom.

The *apple* signified change, and not a covenant with a serpent; rather, the patterning of a male and female human. It represented a wave pattern that involved them in a new form of co-creation. Adam and Eve descended through a portal, which gave them the human DNA, and they stood man and woman on a more physical plane of existence. They were highly enlightened beings. Originally, they brought with them many advanced techniques from the higher spheres for maintaining spiritual control over the human experience, and it was really through successive embodiments they continued to lose their ability to work with their higher intentions. In those early days their physical forms were quite eloquent, unlike the dense bodies of humans now. Before they chose to descend Adam and Eve did not know of disease. They were in an etheric body and shined with the light of their I Am Presence. They occupied a region in the ethers similar to the etheric octaves of the ascended master's retreats, and they both interacted with the Elemental Kingdoms to bring forth the grand design that would one day be part of the human evolution.

As Adam and Eve took on human physical bodies, and their soul bodies withdrew to their higher light bodies their consciousness once occupied, they began to separate themselves from the image of our Creator. It is essential to understand, like you, they had a choice, and God did continue to work with them and to speak to them.

As they relinquished their light bodies they chose to bring forth more life onto the planet. Even though they continued to receive their instructions from the heavenly realms, they were less and less consciously aware of the spiritual guidance, and the Presence that accompanied them on their journey to this planet. Their human form also provided them with a wonderful opportunity to experience the senses and the human thought system earth could offer as an individualized consciousness. What many do not realize is the senses are not experienced in the same manner within the higher domains of heaven, as on earth. At that point the senses began to evolve in a form no one at that level had ever experienced. Desires became part of the human experience, and people lowered their intentions.

The original patterns for Adam and Eve were called the firstborn. They were the first to experience separation from the higher realms and enter such a minor solar system. Adam and Eve's children expanded into the many lands and populated, and since those early experiments many root races visited earth. There were actually multiple sets of 'Adams and Eves,' and others from these higher realms that came to colonize the planet; they had plans to set up a habitat and seed it. Another way to say this is they had high hopes of seeding a colony of people able to maintain the connections with these brotherhoods and sisterhoods of light they were a part of. This worked well for a time, but there were other races within the universe also experimenting, and the Lucifer rebellion was bringing forth additional types of species learning to develop a lower consciousness on planet earth. It was the comingling of the many species, and *thoughts* that broke apart the pure energies intended to allow those on earth to develop as they did on other spheres, and to hold a structure of light. The mental and astral bodies were not given during those early experiences; they formed later as the Divine Blueprint continued to move into the higher octaves. (More information on mental bodies can be found in the chapter, Templates of Creation, page 90. Please refer to the glossary for more on astral bodies.)

In summary, Adam and Eve set out to establish colonies, and were guided by their I Am Presence holding the structure of vast light. This is similar to the experimenting forefathers who left their homes, and traveled on little wooden boats to find hidden treasures in the new worlds. *Adam and Eve also demonstrated the patterns for unconditional love and the pure image of the Higher Self. This is really what should be taken from the story of Adam and Eve.* A valuable lesson they learned is light is a precious gift from our Creator, and in looking to master their understanding of matter in the process of co-creation, some souls have gone too far by creating regions that are too dense, and hold very little light. Adam and Eve can also be seen as agents of God who chose to bring forth life to a distant planet. They displayed unwavering faith they would emerge the victor in each one of you and return home to the heavenly worlds. Through their proper intentions is this enormous gift given to everyone by these enlightened parents who chose to seed the earth. *No sin is passed down to anyone from these divine beings.* Except the story should say that while they chose to occupy the density of earth they could triumphantly re-emerge, and move up through the columns of light, re-establish their light in their I Am Presence, and merge with the Heart of God.

It is also vital to acknowledge that our Creator keeps His promises. Adam and Eve came forth from the Immaculate Concept, as did each of you, and they were returned to their place of glory and honor. They suffered for a short time on earth, but to them it was like a deep sleep. When Adam and Eve returned to the higher realms there were many gifts bestowed on them for their remarkable work upon the world. They are held with esteemed glory in the regions of the higher kingdom where they once again dwell in peace and harmony in the Eternal Flame.

The Tree of Wisdom and Life

Within each person is a Tree of Knowledge, which is actually the Tree of Wisdom. Still, another name for this Tree is the Divine Monad that contains many trees; more simply referred to as the Tree of Life or the Tree of Wisdom, and this is all part of an arrangement of light bodies. As tangible in their respective regions of heaven as the physical body is to each on earth, there are tiers of Oversouls, like overseers. In the heavenly realms we work with the concept of Oversouls that gather light bodies onto themselves that they experience through.

Christ consciousness can best be understood as a light body existing within the Divine Monad, and holding that level of attainment. This Holy Christ Self is the balanced energy belonging to the Trinity, and the Trinity energies anchor to the threefold flame within the heart. During times of prayer and meditation there is a rhythmic pattern that expands the light within. You are then drawn to experiencing levels of love, and consciousness through your Tree of Life that infuses you with spiritual knowledge. As you make your return ascent, called ascension, through the Tree of Life into the spiritual regions, human souls gain enlightenment to the level of the Christ. Within this tree are higher more developed states of consciousness that take the evolving soul beyond the level of the Christ Mind.

Vera's comment: There are many books that provide a deeper understanding of the Tree of Life you may wish you explore.

Transgressions of Divine Law

Sin and Karma

The teachings of karma were not understood and purposely left out of the written word. In its place the word *sin* was used. On earth the concept of sin is really the action or the intention to hold malice, in its many forms, in your heart and in your mind; where you consciously cause harm to another for the enjoyment or the satisfaction of the experience. Willful wrong deeds destroy the soul, yes, that is possible, and this is the concept behind the word sin, and how the divine image is sacrificed within the outer regions.

Negative karma occurs when choices are made that remove and mis-align you with the greater Will, such as when you destroy relationships, and forget your divine origin. Each creation is accountable unto itself. The deeds, good or bad, are balanced through many lifetimes. The human soul must learn it did not incarnate to destroy another.

The violet flame is a seventh-ray aspect of the Holy Spirit. It is the sacred fire that transmutes the cause, effect, record, and memory of negative karma. It is also called the flame of transmutation, freedom, and forgiveness. Visualize this flame to burn negative energy, and you do this by intending or imagining it flowing through the body, mind, and emotions.

Temptation

All experience temptation, and it is a component of the world of form, and part of being magnetic. Temptations are the thoughts and struggles that pull you away from divine light and divine thoughts. Each intention, utterance, and action, releases invisible forms that are currents and vibrations that amplify tones; be it of heaven and divine love or of hatred and bigotry. At some point these currents and vibrations, now magnified numerous times, will return to its creator. I was speaking about forms of temptation when I said, "A man reaps what he sows." (Galatians 6:7) Jesus called the crowd to him and said, "Listen and understand, what goes in a man's mouth does not make him unclean, but what comes out of his mouth, that is what makes him unclean" (Matthew 15:10). Not only will a person experience returning currents from this life, but from other lifetimes. This is the law of karma.

Understand humans are a framework of an experiential part of their soul. In other words, each person experiences only a portion of their soul in which a small amount of the soul's light is actually in human form, until you have a soul merge or soul fusion within your higher light bodies. (A soul merge or fusion is when the human soul unites with the higher components of their soul's light.) Most humans once existed as more light and in less-dense bodies called the garments of light of the Higher Self. These light bodies connect the human to the Christ mind and to their I Am Presence; however, the light bodies moved into the higher realms when the Higher Selves reduced the amount of flames those on earth were receiving from their I Am Presence. This occurred due to the fall of the human consciousness. (Please check the glossary for a deeper explanation of light bodies.)

Another way temptation occurs is when a person is not benefiting from the qualified light descending from their I Am Presence. Instead, they place themselves at risk by being unprotected and misaligned with layers of astral thoughts and menacing energies.

Be honest and get to the core of what you are thinking, and feeling, what you believe to be your truth, and how these misalignments continue to imprison you. Be willing to take that serious walk with Christ and know I will defend you. In return, I teach you to surrender to God's Will as a working action of love moving through each one of you.

Temptation is also a misuse of the God energies, and strips you of your personal power. Those who lack the soul's light are running on empty, and receive very few pulsations from their divine soul. They are ego-driven personalities, shallow in thoughts and actions, and some are bent on destroying themselves and others. At these stages, few even have a conscience to guide them, as the soul of the human is only but a flicker for many. The mind plays out many scenarios between being a victim and a victimizer. Much is misunderstood about the levels of the mind and the emotions, and how to merge these divine aspects of self that are tributaries of light. This is why faith is such an important part of the philosophies on earth, because it gives people an opportunity to heal. Without the Will of God running tributaries of light through the lower chakra centers, a person cannot truly blend with their own Christ nature. Aspects of life may even appear to be spiritual or divine, but the whole personality still struggles with the ego's control and fallen concepts.

I, Jesus, Truly Did Not Die for Your Sins

In this book, I established there is no "sin," only karma, which needs to be in balance. What you should know of sin is the torment it also brings to the soul, for each is accountable for their intentions and deeds. The idea that I, Jesus, died for your sins is painful and an incorrect concept; yet there continues to be reenactments of my final days on earth, and the imagined intentions behind my acts. I will clarify this once and for all, but I know this is going to be difficult for many to believe these words. My beloveds, earth was a dying world and something dramatic had to take place, but

I did not die for the sins of humankind. What I did do was shift the awareness regarding the ability to take on the Christ mind so others could follow in my footsteps, not to the cross, but my path to a loving God. I took this path onto myself, and it was a decision I made on the spiritual planes.

When you first work with me on the higher spiritual planes and at my home in the city of light, we formulate a plan together. Part of this new plan is I hold the intention of drawing the greater light from within you, and I create a magnetic field of protection around your physical body. In a sense, I carry your burdens for a time because you cannot yet carry them for yourself. This is why religion has taught I died for your sins; however, this is not the proper way to understand the teaching. Once more, what did take place as a result of my journey was a shift in consciousness, and I did absorb some negative karma, and this is why many get confused and believe I died for their sins.

I did not succumb to the negative thinking on your planet, and never focused on sin. Earlier in my life I struggled with the same choices some are making in this lifetime, but I chose to be disciplined in my beliefs, and allowed myself to receive the anointing of my Holy Christ Self. Again, it was actually an honor for me to take on the life as Jesus and accept that challenge. The door to humankind was open within my heart, and it was easy for me to come in and to love all others, and I show no favor to any.

The Symbol of the Cross and Sin

There is an extraordinary amount of focus on the passion of Christ Jesus, and segments of my life have been brought to the forefront. For me, this is a distant memory. I am trying to make myself clear this is not something I want my followers to focus on. If anything, I yearn to uplift them, and take them off of the self-made crosses they have created in their own lives. Yet again, the cross I bore was not for anyone's sins because all are without sin when holding the proper intention. As I told you, I did absorb negative karmic patterns; thus creating a positive shift in the energy returning to this planet. Those were challenging times. I ascended and stood before the thresholds of light, and felt peace in my heart as I departed. I was not afflicted by group consciousness; so as I said, I did not submit to negative thinking. I walked earth at the level of an avatar, an ascended master. This means I did not partake of the conscious in the lower mind, and my mind did not experience those tributaries, as most do. I had mastered a great deal in previous incarnations; thus it appeared as though I stood above all others, but this was only in higher consciousness earned from many experiences. Yes, I rose people from the dead, that accounting is accurate, and I walked among the population as a Christ, and communed with my God Presence, which oversouled me. I gave up my life so those drawn to my teachings may know love, and the glory of the higher heavens. I went before you to prepare the way, and to teach you how to hold the patterns of energy through the path of initiation, and become part of the Holy Order of the Body of Christ.

The symbol of the cross for each one does not have to be a path of sacrifice. The Crucifixion symbolized that those in charge did not want change. This still occurs today, but in other forms of persecution, and many who speak the words of truth *now* feel like the outcasts, and pressured to operate outside the norm of society. *The true symbology behind the cross is it represents the outpouring breath, and the mercy of the Godhead to create change in the beliefs of a dying world.* It is why I chose to incarnate at that particular time as Jesus; who was a bold man for the times. I was outspoken, and had a strong will to create change among the clergy who put themselves above the peasants. I lived during a time when there were vast divisions in class, and it is not what exists in the realms of our Father. It is this consciousness that continues to bind earth in the lower octaves. You are each placed on earth to be in service to each other. To ensure you are no longer slaves to your lower mind, I will assist you in removing the cross.

Catherine's anecdote: In my early training with Christ, I saw myself dressed in a nun's habit, watching Jesus carrying the cross. I ran to him, taking the cross and carrying it myself. He took it back from me and said, "Surrender the cross." It took me years to figure out what he wanted from me.

As I reviewed this chapter, I recalled a time when I was shopping for friends stopping over for an Easter message. There was a cake pan in the shape of a cross I was about to purchase when I heard Jesus say, "Don't make me a cross cake." I told him I thought it was nice, but he laughed and replied, "I really don't want you to make me a cake in the shape of a cross." It was very hard for me to give up this idea, but I did and it really made an impact on me.

What Is Original Sin?

Simply put, original sin is only a concept when someone does not hold their Divine Blueprint. This is because the chakras are holding tones, patterns, pollutants, frequencies, and thought forms that cost the person light. In losing the connection to their divine power the human has less of an ability to awaken during that sojourn, and it is certainly harmful to that soul's evolution; however, the power of God can still awaken within the Creator's original seed thought, and raise that individual.

The concept of original sin continuing from Adam and Eve represents humankind's misalignment with the Godhead, and not with the Godhead being misaligned with humankind. Although, not everyone recognizes they are and continue to be precious creations of the higher realms. Only love is within the heavens. Relinquish all thoughts of inheriting the stigma of sin, regarding Adam and Eve. Instead, hold the thought God blesses each birth and every opportunity to en-soul every person with limitless love and understanding of His divine nature. Original sin can also be understood as straying from the spiritual path, and being placed on a parallel path farther from the light, which is unfortunate, for it brings the person deeper in the experience of duality. Reckless behavior, and by this I mean no regard for your intentions, is a sin against the impending light intended to move through each human being. This prevents spirit, which occupies a light body, from blending and occupying the physical form to purify the thoughts, intentions, and emotions. Sin, the way I am speaking of it, is a separation from the divine, but it is not punishable by an individual's inability to receive the full measure of the love of our Creator. *The Divine Blueprint has never been removed, but people are divided and separated from those parts of self where it is housed.* In many cases, they cannot experience it to the degree of one who dwells at the level of the Oversoul.

God's Grace

Mercy

When you turn your eyes upward and ask for God's love and mercy you perform a wonderful service for self. God does not treat anyone like an outcast nor does our Creator treat you differently than He treats me. This is hard to understand, for most have raised me above themselves. *Remember, all of creation came from the Mind of God, and at the moment of the Immaculate Concept every one of you were in that same state of purity as I am.* I dwelled in the mind of Christ and in the Mind of God, and knew myself to be the son of God. For many souls, I represent the sonship, and as the Son it is my job to remind my brothers and sisters they are also the Immaculate Concept. The human soul can awaken to a deeper understanding of its divine nature, as I taught when I was embodied. I showed deep mercy, and this is part of the legacy I left behind. It is what I will for those who love me; to understand God's grace flows through the circuit of mercy.

Worthiness and Spiritual Practice

Only our Creator truly knows you. It is the bond we each have with God, and no one need try to be in favor with our Father to approach Him; He speaks to all His children. From wherever you are on your path ask God to change or set in motion the process for changing whatever is necessary. When a person invites God to be more present in their life they automatically understand what it means to walk in His favor, for God desires each creation to know Him. For some in this dimension their understanding of God is both masculine and feminine; therefore, their consciousness of God is both Father and Mother, while to others, God is Father.

During spiritual or religious services some people praise God for about an hour, and then linger off the path when they return to seeing life through a limited lens. Consequently, they commence contributing to lower aspects that do not honor our Creator, themselves or me. Those who truly place me in their hearts would not fight with others, and certainly would not slander my name or curse with it, nor go to war in the name of Jesus. I do not need anyone to defend me; I could defend myself if I chose to. At this time, there is a need for me to recode humankind with the frequencies of the Christ mind, which is a part of the Christ Oversoul. The code is the remaining strands of DNA I already mentioned that are not currently present in the human body, and it is the doorway to freedom; however, there are other contributing factors as to why certain conditions on earth continue to exist, and why a being such as me is not appalled. The majority do not hold a stature of light that can be given by the mercy of those who have attained it for themselves. It belongs to all of you and exists in a field of light, but until you move through the subconscious mind, which holds onto levels of regret, anger, hatred, bigotry, greed, and jealousy, it is not yet attainable. This is why I offer my mercy.

As I look upon the residents on earth, I understand why many continue to succumb to lower energies, and I recognize the painful experiences they are creating, but are not aware of. I see dark matted clusters in the energy fields around their physical bodies that contribute to imbalances, and shatters them, and I direct sparks of light to those patterns. Many are like a tattered cloth in need of repair, and this is some of the work I do when called upon because

I honestly love, and embrace every one of you. In my eyes everyone is pure, but misled, and this is why I offer my assistance to anyone who calls upon me. Start by feeling worthy and accepted by me. All of you must open your hearts, and ask for knowledge, and that will create the opportunity to return to a peaceful state. In this process you and I initiate our walks together. Then the Christ, the I Am Presence, a council of teachers, and I, assist in separating you from turbulent emotions and thoughts, while quieting them. Beneath everyone's feet is a frequency field that expands around them, and during this process the low-density tones and states of confusion are dissolved. This permits me to encapsulate each of you in light tones, and as you take on additional light patterns the healing begins. A scientific approach also explains this work, which has to do with the recoding of DNA from the God Source. Though for now, I will enfold you in matters of the heart, and focus on your learning to hold purified thoughts of consciousness. In essence, you are allowing the higher components of your soul to contribute more light to your life.

The surface of earth is where one level of your consciousness resides. Available to every individual are wiser states of consciousness. This statement is the truth, but will be somewhat shocking to some and it is what I shared with my original disciples. As Jesus, I was able to view the earthly world, as well as the world my I Am Presence existed in, and you have the same potential. This is why I knew my true kingdom and righteousness was not of earth.

The Altar of Forgiveness

The altar of forgiveness is energy I brought forth to the earth as a way for you to atone, forgive, love, show mercy to others, and to self. Sometimes the notion you can receive absolution is what it takes for you to get you are indeed a divine being.

Always come before our Creator and me with respect for yourself. You all need to become a purified vessel, a house for me to occupy. This means coming before the altar of forgiveness, not as a sinner, but as a child in his or her innocence, and as a creation of God asking to be shown mercy. As I have explained, mercy is a gift from God. Most do not yet hold the degree of development it takes to attain mercy; therefore, our Creator extends it to those who ask.

Sometimes the choices you make are not in accordance with God's Will for your life. This does not mean God and I do not love you; it is just that some of you have more work to do on forgiving others, and yourselves. The man who beats his wife and children, and then asks for forgiveness is forgiven. However, if he continues that behavior he reaps the returning effect of his actions even though God loves and forgives him, and looks upon him as holding the Immaculate Concept of his original blueprint before he departed from the higher heavens.

On this planet, there is much mis-creation and misunderstanding. The wars are fought because you do not see yourselves as belonging to one family, one mind, and one magnanimous sea of love. What I see is the majority of souls still have not been able to develop the levels of love, compassion, and forgiveness for each other that is necessary to carry them to the grand heights where I am. You must rise to the vibration of the light of consciousness within self to birth the higher Will, which was given to you in your moment of individualized consciousness. Each of you is a sovereign being within the consciousness of our Creator, and equal to me. The suffering on this world must end, but first it needs to end within each individual and within each mind.

Penance and Forgiveness

As the Body of Christ, I sit on the right side of God, and I do not dole out penance or punishments. They are forms of ridicule, and I do not scorn the sons and daughters of God. These customs became popular in the centuries after my crucifixion, and are teachings I do not adhere to. I stand before humankind as a representation of the flame from the Heart of God and as an elder brother able to attain the Christ light; therefore, beating oneself, and suffering does not please me in any way.

Even while on earth, I did not give out penance, not even to those I healed or worked with. Penance was developed by those believing their followers were unworthy, and attempted to keep them in the grips of feeling like a sinner. My messages reflect the love of God and my love for all. My words were lovingly given so you may gain the understanding that the people I healed desired and deserved to be treated with respect, and without judgment; as all desire and deserve to be treated. I did not speak of going in a closet or climbing a mountain top, and cutting oneself off from others, for my path was a path of service. This is the information I taught my disciples.

Originally, penance was not considered a form of self-abuse or punishment. It was a technique to blend with the indwelling spirit, and be raised in the light. Penance was really given as a form of receiving God's mercy through prayer, and asking to have consciousness purified. It brought light to the consciousness, and a clearer pattern of energy to face within self those aspects that needed to be looked upon, altered, and refined. Penance was actually a concept to bring about the current of forgiveness within spiritual men and women.

I also spoke of forgiveness and mercy, not punishment. Opportunities are always available to examine your thoughts, concepts, and intentions, and to gain an understanding of the energy that follows the currents you put into the world, and to see if there is spiritual growth, not spiritual unworthiness. When I counsel the heart it is a time for the inner master to help you, the spiritual seeker, in bringing forth the love, grace, and mercy, of our Creator to assist you in expanding your light, your individualized developing consciousness.

Although penance was not intended to be a form of punishment, each time structure comes in it occurs; by structure I mean in the form religions classify sin. Structure has many forms upon earth, but sometimes it is the restrictive mind that cannot bend or connect to an open heart. Each case I hear is somewhat different, even though the action may have been the same. Understandably, some structure is needed to advance the human race, but not all structure, political or religious, has benefited society. For example, it is the damaging stigma that continues on for the person long after they have paid for their mistake. Although, it is important to say here, I do believe in accountability for one's actions. Each divine heart coming before our Creator or me has the opportunity to receive mercy, for by receiving mercy they learn to give mercy.

Sacrifice

When I spoke about coming before the altar of God in the form of a ceremony, I did not mean sacrificing any life. Do not harm yourself or others. I abhor and condemn the use of any living sacrifice, including all animals, as a means of forgiveness and penance. These issues of control occurred because of the doctrine of sacrifice practiced before and after I embodied as Jesus. I do not condone this doctrine. In those days, it was difficult breaking through the minds of the clergy, and explaining to them God did not desire to see the slaughter of animals as a pathway to the heavenly kingdoms. Those who would listen to me, I immersed in greater light, and in a deeper understanding of the divine mysteries. *God created every aspect of life, including animals. Why would He need to have a part of Himself sacrificed on the altar to forgive another?* That is not the path of divine nature, and it would not create balance in any realms of God's Kingdoms. What I taught was on the perimeter of a belief system that was quite old, and this teaching is misunderstood and misused, even to this day. Respect every part of life in all the kingdoms, and come to an understanding it is through balance your world is made whole.

It is time to prepare the mind to accept that penance is not sacrifice, but a time of forgiveness of self, a time to amplify God's love through all hearts, and asking Him to uplift everyone. I brought forth a new way of entering a sacred union with God by going to a sacred space within self, and asking God or Christ, one on one, to raise you to a higher state of awareness. Some experience nagging pains eating away at their soul's light, if this is the situation, go within and focus on my words; they will bring forth a deeper understanding of greater knowledge and wisdom, taking you, the spiritual seeker, to a place of peace and balance. Many lessons still need to be understood by the developing ego communicating to the personality. Although, lessons may come with less of an impact if there is a willingness to grow from spirit guided experiences that direct soul in developing with less distortions. This is part of the energy of redemption that comes from the seat of mercy.

Understand, my beloveds, you all are forgiven as soon as you ask, and forgiveness of self is also necessary; otherwise, the one asking might not vibrate high enough to recognize their prayer for forgiveness is answered. That would be a shame because forgiveness prepares the personality for the next level of opportunity to deepen its understanding with its I Am Presence and our Creator. During prayer or times of deep sorrow many masters assist the developing personality in recognizing the importance of right thought and right actions. If those seeking me understood I am present in their lives and continually offer guidance, they would freely speak to me, and commune more with our Creator. *God blesses and raises each soul who has chosen to love and bless creation. However, those who choose to prey on others are sealed within a limited field; so they can understand what it feels like to have those dark experiences returned to them. Some have called this harshness a punishment, when in fact, it is a self-created state of the lower mind involved in co-creation at that level of frequency. It is unfortunate a large number of souls reside at these levels.* Too many upon earth and in the lower astral planes are not yet choosing love, and respect as a vibration they desire to hold within self. Instead, they create an environment where they exist with others who also choose the expression of limited light reaching them. At any moment, a resident of these realms can ask for knowledge or a rebirth in to greater possibilities to understand their divine nature. This request is usually granted because higher states of consciousness are always given to those who desire it. If you choose to pray for those souls then imagine shooting arrows of light toward them, and this will assist them in asking God for an opportunity to grow out of their current stage of consciousness. Again, I am mentioning there are souls existing in different levels of learning, and some have almost no light available to them that will hold a conscience, but this does not mean they cannot ask to be made whole once more.

The *etheric duplicate*, if it were visible to human sight, is a mirror image of the physical body located in the etheric or astral realm. While incarnated you appear in the astral and etheric realms the same as you are in your current life. This is because the ego is still attached and you have not yet ascended. Limitation in consciousness has been occurring on earth because the etheric duplicate, at this stage of development, has many astral and mental bodies to clear. Prayer and the light must first connect to the etheric duplicate, then to thoughts and emotions that must be cleansed in a higher light. Actually, the etheric realm is where healings begin before they are realized in the physical matter body. Another way to understand my previous statement is the lower chakras—energy centers located within the etheric duplicate—are not open to the flow of higher light, which prevents the expansion of thoughts, consciousness, and blocks healings; this is also why many do not have an aura of protection around them. The lower astral plane surrounding earth is supported by various acts from beings such as those holding lower vibrations like violence, and can cause harm to themselves, and others when they find a "home" in a weakened mind, and in unbalanced emotions. I cannot impress upon you enough to deepen your desire to receive your Divine Blueprint; this is also when humans know they are a son or daughter of the Most High God.

My will is for everyone studying this material to have a true understanding of the Christ energies I held as I walked earth. Without forgiveness of self and others there is no measure of mercy that will stimulate the required healing process. *You cannot love our*

Creator without understanding He exists within all creation, and this includes every single face you look upon.

The Ruby Ray

I hold frequencies within me called the ruby ray, and it is a pattern of light I release from my heart. I will give you something now. Instead of focusing on suffering and penance, allow me to share this ruby ray from my heart, and I will seal you within my love, and within my Presence. Humankind was always intended to be free. No one ever chooses to incarnate and then suffer. When you embrace these concepts and enter the columns of light the ruby ray will expand the range of frequencies I hold. Move the ruby ray into your heart, but also see it moving through the whole body, and your emotions. It will assist with clearing disappointment from the mind and heart, and help dissolve the lower consciousness; so you can dwell in the divine light, as it is part of the miraculous body I hold. It also allows me to align with you, and for us to feel a deeper connection. Please remember, when I come knocking at your door, I will only enter when you give me permission.

Atonement

Atonement to me is not a debt I am waiting to receive, and I now give absolution to anyone holding this perception. This thought process was not part of my original teachings; it came after the Holy Wars. I honored the beggars, lepers, and those from all walks of life; I never stood apart from anyone. I treated each one as my family, for in them I saw myself. What I aspired to create was the stirring within causing the door to open, and perhaps they would ask a series of questions that would take them beyond their current beliefs. Back then, there was a great deal of discussion and drama about bowing down to those who were seen as holding a higher position. I did not indulge in such behavior nor did my followers.

My instructions were for the pure of heart that, for a very long time, had been beaten and held down by a caste system.

Each person's divine soul is somewhat restricted because it does not fully interact with its earthly personality until it, the personality, reaches a certain level of spiritual enlightenment. This occurs since most humans do not have the full measure of higher light bodies attached. In this time cycle my message of atonement is not that I believe you are sinners; rather, I am attempting to open a gateway because the human ego and the teachings familiar to the majority have placed you beneath me.

The Holy Spirit is capable of completely filling the mind and heart with a higher consciousness. This is a process we go through together. As people strayed off the path they had regrets; subsequently, there needed to be a means to have them accept that they could receive forgiveness, be atoned, and metaphorically be washed clean and welcomed back in the fold. In most of your past and present lives your emotions get trampled on; therefore, it takes the concept of being forgiven to open your mind to the understanding you too are divine. God speaks to all who call upon Him, and always raises them to the oneness we eventually share.

Prayer and meditation was introduced as another way to atone; so humankind could comprehend the meaning of unconditional love and forgiveness. Through wisdom you will learn to receive these gifts from our Creator and feel justified in knowing you are also the son or daughter of the Most High God, and in whom God is well pleased. In the process of evolution you will draw your strength from me, but do not see me as a mediator between God and you. Quite honestly, this concept is incorrect, *for each soul stands as close to our Creator as I do.* See in me a portion of yourself, of what all of you are intended to become.

As the Christ, I oversoul my followers and I am generous with my gifts, and as the Redeemer, I am also the gate those leaving earth pass through. In time, through the energies of atonement and forgiveness, group consciousness will be in attunement with my limitless body of light. The Celestial Christ is the divine nature of the spirit that pervades all living consciousness, and as Jesus, I said, "I am the gate; whoever enters through me will be saved. He will come in and go out, and find pasture" (John 10:9). It is within each of you to allow the gate to remain open or closed. I bring forth a variety of gifts from my kingdom to earth, but the exceptional gift is to be oversouled by your personal Holy Christ Self, which is the bridge to heaven. Mother Mary and I work hard to maintain the Christ light for all spiritual seekers. We clear a path and take you by the hand through an immense gateway of light, and you will come to know the truth lies within.

Mother Mary on Prayer

The Power and Importance of Prayer

I was blessed to be the mother of Jesus. As the Blessed Mother, it is important I teach those who call upon me about prayer, which is a tribute to their divine nature and an opportunity to gather more light unto them. You obtain light and grace through prayer work needed for your next experiences, and this facilitates your receiving your divine image. Prayer, in the manner I am discussing, is time spent with God to uplift you and not a period of embracement; however, it is when you commune with your higher soul's vibrations, your I Am Presence, and with our Creator. Many come to me in prayer with tear stained eyes because the poverty of their quality of life, be it health, the spirit or finances, has left people feeling defeated. The human condition, in its many forms of despair, was created because earth has been subjected to undeveloped rulers or overlords during many cycles. These overlords have allowed satanic-type cults to develop here that opened the door for lesser beings demonstrating fewer light currents to occupy the hearts and the minds of those incarnated. This is why the higher soul does not occupy human thoughts or emotions before a soul merge occurs. To reiterate, your soul and spirit reside in a corridor of light located in the light bodies, which are part of the Higher Self and the I Am Presence. Through this corridor of light fragments of purer qualities of thoughts and feelings merge with the personality traits held during your embodiments. It takes a highly developed human being to draw down and merge with the qualified light that is the higher soul or your understanding of spirit. The ego has replaced the attunement you had with your Higher Self and numerous light bodies. You, as a developing soul, experience numerous awakenings before reuniting with the Christ Oversoul; this is the work of the Christ. The soul merge is not your final destination, but it is the journey to understanding self as the beloved returning to the God systems, which are filled with joy.

The terms in this book should not cause anyone to close their mind. Allow the words to resonate at the altar within. In other words, an altar should always represent the purity residing in you. The altar is to be understood as an opening to a corridor of light your personality uses to bring higher components from your soul's essence able to contribute to your heart and mind. This is the same concept of going on a spiritual pilgrimage. "See" the person you intend to become and imagine being around people you most like to spend time with who will honor and respect you, and then proceed on this journey in good company. This process will create a shift and assist in raising the experience and the light within.

There are many levels of understanding, even in the scriptures. Your Higher Self has the ability to reveal expanded understanding and indepth wisdom, which is meant to bring knowledge to you. The journey spiritual seekers are taking in the thresholds of light follows in the footsteps of my son, Jesus. This still needs to be accomplished, and if this were not true humankind would be with us now, and holding a refined body of light. Far too many people have a poor self-image making it difficult to carry the filaments of light coded in the higher components of the soul, and this affects their ability to co-create. In other words, they don't always have enough light to bring their creations in to manifestation, and this further lowers their self-image. I, the Blessed Mother, have visited earth on many occasions to reinforce God is love, and He has not withdrawn from the lives of His creations. Your suffering is never what our Creator wants from His creations. Celebrate life and commemorate even the smallest joys. This is how you return your love to our Creator, and ask that all hearts and eyes be opened.

I have several cities of light where I reside and continue to contribute my work for the good of earth. The one I am sharing with you now is located in Italy, beneath Vatican City, in the tributaries of light that exist in a higher dimension, and there is a seal one can pass through to gain entrance to my chambers. I chose to have a home there to support my son's work, and to oversee the pillars of light anchored to the earth at that location. This is why many experience visitations from me, and why I remain close to the planet during this important cycle. The sacred sites where I appear hold tributaries of light, and connect to power sources at my cities of light. I do this as part of my healing work with the planet. I remain with the faithful, and assist them with handling the pressures of their lives. I hold the original Divine Blueprint of a pure mother's love for everyone who calls upon me, and has an open and receiving heart. I bow before each of you, for within you, I see your illumination, which is the seed of God in the higher soul that exists within the light bodies, making the soul merge the true blessing. Without a soul merge humankind will continue to prey upon one another in response to savage energies that are still part of the group consciousness connected to earth.

I am veiled with the light of God. For those on a Christian path or if you hold a belief in me, I am present during the christening experience when the veil of light is placed around you. The essence of the Divine Mother is given so all of you will know God always remains with Her children.

Catherine's anecdote: Mother Mary explained that she always appears wearing a blue veil to represent her work as a member of the Order of the Blue Rose; an order she says originated from the Order of Melchizedek. Mother Mary speaks about the Order of the Blue Rose as an ancient healing order she, Jesus, and others have brought back to earth. In 2005 I was initiated in to this Order of the Blue Rose and given permission to initiate others. Mother Mary told me the image on her miraculous medal connects those using it in prayer to this healing order. I see her as she appears in Medjugorje, and Mother Mary told me Jesus and her have several bodies they can appear in. Mother Mary also told me when Jesus would first come to me he will look like the picture I had in my home; the one with his face turned to the side. Since I did not grow up with that image, I asked why? She told me that was the closest image to how he actually looked as an adult. The likeness I am speaking about is titled, The Head of Christ, by the artist, Warner Sallman. Only on a few occasions did he look different from that picture. By the way, Jesus has a wonderful sense of humor, is usually laughing and filled with joy.

When I began my path with Mother Mary in 1990 she took me to her sanctuary, which is a city of light. I was raised Catholic; therefore, when Mother Mary first began to appear to me, I was confused and kept falling to my knees. She would pull me up and say something like: You are here now, and I don't want you to kneel before me in worship. Then she said, "Now, I need to show you what I do with the prayers we receive." She told me I needed to learn this because I was now able to work as an assistant in her sanctuary for her work with earth. I saw all the energy of these prayers before me, and Mother Mary went on to explain how she and the saints divide the prayers. Many prayers are answered by the angels, some Mother Mary personally handles, and other prayers continue beyond her sanctuary to be dealt with in the higher positions of the Godhead. Mother Mary assured me all prayers are heard and answered to different degrees. To decide the destination of each prayer and to choose who acknowledges them has to do with the intention, devotion, and depth of each prayer. During that training, I remember I often saw Mother Mary seated at a table counseling people who had asked for help.

The Rosary

For those who were taught they were sinners and in need of for-giveness, I gave the Rosary to present a way for them to pray. *You, my blessed children, are not sinners.* It is also a gift I chose to give to those who are comfortable with daily repetitive prayer, and a means to teach them God is forgiveness, love, and mercy. The Rosary is one path that brings those to my inner sanctuary that are requesting my assistance. You are beautiful creations cloaked in innocence and darkness, but many are also awakening to the call they hear within. Saying the Rosary in conjunction with holding a gaze on the three-fold flame removes the person praying from bondage, and releases a magnificent light to them from their I Am Presence. Our messen-ger Catherine and a few who work closely with her are comfortable with saying the Rosary; however, many are not, and that is okay as long as they pray in their own way.

I will continue to escort those who choose the path of the Rosary or direct prayers to me. On earth there is a saying, "Birds of a feather fly together." To have the Immaculate Virgin Mary as your friend, your mentor, and your mother, means you fly where I fly. Let it be written and let it be done. Each is cherished within my heart.

Catherine's anecdote: I have had many interesting experiences pray-ing the Rosary. Twice Mary Magdalene came and prayed the Rosary with me, and then took me to see Mother Mary who was surrounded by flowers and angels. Mary Magdalene told me angels always accom-pany Mother Mary, even when she visits earth. While praying the Rosary on another occasion an angel came and said, "Catherine, do you think Mother Mary prays the Rosary?" I told the angel I never thought about that, and I asked, "Does she?" The angel replied, "No, she prays directly to God." This reminded me of a time when I first began receiving visions of Mother Mary, and I was concerned she was a dark lord trying to fool me. Mother Mary told me to keep praying to God and when she came again I would know He had sent her to me.

Prayers and Chants

Prayers from all sources are welcome by God, and can be recited by anyone. Many ways are available to open a line of communication with the divine realms besides pray, such as meditation, contemplation, chanting the sacred names of God, chanting Om or holding a focus on the flame within through a strong desire to know self, and that is my greatest wish for everyone. *Strive to know self. Even beyond the limitation of what a particular sect or religion deems to be its highest teaching, and ask to know what cords of love are intended to flow through your soul from our Creator. Set no limit of what is handed down. This is a bold statement and a daring choice that can raise the human soul above the boundaries of the norm.*

At times, my messenger listens to some sacred Sanskrit words thought to be a Buddhist chant, Om Mani Padme Hum. If this method of prayer or any other appeals to you, begin to hold these frequencies within your spiritual heart. Whether a person chooses to walk with the Beloved, say the Rosary or chant a sacred Sanskrit tone, understand it is a means of asking for and receiving more light that will assist you in resonating to higher, purer, sound currents.

Vera's comment: Om Mani Padme Hum is pronounced as *ohm mah nee pahd may hum.* This Sanskrit term has a Hindu background, and it is said the Buddhist changed the pronunciation slightly. It is believed to be such a sacred chant it cannot be properly translated, and merely seeing it in print has a positive effect on the reader. This chant is primarily used in preparation for meditation or in adoration for communing with our Creator. It may also be recited as a sacred prayer, and anyone can use it to connect to a higher power.

Open Your Heart and Pray

During the days when I walked the earth, as in current times, there are people who choose to overindulge in the lower mind activities, such as drinking, violence or sexually related indiscretions; yet they never utter a prayer. They develop a habit where they over-stimulate the lower senses or pray so verbally it is mindless empty words, and not deeply felt within. They then experience feelings of isolation, anger, and limitation, which are all fear-based. *Fear comes from levels within the personality that have not yet dissolved enough of the lower astral energy fields.* These are warning signs that folks are not close to God.

As Jesus, I prayed deeply, opening my heart, mind, and ears. I not only prayed to God, but I also listened for His answer. God speaks to His children, but you need to have an open heart and develop the hearing aspect within self. While most prayers are primarily centered on immediate needs, concerns should move beyond a limited view of reality currently seen as friends, family or loved ones, expanding your intentions to include ways to improve the world. This causes a shift in the personality to now be guided by the divine soul, not only by egos, placing you in alignment with your Christ nature that sees all on the planet as connected, and an intricate part of each solution. All beings are part of the Godhead and affect the world as a whole. Thoughts that not everyone is a part of creation are what caused slavery and caste systems. This form of thinking brings forth rivers of tears, and does not serve the messages I brought. Nor does it honor anyone when images of separation are created. Prayer was introduced to the inhabitants of earth as an opportunity to be counseled from above. During prayer, light from the Holy Spirit is focused on those praying, and also to the souls or situation the prayers are directed toward.

Not all, but the majority who call upon me have challenging existences. Some are involved in lives that stem from tragedy or are filled with anger, jealousy, greed or they are under the influence of substance abuse. When you call on the Christ, I move close, and draw you up through the energies of the threefold flame within the secret chamber of the spiritual heart center. I develop within you ribbons of light and enhanced understanding. I also charge you with light from my sacred heart, which is a pattern of love from our Creator, and I deliver it to all who make the call. I teach you, step-by-step, to overcome the conditions of earth. You hold onto me, and I hold onto you, and I start clearing your thoughts and emotions. Taking on a body of flesh created levels of experiences people, as divine spirits, were not familiar with or prepared to undertake. This brought about the need for an ego to be part of human thought. In time, the forces of light intended to guide humans through this journey began to disintegrate, and the lower mind penetrated the mental activities. These frequencies took hold, and the memory of who you really are did not dissolve, but became veiled or hidden from most. This subject I am speaking about right now is vast in its understanding and application. I recommend those of you interested first learn to hold the intention of discovering yourselves as a divine creation of God. Hold that thought for several weeks or several months, allowing the brotherhood and sisterhood of Christ to deepen your understanding of this concept before continuing your studies.

Negative karmic patterns delay the progress of the human soul returning to heaven, and this is an important teaching that was lost in the shuffle. You cannot just bend your knees, bow your head to pray, ask God or Christ for forgiveness, and then return to the same low energy patterns of destructive intentions and behaviors. I spoke about learning to know self, and going within to discover what your deepest thoughts and feelings are. If there is negativity in your lives, see prayer and forgiveness as tools to release it once and for all. Prayer is intended to connect you to your divine soul, your spirit, to God, and it is an opportunity to transmute lower energy. Your higher soul qualities open the heart, calm the mind, and bring about healing, and prayer becomes the open door that makes it possible to be aligned with the higher realities called the heavens. As you pray radiant light surrounds and protects you. My blessing is always that those who ask will receive a fresh start, a new beginning. Prayer is an opportunity to dismantle the old thought forms, and regain balance and authority over life. Prayer has been called the armor of Saint Michael the Archangel, and when you pray; indeed, he and a team of angels and guardians do come to your side.

Take time daily to commune with our Creator; prepare to be still and listen for God's reply. Trust the impressions received during meditation and prayer, and "expect" answers to your requests. Prayer is not meant to be strenuous. It is a form of surrender to the governing powers intended to oversoul you, and they are able to see life situations from a higher vantage point; so they can direct you through what may appear to the conscious mind as turbulent waters. After praying feel as if the line of communication is open between you, God, and your I Am Presence. See this relationship continuing and intensifying, bringing that energy to all parts of your daily experiences, as this will strengthen your ability to remain within the higher currents of light. While in prayer it is important to feel grounded; that the prayer anchors you to the earth. If you feel yourself becoming disconnected, be still, take several deep breaths, and then ask for guidance and direction. The more you practice the more you will develop trust that there is a divine essence within that intends to take action, and a solution is on the way.

The Sign of the Cross

Many make the sign of the cross when they pray; yet they do not realize this is a blessing, and it does not belong to any religion. When demonstrating this sign you are attuning to the Trinity energies and asking our Creator for a blessing; be aware this gift is received each time you make the sign of the cross. It is also an occasion to ask our Creator to increase your understanding concerning areas of your life you wish to improve.

The sign of the cross is performed while simultaneously reciting the following prayer: In the name of the Father, the Son, and of the Holy Spirit, Amen.

First touch the right hand to the forehead as you say, *In the name of the Father,*

As you touch the solar plexus, which is located midway between the navel and the base of the sternum say, *the* son,

As you touch the left shoulder say, *and of the Holy,*

Touch the right shoulder and say, *Spirit,*

End by reverently putting both hands together in the prayer position. (Putting your hands together actually activates the threefold flame in the heart.)

And then say, *Amen.*

Removing the Fear of Death and Judgment, and Uncovering the Mystery of Ascension

Death and the Heavens

I f you and your loved ones live a life devoted to love, and make a conscious effort to understand your intentions toward the world, then no one need fear dying or losing someone, since all of you will go to a better place. The heavenly realms are beyond the firmament, which is a veil that separates the heavens and earth. This is a place of divine love where all the residents share in the beauty of creation and live in joy. After leaving the planet, many souls enter thresholds below those higher states of consciousness. They enter etheric regions close to the earth that are a familiar frequency to what they just experienced causing them to reincarnate to learn lessons not understood in their last lives. Few souls go directly to the higher heavens because they have not yet developed the ability to unconditionally love all of creation or they did not complete the settlement of their debt for any negative frequencies they contributed to earth's patterns. Until they do, they cannot cross the higher gateways called *the ascension of the light*, which are the true heavenly worlds I spoke of; however, between the higher heavens and earth are many beautiful resting places to enjoy and spiritually grow. All who love Christ will be with Christ; I will continue to teach my followers, and my past, present, and future disciples, and prepare them for the higher heavens. Some souls reside in the mid to upper astral worlds, while there are those who choose to enter the quite dense lower astral regions because they do not recognize the creative force behind an unjust mind. Others have refused the righteous path, and there are temporary places inhabited by such souls who decide not to respect life. Teachings given to humankind have understood the denser realms as part of a lower astral plane called the purgatory worlds, but they were not created by God who loves every creation; rather, by the negative flow that exists within souls choosing to become a part of its creation. Also, some souls are trapped between earth and the lower creations, but this is of their own evil doing. Many times these personalities have distanced themselves from their soul's light or the emanation of God within, and they ceased to evolve; however, they do eventually dissolve back to Source. Consequently, prayers are needed to ease the cause of this confusion.

Simply put, you enter a region of similar vibration to what you held when you crossed over from earth, and there is separation in those realms. In other words, if you have a selfish disposition, you will reside with those of like nature, and not co-habit with generous souls. If a criminal is not remorseful, and continues to hold malice toward others, then he too will dwell with those of similar character. On the other hand, if you are a person of integrity that chooses love and service, you will abide in a much lighter region where others share your qualities, and you will have earned positive choices, and experiences. Also, there are always opportunities in these realms for education. For instance, if the desire is strong enough souls can continue to rise in the vibration of spiritual energy and wisdom, and make their ascension.

Many leaving earth continue on in their former life expression before they take on a new embodiment, and this is why death is not difficult for them. Besides, the human soul is somewhat of a memory bank at the moment of death, and it takes several months of earth time before the new arrivals are ready to make these types of decisions. For a while they get an opportunity to refresh themselves, but they can also experience *the call* in that dimension. In the mansion realms souls receive support, and assistance in completing the required education to advance in gaining enlightenment to make their ascension through a higher portal, and will not have to return to earth or another purgatory world.

One cause of earth's cataclysms is, on occasion, when groups choose an opportunity to be removed from earth, and brought to a protective zone of light in the fourth dimension to prepare for ascension. However, the transition from one plane of reality to another through the path of a disaster should not be looked upon as a gift, for only in rare cases, when the soul is misaligned in the human experience, does it prefer this as a form of departure. *A popular belief is that everything happens for a reason, but is important to understand that accidents do take place.* (Please refer to number eleven in the chapter, Christ Answers Frequently Asked Questions, for more discussion on this topic.) There are times when a soul will open to a particular karmic pattern, but does not wish that experience and will choose to be part of a mass exit. Once the soul has left in this way it works with teachers in learning to see its karmic patterns, and what opportunities are next. It is best not to judge such events since you do not have the soul records of those leaving through disaster to verify their soul's motivation. The shock to the system from a sudden death due to an earthly disaster is sometimes difficult, but the souls who meet the karmic requirements to gain further enlightenment do have a joyful experience. For others, sudden death can be frightening because they do not recognize they have physically passed since they appear as they did when in human form, and they have the same thoughts as before they died. In the moment of clarity about their situation some souls realize how fragile life is, and this creates sadness because of the sudden separation from those they left behind or from things they no longer have, and they suffer such a sense of loss that many sometimes experience an urgency to reincarnate. Nonetheless, there are a wealth of wise teachers, and masters assisting souls in making decisions when transitioning from the earth plane to the dimensions not visible to earth. Most that cross over, due to disasters or by natural causes, choose to rest between lives. (Not often, but some people do experience warning signs an earthly disaster will occur during a certain time if they visit an area, ride in a plane, train or automobile, and this has happened to our daughter, Vera.)

As long as people hold judgments within self, and dwell in lower consciousness, they will not acquire the wisdom of their Holy Christ Self. The Christ can only descend so far. It is up to each individual to develop the spiritual energy within to move into the higher heavens. I carry within me a torch of hope that more people will open their hearts, and allow Christ to enter; so they too may come to dwell in the paradise worlds surrounding the Godhead. Those who ask, I assist in harnessing and holding the higher energy vibrations. It is a union we create together. Some of you will find peace in my words, and my ability to work with you is like cutting a stone in to a beautiful gem. Those of you choosing this path will learn to walk in tune with my frequency, and deep love, and I will reveal to your outer consciousness the greatness also dwelling within you. Then the spirit you are, that abides within, is released, and activates the process of ascension.

Ascension

The word *ascension* probably sounds mystical to some readers, for it is not a familiar term within most religious sects, although all saints and mystics have experienced this. Some have referred to this process as the Tree of Life. If you understand that familiar teaching, it is through the center pillar the human soul makes its ascent. The prism of light will descend around the advancing soul, and they will harness a greater spectrum of light emanating from God. You will come to a summit, it is the fifth dimension, and from there you are guided through and brought upward, spiraling into an ascension wheel. In this wheel there is enough of the soul's higher coding to pass through the gateway, and make the ascension. As Jesus, I taught my disciples what I am teaching you now, to enter this spiral of energy and light; as a result you will experience the heart energies of your own God Presence, which draws you into the higher light bodies where you once existed with God. Ascension is also the meaning of the word resurrection, which is a seed thought form anyone may ask to have awakened within them. It is part of my work to create the remembrance or the awakening of the process of ascension; so the Will of God can descend. When this remembrance is stimulated it creates the opportunity to awaken and move souls through the energies of the Tree of Life. Not everyone has the desire to ascend at this time, even so, it is intended that eventually most of you will.

There are still greater concepts to be understood than those written in Holy Scriptures, and a grand mystery is unraveling on earth about the divine origins of who you truly are. Do not be afraid to engage in this research. The mystery is a spiral of ascension that, in time, will return home those who are prepared.

This particular universe is working with a hierarchy that offers itself to all of you as an expression in accordance with the Will of God. The Higher Mind qualities are experienced with precision, but it is important to understand we are all intended to be part of this extraordinary gift of expression. Everyone's I Am Presence dwells in these heavenly kingdoms, and identifies with the sonship and daughtership of the Trinity. The sons and daughters are the outward manifestation of the eminent expression and Will of our Creator to experience their love in form.

The Karmic Board Defined

There is a grand system in place in the higher heavens called the Karmic Board. This justice system was established in this universe to preside over the people incarnating to this circuit. The Karmic Board does not judge anyone. Its members offer many dispensations and opportunities to advance the soul into the higher corridors of light. When it is appropriate, they remove the seals given during prior incarnations for the souls own protection.

After death developed souls go before the Karmic Board for a life review. Again, while they do not judge anyone the Board discloses the destructive and constructive patterns each soul created, and whatever joy or damage they are responsible for placing on group consciousness, and how this affects all those dwelling on the planet. It is where the ancient concept came from, *"your heart is weighed against a feather,"* meaning souls do not go to heaven unless their heart is as light as a feather, and cannot be weighed down. What releases this portion of the soul and makes it light is the qualified light within the heart center.

Unfortunately for many, when they come before the Karmic Board they experience grave remorse. What upsets them is not something the Board places upon them; rather, it is in the reviewing of their lives they now see the affects of their earthly patterns, and this is overwhelming for the soul to experience itself in actions that caused harm to another. In those moments, the soul witnesses the level of its intentions. Now that the soul is in a more awakened consciousness it grieves for the damage it caused, and desires another opportunity to rectify those actions. As previously stated, there are many in attendance assisting the soul in understanding the patterns it held during its previous lifetime, and to help decide what must be done to correct those actions or how to prepare for the next incarnation, if another is required. This is a serious time in the soul's evolution, and after a period of rest and training the soul may request another embodiment.

Those few who hold the energy of joy, respect, divine love, and mercy, on earth will hold these same frequencies when they cross over. They will look upon their actions and interactions with other people as joyful experiences. They have held pure intentions of love and light, and they will come through to the other side experiencing goodness and love for themselves. This is why everyone should radiate joy. At the moment of their death those who hold deception, anger, and hatred, in their hearts will dwell among those who hold similar frequencies; however, they can ask for mercy. Often for those beings it is harder to move through the columns of light that, when called on, descend from the heart of the I Am Presence as a form of protection for the lower bodies. Prayers are needed to help guide those souls to an awakened consciousness.

I always sought the opportunity to teach humankind to remove the obstacles on their paths; so when souls are called before the Karmic Board they are not met with difficult consequences or with pains of resistance. To know you have loved everyone to the fullest measure, and your heart sings with joy for the experience to love and be loved, is the message I hold.

Judgment Day

There isn't any judgment day; rather, it is the balancing of cause and effect before the Karmic Board, which I just spoke of. There truly are no accusers and your Christ Self stands beside you. What happens is you are given every opportunity to review your life, the affect you had on others and on the world, and to cast light on these situations to bring them in balance. The Christ also intercedes for you as this is part of your life review, and less about judgment. I, Jesus the Christ, am incapable of hating or judging anyone. I merely view stages of growth within each of God's creations

The Halls of Judgment

No one should ever be afraid of our loving Creator; God does not deal with His creations with a heavy hand. Several prophecies within the Old Testament need to be updated, and this is one of them. In ancient times, there was a tabernacle in the astral planes called the Halls of Judgment. The Karmic Board brought forth a dispensation from the Halls of Justice and closed the Halls of Judgment, replacing it with the Halls of Mercy.

The reason the Halls of Judgment existed at all is because the light within the threefold flame was reduced to those on earth by the I Am Presence and the Higher Self. The human soul could no longer connect to its higher soul components, and the soul energy receded. The Halls of Judgment also existed because unclean spirits began to inhabit earth, and subjected the people to their will, but only those who were truly wicked moved through the Halls of Judgment. Not that anyone was harshly judged, but it was a necessary part of their evolvement. In their life review some did not choose to accept the light; consequently, they were not allowed to continue to evolve in human form. Many of them became the alien races that still do not work in the light.

See Christ in Everyone without Judgment

This is a good time to address how to move beyond personal judgments. Simply put, speak to others as if you were speaking to me. Always see the Christ in each person's eyes, and you will understand the sense of brotherhood and sisterhood I experienced when I was embodied as Jesus. I saw in others what I saw in myself, and respected them without judgment. Always expect to see God qualities in everyone. Along these lines, teaching by example is a wonderful way to work with children, and then they will organically develop their own God qualities without their parents or guardians enforcing it upon them. Do not focus on expecting to see disappointment in another or thinking he or she will let you down. If someone chooses to be that type of energy, let them go. Always imagine meeting people on their highest level. Anticipate seeing the halo of light above their heads and around their hearts, and this will aid them in developing that light from within; good relationships are developed in this manner. It is how heavenly circuits work. If some individuals, for one reason or another, cannot meet you at this level of mind and heart from their own Christ nature, they will simply not be there.

That said, as a person opens to the energies of the Holy Spirit they spin in such light and joy their expectations of others are not always met. This is where discernment plays a role. You see, not everyone is necessarily ready to take on a higher consciousness. They have not met the master on the path. Still, as the budding master, you are asked to love and respect them, honor their freewill, and allow their expression of self to be at whatever level they deem right for themselves. I, Christ, am not burdened by this. I see all as my children. However, those souls do create a weight on society at the level of group consciousness. Subliminally there are times you understand this; nonetheless, it is natural for souls in the process of learning mastery to feel resentment toward those brothers and sisters choosing to hold more darkness than light. In these cases I stand beside you, encouraging you to still see them as creations of God. Understand it is a part of their evolution and their freewill when they choose to destroy the light; instead, of holding onto it. We, in the heavenly realms, join you in prayer to assist them in awakening, but we cannot interfere. It is why intentions are important.

Know we hold a state of grace and a higher state of mind for them, and when they are ready enormous light will adhere to them. Do not pass judgment. Only see the light of Christ offering itself, and indwelling in their minds and hearts. For those who are not yet ready, this allows them to receive the message to prepare to awaken another day or perhaps in another life.

Refrain from Judging

This brings me to another topic: what causes one to walk away from the light? It is judgment, which creates limitation, and this is another reason why I chose to speak in parables. Most people could not yet hold enough light in their lower bodies to remain within the light of their Christ Oversoul. The mental bodies are extremely active and fierce at times. This is additional motivation as to why it is essential to discipline the mind, because it affects all lower bodies. It is important to understand we do not see anyone through the eyes of judgment. The majority place blame on others for one reason or another, which is a form of control. The mind has to be strengthened and prepared to restrain itself. Levels of conscience are developed within the human soul, and this is what eventually will guide that soul toward holding more light. I am not speaking of children, and I am confident when they are observed misbehaving that no one will mistake them for dark souls.

The verbal word is enormously powerful and emits a frequency into the ethers, and could actually affect the light of another who is in a weakened state. This is what occurs when dark beings get hold of a weak-minded human. A different issue is many are filled with anger and resentment toward fellow beings, and you draw additional frequencies to you from unseen regions holding the same energy. Some people come together and praise me, but they do not honor me, themselves or others when they are not being the living example of my words. I exist without judgment in absolute unconditional love; equal for all evolutions of life. I do not hold any races or nations above another. What's more, the animal kingdom is suffering greatly under the humans, and you must genuinely understand that these creations also come from the hand of our Creator.

I came forth to assist in the creation of a vast understanding of the tributaries of love. Since then, an overwhelming number of souls have tried to fashion their lives around my teachings, but in order to do that they need to immerse themselves in deepening their relationship with me. Regrettably, too great a number of souls come before me while still misaligned within this field of judgment, and they take my words out of context, and do not realize it is never the goal of a higher being to destroy relationships. My walk on earth was short, but I contributed to humankind, to understanding life, and to spreading a message of unconditional love. My words have brought forth positive changes on earth, and as I keep reiterating, a considerable amount of what I taught has been lost, misconstrued, and manipulated. Yet, the original texts were given to unify the people under one God, a loving God. I gave a large range of very deep talks, and as my following grew there was a wealth of people that permitted the light to course through them. They drank from the same cup I drank from. A substantial number of scholars examined the meanings behind the scriptures, and what saddens me is, not all, but most sects still construe my words as creating division. Consequently, what humankind now has is a shallow doctrine of the truths I gave in my original teachings.

The Initiate

The Way of the Initiate

The path of initiation is part of my work as the Redeemer, and this is a powerful teaching I am now bringing forth. While I was Jesus, I was an initiate on the path, and you now need to see yourselves as initiates too. I experienced powerful initiations on the spiritual planes, which are dimensions of consciousness on other planes of reality, and throughout my life that brought about changes in my awareness and my consciousness. I took on the Mantle of the Christ, which is certainly an endeavor I hope many of you will experience for yourselves at some point in creation. Unfortunately, a large number of people stray from the path of initiation since it causes necessary upheaval in their lives. The turmoil only occurs because negative thoughts and emotions are released, and this is essential for the purification of the denser planes earth is on. Dormant within each soul are patterns that cause certain recurring conditions, and this happens because the human soul does not fully comprehend the creative process. Beloveds, each soul needs to formulate a new thinking that moves away from worshiping me, and places the focus on the fact that each of you is created with the same original seed memory I was created with. *I am an example of the human potential, and this initiation is open to everyone.*

The Initiation Process

Initiation is a tremendous principle at work within the universe, and as I have said, this process is part of my responsibility as the Redeemer. Many of you are holding dense karmic patterns, and it is one of the reasons you cannot behold my vision any longer, and why initiations are necessary. I intend to teach all of you to hold onto the illustrious light and to share with you a part of your Divine Blueprint as you continue to develop a relationship with Christ. There will be numerous initiations I will bring you through, and they will start with opening your spiritual heart, and in due time, I slowly remove the veil, and reveal myself to you.

It takes seasons to work with me, and to understand this is a bridge we create together. I recommend you become familiar with my light patterns; so you will recognize them when I am close. I pattern your Christ Self after my frequency, but this does not mean your Higher Self is beneath me or lesser than I am; however, for a time, I enter the position of command that once again brings to mind my other title, Savior. (The Blessed Mother also works with you in a similar manner.) Within each breath is a momentum of light given to you by God. By elevating your thoughts you qualify that breath energy, and it becomes the fire breath of the Holy Spirit. When your own God Presence works through you it creates a piercing light, and an opportunity for me to descend to the earth plane and embody you, but I do not control anyone. Freewill is a precious gift from God given to all of creation on this earth plane.

There is a special relationship that I, Christ, aspire to have with you. I am the breath of life, and I become the substance that is the action of the Will of God flowing through everyone. Your soul dwells in the higher kingdoms where I abide as Lord. Again, I am not ruler over anyone. I am the Good Shepherd returning my flock to their original Divine Blueprint emanating from God, and I come forth with a staff as a symbol of power that is released unto each of you. Many corridors of light exist, and once again this refers to dimensional layers in the higher octaves each soul needs to transcend, and another reason why initiations are essential. Your energy field appears as columns of light holding a particular vibratory pattern, and controls your mental, and emotional attitudes. For a moment, imagine you are in a column of light where I am standing beside you holding a frequency for you to enter. These are the descending columns of light from each person's I Am Presence I encapsulate. When the process of initiation occurs your consciousness expands through these columns of light. The first level of initiation is the soul merge when the aura becomes very bright, and sometimes the light you experience is similar to a feeling of heaviness or pressure. This is also when you open to receive the Divine Blueprint of the Will of God.

Throughout this whole process I am communicating with you; therefore, fear not when first I speak. As we deepen this relationship, some will come to know my sound tones. For a time, you may want to work with me in solitude as you develop an understanding of my essence. I represent a brotherhood and a sisterhood of those who are Christs. It is what I mean when I say you are also intended to sit at the right hand of God, and all of you, every soul, are part of the sonship and daughtership of the Trinity.

An Initiation

In this moment, if you feel open to this suggestion then ask that your heart be filled with joy, and allow a prism of light to be focused on you. As you attune with me, I place the Seal of Abraham around you in the form of the Star of David; you encounter this on the spiritual planes as an initiation. The Seal allows currents of energy and light to flow in you from your Oversoul, from my sacred heart, and the Sacred Heart of God. Know I am giving you a blessing, and an invitation to join me at the level of the Christ.

The Divine Blueprint and the Oversoul

T he Divine Blueprint and the Christ Oversoul are concepts some may not be familiar with, especially if you are
coming from a religious background; yet it was all a part
of the work I began more than two thousand years ago.

The Divine Blueprint

This Divine Blueprint we each have comes from God, and is not
referred to by any secular name. It is part of the Divine Mind,
and the Divine Will of God that flows through all beings of light;
through a prism of intense light. This teaching, of receiving the
Divine Blueprint, is the hidden concept held within the rituals of
baptism and communion. As Jesus, I remembered my Divine Blueprint, and embraced it. I beckon all who feel *called* to explore their
divine nature, and ask to be guided to the knowledge, and understanding of the mystery of their divinity. Many are working with
alternating frequencies that create karmic patterns and resistance,
and then my followers come before me, not as an equal as they
should, but as a child in search of guidance. *I tell you truthfully, your
soul was cut from the same light I, Jesus the Christ, was cut from.*

Your Divine Blueprint contains the missing strands of DNA
you held prior to the fall, and it occurred before humans obtained

an ego. During these earlier cycles, when humankind did not possess an ego, they were guided by spirit. The Lords of Karma explain that the DNA strands were removed during a low cycle on earth because the heart flame had become dim in those embodied then. There was a group consciousness of desire, including near animalistic types of sex, and these perverted acts were not what the spirit wanted, and then honor was lost with God. This created very low energy; consequently, the planet was very dark. Prior to the fall the DNA patterns were intact, and humans dwelled in a heavenly state of consciousness guided by their divine soul.

Your cellular memory still holds your Divine Blueprint that is your divine inheritance. Disrespect toward self, and the world creates negative karmic patterns, and prevents entrance to the thresholds of light located in the spiritual heart center. These thresholds of light hold the Divine Blueprint, which is in fact the Immaculate Concept. The process begins when the I Am Presence focuses the Immaculate Concept image through the Higher Self to those embodied on earth or in another realm not fully purified or sanctioned by the Father's will, and this restores the Divine Blueprint holding the divine image. Once accessed, other masters and I are called to action; however, we are only able to bring the majority a small amount of your Divine Blueprint into the lower dense octaves. This is the reason most people are only beginning to embark on this grand journey with us. In other words, at this time there are not many souls able to carry these currents because higher spiritual intelligence has not yet returned to the masses. Souls able to carry these currents, and function within their garments of light worked very hard to make this possible. Humankind is holding multiple levels of consciousness, and spiritual knowledge, and this is a major reason earth is out of balance.

The Divine Blueprint also prepares you for ascension into the higher heavens, but as I have said, I do recognize not everyone may hold the desire to ascend now, although most eventually will. When answering the call to work in service to God, and develop an understanding of the Divine Blueprint the arm of mercy is given to you, and judgment is removed. When I speak of judgment it is not God or me that judges; rather, how you chastise yourself. Your core beliefs are where I encourage, and assist you in releasing the pain related to any system of judgment. Forgiveness is a tool we use on this planet to assist you in breaking free of the lower mind locked in the astral corridor, and then self-criticism gradually lessens with increased spiritual awareness. When your mind is in the currents of forgiveness, and respect for self your vibrations are raised, then order starts to return, and you are more in control of your life.

You are but an embryo. For many, the columns of light have not yet penetrated the lower emotional and mental bodies nor begun to filter through the physical body. This is also why some experience disharmony in its various aspects. As I work with you, I prepare you to receive qualified light, and you hold an expanded understanding of self. I assist in qualifying the light around you, enabling you to hold more tones of appreciation, more expressions, and qualities usually attributed to angels. Many will even feel or identify with being an angel, and this is extremely joyful to us in the heavenly realms. It is the rebirth process experienced, similar to when some-one believes they are reborn in the knowledge, and understanding of the Christ. It is a bridge of light I assist you in crossing. I levitate the energies within your aura, and attune them to the Higher Mind that then communicates to you in accordance with your level of understanding. This may create issues for many because you some-times resist letting go of old patterns; however, you all have freewill through your thoughts, and actions to mis-qualify the descending light to you. By doing so you create holes in your aura that in turn allows negative emotions, and thought forms to be experienced by you. Always focus on triumphs, never failures. This does not mean there will not be challenges, but when the focus is success it is easier to move along that current, and each time this attitude is repeated it becomes easier to succeed. Hold success as a diagram you wish to experience, and the universe that operates according to God's Will can manifest your desires. *Success is always God's Will for everyone, and when this technique is practiced the opportunity to achieve your goals occurs more often.* This ability to create what you wish to experience with ease and grace is within everyone. Your outer manifestations are really affected by personal beliefs, your level of intelligence, group consciousness, and karmic patterns. Frequencies of creation are all around, and doors continuously open and close.

If it is comfortable draw upon my strength as the Redeemer, as a symbol, until you receive enough of your own Divine Blueprint. This will assist you in accepting responsibility for your actions, and intentions. The threshold of light you work with is your specific energy signature or level of light you are currently holding, and present to the world. When you are oversouled your light is raised, and you receive your own divine pattern, and for those who have earned high levels of light it will be the Immaculate Concept.

As spirit is released from the higher soul, and the Breath of God is allowed to expand within, you will dance within the light. Again, rely on my strength as the Redeemer, while I assist in recoding you to hold more of your Divine Blueprint. It is then you will dwell in the luminous system I exist in, and the Holy Spirit will descend upon you. A wealth of opportunities will continue for souls on earth to open the door for surrender to the divine. In the evening or morning, enter the chamber of the spiritual heart and receive a blessing from our Creator. This will clear the memory banks so each day will begin anew. Value the sacredness of the divinity inside, and for receiving your inner light, and ask to see significant, positive changes in your life.

As I communicate through these gateways do not create limitations. This occurs when I am placed in a box, in a religion, in a faith, but truly, I am above that. I speak to each as brother to brother or brother to sister, and ask that you have an open heart, an open mind. *It is not necessary to belong to a religion to find me, although I am in all religions, and in all faiths. I am everywhere.* All who love God, love mercy, and love each other are holding my frequency of light. As you experience more joy, and gratitude an expanded light flows through the body, and these feelings, and thoughts contribute more light to your soul. This is how spiritual seekers move along a path of initiation with the elders of earth, and receive superior wisdom. Light needs to flow freely through you, and then anchor it beneath your feet, and as this occurs your experiences will deepen. The following is a prayer I wish to share:

> I am in the arms of God. I am a (son/daughter) of Creation. The powers of God are my inheritance. I unfold the light of the Christ Mind, and desire to receive my Divine Blueprint. Amen.

Christ Explains the Oversoul

The Oversoul or the Mantle of the Christ is a memory capsule placed above the crown center chakra, and it is a consciousness; part of the Divine Mind of our Creator. The Oversoul is also a vast light that beckons to all life streams, and it is the divine nature of the spirit permeating all living consciousness.

Humankind exists in a world of structure that is not the form where soul easily finds peace. This is reason enough why people need to be returned to the Christ Oversoul; it is everyone's birthright. Beloveds, the human mind holds limiting concepts. It is called the lower mind, and within it you hold the denser energies, and reasoning powers; thus allowing it to be trapped in limiting thoughts that desire less than divine forms of creation. To know God's freedom you must expand in to the purer frequencies of the Divine Mind. This brings you through a portal of light into the area of the Christ Oversoul, which houses the Christ mind. From there, together we take the journey toward the heavenly realms I spoke of. Trust in me, I know the way home, and will safely lead each of you there. Walk the path asking to know Christ, and to deepen your understanding of your place within the Oversoul of the Body of Christ, and then you will not depart from the purpose of the Divine Blueprint.

When I stepped out of the holy sepulcher, I became one with the Celestial Christ, Emanuel. The Celestial Christ vessel is an Oversoul. It attunes to the Diamond Mind of God and creation, and holds the son and daughter energies. A large amount of people refer to, and understand this as the Trinity, and as Jesus, I held an attunement with these energies. It is the consciousness I dwelled in, my Mother Mary, and innumerable others experienced, and what I taught my disciples to reside in—to the level they were able. Many other masters who came before and after me knew, to varying degrees, they too were divine creations. As the Celestial Christ, I oversee all who dwell on earth. In due time, I will reveal more about a *treasury of light* that will give the true picture of humankind as being part of this divine family. It will be revealed as a time capsule to assist humans in understanding their divine origins.

From when I was a small child my yearning was to know, and become one with God. My heart was pure, and my yolk was light because I had very little karma. *I am not limited to the followers I had as Jesus or to the personality I held as him.* I am a consciousness, the Oversoul, which he, Jesus, united with while he was embodied. Of course, that was his Divine Blueprint. The Body of Christ over-souled Jesus, and drew him into the eminent flame. It is through the Christ Oversoul you become enlightened. Remember, there are more Oversouls available than the Christ Oversoul for each of you to receive that were given at the time of creation. For now, hold the idea of becoming a Christ.

The oversouling Process, Receiving the Christ Oversoul or the Mantle of the Christ

In time, the following is what occurs when you receive the Christ Oversoul or Mantle of the Christ, which will completely surround you, as it did for me. When I step forward, and become the teacher, I create a bond of friendship between us, and stabilize and focus light to you. The process is an exchange of light I give, and has been depicted by artists in the drawings of the sacred hearts of my blessed mother and me. I, as the Celestial Christ, have the ability to dissolve your karmic patterns through the form of blessings, and dispensations. This is another reason why I hold the titles Redeemer, and Savior. A prism of light is placed above you, and eventually you are taught to expand in it, merging with your Higher Self. At the center of each being is a magnetic core and it holds certain sound frequencies. I awaken these higher tones within you for our work together. The magnetic core is in the spiritual heart center, and it extends to the solar plexus area. During this union an expansion of light occurs, and this is the true meaning of communion with Christ. Through this process you join in communion with me, and it is how you enter my kingdom where I am Lord. The next step is when I surround you with a protective garment of light, and expand that light to hold more of the radiance of our Creator. This broad spectrum of light comes through a doorway in the Christ Oversoul, and it means I hold the proper intention for our work together. *Simply put, to be oversouled is when you allow the Christ to combine its energy field with yours.* It raises your vibration even when I am only temporarily close. The Oversoul represents the combining of light frequencies, a blending of the energy fields, "as above so below," that create an alignment with the Celestial Christ who overshadows, and raises the human soul. The process of being overshadowed by Christ prepares you to receive the Mantle of the Christ for yourselves, which is a portion of your Divine Blueprint, then your divine nature returns. Hence, this expansion of light is termed the Higher Self, and it has a heightened consciousness able to present answers to daily problems your egos are not always capable of solving.

Within the Universal Mind is a structure used for creation called the Antakharana, and it is a bridge of light consciousness uses to transcend. It is also called the rainbow bridge or the web of life. This bridge is a net of light, spinning spirit, and matter, connecting, and sensitizing the whole of creation within itself, and to the Heart of God.

When you go through this progression there are many changes in consciousness as well as spiritual choices. God allows me to work with those asking for assistance in clearing their memory patterns as a part of the uplifting, and expanding techniques. When you are involved in situations controlled by the outer world, step in a circle of light, and invite me to guide, protect, and surround you, and always ask to gain higher wisdom from this union. At first subtle changes may be experienced, and those in deep despair might feel lighter, and more hopeful. You will learn to draw your breath and energy from your own Holy Christ Self. *Between worlds is what is analogous to a curtain or a veil, and to remove it faith is not enough.* You must listen to the still small voice within the center of your mind. It is where you are nudged forward. It is the call. The majority of beings have too many distractions to hear me or our Creator whispering. The Christ is an open doorway, an Oversoul, part of the universal design to uplift humankind; so once again you are aware of the divine plan operating in the higher dimensions.

Everyone has a God Presence, which is a being of immeasurable light and joy, and a reflection of the prism of the light of God. Think of your God Presence as being a bright star that expands within your spiritual heart. On each point of the star is a quality of God, such as God patience, God love or unconditional love, humanity, and service toward others, divine will, divine thinking, compassion, and goodwill. Focusing on this will bring you proper causation to receive your returning current of qualified light in the physical realm, and assist you in maintaining it. When discord is experienced bring your mind back to a quality God holds, that I hold, and is in service to the planet. As you allow that prism of light to flow through you, thoughts will clear and you will become a magnet for the joyous expression of light.

Each person's soul needs to be affected by the currents of light of the Oversoul of the Christ. The Christ can be understood as a collective, consisting of a brotherhood and sisterhood. When you hold the Christ patterns of light you are redeemed of all karma, and mercy is poured forth from my heart onto yours. As I oversoul you there isn't room for any of the fallen lords or systems of lords, still desiring to control the inhabitants of this planet, to enter your energy field. Even children need to be taught how to recognize the different powers existing on earth. They need strong examples in their lives, and every adult has a responsibility to be that.

Everyone who sincerely calls to me takes on a childlike innocence in the pureness in which they were created. In the beginning, they turn toward me, as I have chosen to be that example. In due time, I teach you how to go within the stillness that is the purity of your own soul's perfection, and I open a gateway, and assist your I Am Presence in finding fertile ground therein. I remain a constant presence on earth. I do this by emitting a frequency to you, as spiritual seekers, and to all my past, and present disciples. I have enough love for all, and stand ready by each person's side.

Vehicles for Spiritual Awakening

The Cube in the Heart Center

Each developing soul needs to be in balance with the frequency of energy and light that resonates to a sound current within the heart of Christ. It is within each soul, and is known as the white cube. It is another gift from our Creator. The cube within the spiritual heart was veiled for some time, and the dormant additional DNA strands humankind once held are stored in it. During this cycle, more souls will have an opportunity to once again hold this pattern, and it is through the Christ Oversoul they will have the awakening of the cube within. It exists beyond your range of emotions, and assists one who is on a path of self-mastery to refine enough light to work within this mechanism. It is also used to connect to the energies of the Rays of God as they enter earth. The white cube holds a frequency for a pyramid of energy called the capstone, which high initiates have above their heads. No one gains entrance in the white cube or holds these energy vortexes until they retain a sufficient amount of unconditional love toward their fellow man. The white cube held in the heart of an advancing initiate allows them to communicate with and to visit the higher worlds, and gain access to many doorways to the higher heavens. The communities of light and the beings residing in these kingdoms appear to possess miraculous gifts the masses on earth do not have. Through the white cube initiates also learn to *bend light*, which will be discussed in a later book.

As the human race continues to develop spiritually this cube, holding the additional strands of DNA, will be revealed within the hearts of humankind. The cube is anchored to the threefold flame and will expand the ribbons of light to the Oversouls. The Higher Self will use the cube to return the original strands of DNA for the purpose of maintaining its currents through the human form on planet earth. Hindrances on earth are many, and there are obstacles not of an individual's own making, but the returning DNA programming will help remove some of them. The returning DNA also restructures the physical form, evidenced by the fact humankind has already begun to notice that the population is healthier and living longer. In time, human decay will slow up even more as earth's inhabitants learn to harness greater light. In fact, earth is going through an evolutionary process too, and its magnetic core is changing, giving me a new opportunity to work with people in a more personal way. When a greater amount of humankind can hold the higher coding it will be possible for additional enlightened souls to incarnate here. This will create a different polarity and a shift for the coming of the heightened Golden Age.

This is why I came to earth, to be among those who would become catalysts for a new beginning. I work through a magnetic core or grid coding the frequencies of love; with greater love comes wisdom and patience. For those capable of receiving the cube the veil between heaven and earth is beginning to disappear, and a new structure of light is returning to the planet. Do not be enveloped in fear and judgment. Set your differences aside, and choose God first in your life. Possessions are not going to remain with your soul, and some put too much value on them. Be conscious of your intentions and everything you think, say, and do, because every detail is written on a scroll called your Book of Life, and can be found in the akashic records. The spirit within is the true gift, and the gem most valued.

The Star of David

The Star of David is actually a vehicle for the Higher Self, and God consciousness utilizes it to work with humankind. It should not be seen as a Jewish symbol. One of the ways you are taught to gain wisdom, and move to higher positions in the Tree of Wisdom is by working with the Star of David, which is your Divine Monad. Within your Divine Monad are many trees, referred more simply to as the Tree of Life. The star will descend through the tree in a spinning action and elevate you, and eventually this ancient symbol will create a spinning action around the physical body that brings enlightenment. In time, the Star of David will fill with greater light from above, and the Seal of Abraham will be opened, which is an activation of a level of initiation, a passage of light, and the release of the Holy Spirit. Then the mighty I Am Presence you hold in the higher heavens will filter through the human body and mind, and you will come to know our Creator and me through increments of light that will develop within.

A more indepth look at this process is to know that the Star of David is a method of teaching, "as above so below." The Seal of Abraham above the crown activates an elevated chakra system from a higher light body, which is outside humankind's current level of awareness. You pass very quickly through the Seal of Abraham, and gain access to the Star of David: a six-pointed star that grounds you in the fifth dimension. Anytime human consciousness merges with a higher portion of the emanations of an Oversoul, a certain amount of the light of the Will of the Creator is given to the lower body, mind, and heart system. In this case, it contains a portion of the Divine Blueprint. Another way to say this is the Christ Self is attuned with the I Am Presence, making the Christ Self, and all connected to it, a part of the Trinity.

The Star of David should not be thought of as flat when it passes through the body; instead, see it is as multidimensional and penetrating the physical form. The star becomes a tetrahedron as it expands consciousness through a portion of the Tree of Life. From here you may better understand that an Oversoul is like a tree within the Divine Monad; the Divine Monad being the roots of the tree. Once the star tetrahedron reaches its highest level of ascent, additional light rays continue to expand from the heavenly regions, and you take on more advanced structures of light. This is all part of an arrangement of light bodies. The tiers of Oversouls, (once again, like overseers) gather light bodies onto themselves that attune to them.

There is actually cosmic order to the universe. It is difficult for those who reside below these levels of enlightenment to pierce the veils that are garments of light; however, each time a soul penetrates these thresholds they gain a deeper understanding of the process.

The Seal of Abraham

The Seal of Abraham is now being returned to humankind as part of the covenant spoken about in ancient days, and it is given as a symbol of faith. It comes in with the Good Shepherd, and has been on earth for quite some time. It is part of the Oversoul within the tributaries of the Christ Matrix, a grid from the Body of Christ, utilizing, and developing the Christ energies. The Christ Matrix is living energy that can support, and assist you on your personal journey.

The Seal of Abraham is an opening to a portal of light being utilized by the I Am Presence. The seal's piercing light opens to the heavenly kingdoms and the paradise worlds, and there is an inflow of divine love from our Creator. The attunement to the Seal of Abraham causes a continuous current of the higher light within the Christ Matrix or the Oversoul you hold as a Christed being. The Hebrew fire letters represent the value of a letter and a number in the Hebrew alphabet, and they are coded with the tones to open the Seal of Abraham. It is why ancient scholars who studied the Hebrew fire letters were able to penetrate the kingdom of God. Prayer also assists in opening the Seal of Abraham.

As stated in the previous section, the Seal of Abraham actually appears in the form of the Star of David. Visualize the star above your head, and anchor it about a foot beneath your feet to ground the energies of the Oversoul to the physical body, allowing more light to travel through you from the regions of light. That purer light exists in eternity, and feeds the flame within the heart with the sparks, and the divine personality humans were intended to hold. When this happens the outer garment you wear, your physical body, will be free of disease, and able to fight off latent energies still surrounding the world. The Seal of Abraham delivers an additional spectrum of light to the body. It is a higher pattern of energy I give to spiritual seekers during their initiations, and it opens the gateway for the energies of the Holy Spirit to descend upon you. During this process, it is the raising of the threefold flame that ignites the fire allowing the Seal of Abraham to open. It is how you embody the light of the Christos, and the action of God within self.

The Christ energies have been on earth for quite some time, even before I incarnated as Jesus the Christ, and humans were already receiving the light of the Christos. During the time of the Old Testament, as well as Atlantis and Lemuria, there were those who were encoded with the Seal of Abraham, and utilizing the flow of light of the Christos.

The majority usually embark on a journey of the mind to understand the teachings attributed to me, which brings them a certain amount of contradiction, and controversy. Instead, I invite you to read scripture with an open heart, and allow me to fan the flame, and I will bring forth deeper understanding, and greater attunements. In the process of rebirthing this consciousness, when you study, whether it is the Old Testament or the New Testament, the words in the Bible will unfold, and the secret meanings coded in these books will be understood.

Many of you are also learning to hone your skills and your spiritual abilities. Make an effort *not* to focus on what you do not have, your faults or the faults in others. Far too many experience enormous loss and hardships, and your suffering is not our intention. Do your best each day to love yourself, and expand that vision to all others. See the goodness that lies within and trust in yourself. The words I spoke were simple. I held enormous love for all who came to listen to me, and I still see humankind as my flock. I will remain with humankind until each of you return home to the higher heavens.

Communicating with Christ

Intuition

Intuition is wisdom and always accurate, listen to it and you will never take a wrong turn. (*Vera's comment:* Where people get confused is their incorrect interpretation of intuitive thoughts, especially when under stress and emotional.) Develop listening skills, because you are regularly receiving messages through intuition and your mind, and then trust that information. Our Creator does not speak in a thunderous voice and neither do I. If you pay attention and expect a response, we can be heard or experienced by most in prayer and meditation; the latter is a tool that aids in developing intuitive abilities.

Intuitive messages first enter through the third eye located in the space between the brows. In order to enhance intuition, other master's and I assist you in drawing in more light through the opening behind the navel, where the soul body attaches to you. This location is the reason intuition is experienced as a gut feeling.

The Third Eye

When you are ready spiritual visions will originate in the third eye located on the forehead between the brows. Higher visions come to those who are holding like energies, and can visit or see elevated levels of reality; however, not all spiritual seekers have this gift. During prayer and meditation focus on the heart center, and gradually move up to the third eye. When you feel you have reached a higher state of awareness the third eye will open and become the window to higher communities of light. Until such time, the forced opening of the third eye is not a good idea because it could access an astral level, a lower dimension or even cause subliminal thoughts to rebound in to vision. If the chakras are not completely balanced the spiritual seeker runs the risk of seeing a lower vibration existing in another reality or coming from subconscious thoughts not yet cleared by balancing the heart energies with unconditional love. For most, the third eye is sealed because painful memories from previous lifetimes are still within their energy fields. This is why a filter is placed there; so disturbing past life thoughts and memories do not reawaken and send images back. Also tied to the third eye are astral plane visions and voices of the deceased who have not chosen to go to the light; there are numerous reasons why some choose not to cross over. For example, they may remain to protect a loved one or an area. Still, there are others that are violent in nature, and terrorize souls through psychic attacks.

Those who prematurely awaken the Kundalini may see visions through the third eye reflecting back painful thoughts, memories or frightful areas, intended to be veiled. Again, this is due to the fact they are working with an unbalanced chakra system needing to be cleared and balanced through their feelings and emotions, and this also comes under the heading of psychic attack. It is one of the reasons to balance karmic patterns, and stay focused on pure intentions to hold and work with the light.

Vera's comment: There are teachings that encourage students to incorporate the third eye when practicing certain techniques, and they are protected by the master teacher. If you are not under the umbrella of such a master, please do not amalgamate the third eye in your spiritual practice until the development of the threefold flame, which is the foundation in all of the teachings through the Christ Matrix.® Jesus always suggests integrating every practice with the development of the threefold flame.

Conquering Self-Discipline

Do you long to be settled in your life and exist in peace? Or do you want or even crave the drama, and chaos? This is how honest you need to be with yourself. I am not pointing a finger at you. I am saying it is time to mature spiritually.

In a sense, everyone is a case study to their teachers, ascended masters or divine beings assisting them throughout this life. What we see is you make it more difficult than it needs to be, and usually as a result of misunderstandings guided and directed toward you by fallacies within your own thinking. Far too many are burdened with and accustom to particular patterns that no longer serve them. Do you enjoy holding onto anger or fear more than the freedom of a sense of peace, balance, and harmony? Do the latter currents create boredom? I ask this because some developing personalities yearn to stir things up evidenced by problems stemming from a cold heart, holding jealousies, and emotions that do not serve them. Some souls live an existence I consider to be a nightmare, and there are those who paralyze their own lives. Understand, when the mind and ego tire of the negative currents presently creating your realities, you will make the changes necessary to turn things around, and bring more joy in your lives. For some, this may not happen for several lifetimes, and for those who are ready now, I suggest you lighten up; we seek to set these people free. Assist us in assisting you by recognizing patterns that no longer serve the light, and this means really getting in the corners of your mind to see what you hold in your heart. Some of you are very proud, and this also needs to be addressed. For us, the reward is seeing you experiencing peace, harmony, and happiness. It is why you call out my name to help with releasing your burdens; in truth and in service, I send forth a brilliant light to help dissolve them. This also requires you do some work by turning inward and making the necessary changes; deciding what will stay, and what you are ready to release. Together we will consider every aspect to move you forward.

The nature of our Creator is to love you, and bring peace and joy to everyone. We, in the higher heavens, generate enormous love for all, knowing each and every person holds their own destiny in their hands. If you ask, we will intercede, and assist in removing negative blocks, and your Higher Self is that bridge, as well as the key to eliminating all fear. The essence of divine love given by our Creator, and ignited by the energies of the Holy Spirit, is intended to awaken divine love within you. To realize this you need to be still; however, many are seeking attention, and do not always recognize this creates a great deal of drama. The noisier you are, the less likely you will hear the Christ speaking within. Soften the frequencies within your mind and listen, and some may also benefit by slowing the pace of their lives. Daily create a line of communion where you speak to our Creator, a place where the Dove, the Holy Spirit, can enter your heart and mind. The Holy Spirit holds the vibration of God's pure love; so when it enters your heart you will know peace, mercy, and divine love.

Developing the Mind

Developing the powers of the mind is what is missing from western traditions, and the reason many people cannot pull their lives together. This is because most of you were not taught proper concentration techniques to strengthen the mind to hold a focus on thoughts that reinforce an alignment with spirit. In other words, most people do not have the discipline to still their thoughts long enough to create the space for heavenly hosts to ignite them with the light. This is such a shame since it is a blessing a large amount of folks ask for, and it would greatly assist them on their path. It is serious work for us. Unfortunately, many bind themselves tightly, do not allow us to speak to them, and are not open enough to receive a response to their prayer requests. Consequently, they end up experiencing numbness. I always aspired to bring peace in the minds and hearts of those who call me teacher, and I am still doing that work today. It was part of my teachings the church and its many branches kept secret. This is why the majority of those who seek me do not approach me with intelligence, because they involve themselves in a belief system that is only a small part of what I taught. Yes, their hearts need to be developed, but their minds have to be strong; they must be able to stand up to the momentum of light entering from the Christ Oversoul.

When reading the Holy Bible or any spiritual text such as this, allow me to work the words through your mind and heart, and ask to receive whatever portion of the teaching you are ready for, and permit me to raise you into that Divine Mind I hold. Activate this process by accepting the thought, you too are divine. This is actually how you witness Christ.

The *gate of tears* is not what I sought to take my followers through. I did not desire to share the burden of my ridicule with anyone, for I alone chose to bear it. Possibilities abound, and there are choices to make every day. To bring about quicker resolutions to current problems, I suggest adopting a stream of thought that is part of a consciousness dwelling within a higher vibratory pattern. *Concentrating on misfortunes accumulates and directs more of the same toward you. I am not placing fault on anyone, but this is what occurs with disease and misfortune.* Where you place your mind, thoughts, and energy, will return to you. In a sense, you become a magnet for what you least hope to experience. Faith is what many exist on, and it does form a small opening I can work with. Singing to God, other masters, and me, also creates an opportunity for light to enter even the darkest minds.

Sitting at the right hand of the Father is not a gift I alone was to receive; it is a gift for all of God's creations. This is a distinguished honor I will share with each one of you when you are also able to hold the pristine garment of your Immaculate Concept. To understand self-sovereignty as a son or daughter of the Most High God begins with learning to respect, and honor your decisions, and yourselves. Choices made two years or a few months ago are not necessarily decisions you would make today because many of you are evolving, and this growth is part of the intended healing process. Each day observe how your intentions, and actions create the experiences you are now living.

Stillness and Meditation

There is a period of stillness that occurs when entering the Mind of God. The-personality, including feelings and thoughts, resonates with the Christ within. The inner spiritual being you are intended to be lights up like a Christmas tree, and holy is the tabernacle within. It is the reason some of you are becoming a chalice unto our Creator. The busy lives you lead, if you allow them, will remove consciousness from this holy union; therefore, you need to be quiet and listen. Meditation is the perfect tool to perfect this discipline since it is a time to be still. The masses do not have awakenings because they are self-absorbed, and ruled by their egos. They do not look outside the boundaries of themselves, and many develop fear in venturing farther than their circle of family members and friends; they hold the consciousness all others are outside of their unit.

When you decide to take on Christ consciousness stillness comes over you, and you experience peace within. Also, there is an inner knowing you are governed by a luminous light, and that light expands dimensionally within you. In the stillness you will find vast knowledge, understanding, and wisdom. To reach the stillness of meditation develop concentration and practice receiving thoughts from your divine self, who is the divine being that holds the Divine Blueprint. Intend this, and the action will create an awakening for the energies of the Holy Spirit to descend, expanding ribbons of light and love within and around you. In time, each and everyone will become a Christed being, and divide the waters, hear the inner call, and recognize truth within self.

A Meditation: Merging with the Christ Heart and Mind

I invite you to meditate on this process and play relaxing music, if you like. Enter the stillness by taking a couple of deep breaths, slowly inhaling, and exhaling. As you breathe focus on my face, the face of Jesus the Christ or the Blessed Mother. Visualize being guided to a corridor of magnificent light where there are cells of memory. Feel as if you are in harmony with our love flowing toward you, and there is nothing between us. Do not allow doubt or fear to enter. If negative thoughts distract your attention, see them moving into a violet sphere, and just tell yourself you will deal with them later. If it helps, see yourself entering the doorway of my sacred heart, if that is a comfortable thought or hold that intention. The sacred heart is a symbol of God's love reflected onto the world. Feel as if you are merging with the heart and the mind of Christ, which is your sanctuary where you are honored, respected, loved, and not judged. See yourself as we see you, as a beautiful being of divine love and light come to witness the goodness of the world, and to be part of the salvation of humankind. Feel our love and peace entering you, and your inner knowing awakening. Take several more deep breaths, deep cleansing breaths. Focus now on your heart center. Imagine the beautiful threefold flame within your heart, remembering its intertwining flames of pink and blue, with a golden yellow center. See the violet light around the flames. If you are not visual, intending these images has the same outcome. Just breath love in your heart, for it is a celestial corridor of beauty, and it is how the higher component of your soul first communicates to you. It is also the threshold to the Divine Mind, and it connects to the heart of the Christ, which is connected to the Heart of God. Now sit still for as long as you like before continuing.

Make it your purpose to be a guardian of this planet, and to be an extension of God's love, mercy, joy, happiness, and goodwill. Notice if others attempt to control you, if so, you have the choice to release them in the guidance of their God Presence, and then ask for the best outcome that will bring about the most joy, love, and respect for self, and all others. Then do not worry about the outcome. Experience God's love, and believe your image is perfect, just as our Creator is perfect. Know that all outer circumstances are temporary, and they will not be sustained in spirit; negative karmic patterns are dissolved in this beautiful light, and wisdom replaces troublesome currents.

Be present in the experience of enjoying life more by uniting with God, and taking pleasure in being part of an Awareness experiencing Itself receiving blessings. If you see or feel any resistance to know our Creator, rest assured the Holy Spirit is dispersing it. To reiterate, God truly does not want to be worshiped. Our Creator is love, and patiently waits for our love to be returned. As I have already stated, by respecting yourself you respect our Creator, because you honor God through love and respect. If you are having problems or issues respecting yourself, ask for a healing. See yourself living a virtuous life you can be proud of, and initiate discussions with others to work out agreements that bring everyone peace.

God is generous with all of His creations. Experience yourself entering the mind of Christ where you will understand the divine Will of God speaking directly to you. The Mind of God enters you through a prism of light called the *Abba Nartoomid*, which is a bridge of God's limitless light. Settle down in the energies of the Christ and continually ask to be in attunement with the Christ mind. Finally, ask the Holy Spirit to remain with you always.

Catherine's anecdote: Years before my conscious work with Jesus, I meditated before a picture of his sacred heart, and would practice moving my consciousness inside of it. After a time of perfecting that mediation, I felt I was with him. Years later, I did ask him about those experiences, and he told me his sacred heart is the doorway to his inner retreat, and I had discovered that hidden mystery.

Heavenly Guidance and Direction

Angels and Archangels

Not everyone is open enough to accept this message, but it is a gift from me I wish you to be aware of: *angels guide your path.* I, Jesus, send forth legions of angels to assist me in my work with humankind, and I also send dozens of angels to surround each one of my initiates. The angels communicate by conveying your requests and dreams, and then I fulfill or align you with what I see you need to receive. Angels also assist in speeding up the light entering your aura, and support you with maintaining the energy patterns coming from my divine heart. Like eagles, the angelic forces soar toward the earth, and as they do they create openings to elevate your attunement with the Christ.

The archangels come from the Godhead, and they serve in unconditional love. When you are working with high intentions you will attune with beautiful archangels, and they help guide your patterns to the various Oversouls. You may not be conscious that the energy you feel is of an archangel, but you may be very familiar with their frequencies. In fact, angels and archangels have remained with most of you through many incarnations.

Guardian Angels

Many are interested in understanding guardian spirits and guardian angels. I enjoy teaching about these divine companions, and most awakening souls identify with them. They are as near as any ascended master teachers, and these divine companions are your closest friends, and really listen to every word you speak. Actually, I worked with many of the angelic realms while I was embodied as Jesus.

Beings from the angelic realms have the purest hearts and intentions, and the mind of an angel is attuned to its Presence, and holds its I Am Flame. They were created from the Diamond Mind pattern of the Godhead, and all angels are required to hold a frequency within of the Holy Spirit; this is why humankind thinks of them as having wings.

The angelic realms are vast, but for now I am going to speak of those that surround the Temple of the Presence. Angelic beings are the primary caretakers for the ray energies they are assigned to, and for spiritual seekers learning to master the qualities of particular rays. As I stated, many of you have angels and archangels that remained with you throughout most of your lifetimes.

When you are ready, angels also help by speeding up the sound current, thereby assisting you in maintaining the frequencies of your Divine Blueprint, which is part of the Oversoul. God created trillions of angels, but most have not desired to enter these regions because of its contamination; therefore, humans should be most grateful when approached by angels that have chosen to serve here. Many guardian angels increase the light held in the auras, not only around people, but around the planet and the solar system. Their work is part of the special love they have for the offspring of God, and they are present in every spiritual community. Angels are also learning to expand, and master their understanding of the human race they know to be divine.

Their heavenly homes are quite different, and they hold many more additional strands of DNA not available to the human during this particular time frame. Some of you will have an opportunity to enter an angelic Oversoul if your I Am Presence gave you that Divine Blueprint; however, not all humans carry that imprint or were meant to, but this does not mean all humans are not also divine in nature.

Guardian Spirits

Many guardian spirits are on paths of ascension, and will be the spiritually awakened children incarnating on earth someday or they have in the past, and remain in service, while others come forth from angelic realms. Some guardian spirits already come in as children after being sentinels to their parents. This is noticeable in offspring when they continually offer wise advice to parents, and occurs because of the bleed-in memory of when they were in a position of guardian. Many are from the higher fourth through sixth dimensions, and experience freedom humans do not since they are not bound by earth patterns, and able to come and go as they please; therefore, they are much more joyful than those in human bodies and consciousness. And there are those that come from the pure light or even the heavenly realms, and they are heightened in their awareness. They aid the ascended master realms by bringing in our messages, and assisting those on earth in establishing communication with their Higher Self or levels of Oversouls; an awareness more will hopefully ask to work with. To be clear, the guardian spirits do not replace your Higher Self or your I Am Presence; rather, they work in unison with them, and with your ascended master councils. Like the angels, many guardians are very knowledgeable of the qualities of a particular ray. Some hold more of the general rays or an alignment from a particular planet, and some do not.

When someone is ill guardian spirits sit beside them, and take this opportunity to learn patience, and deepen their love and respect; this helps them in understanding human concepts and customs. They also prepare souls to leave this embodiment. From this close association, of watching people develop and learning lessons, they become wiser in understanding how to function on the earth plane.

Fallen Angels

Fallen angels are those who chose to follow Lucifer and Satan in the rebellion; consequently, their consciousness fell to a lower level of vibration. Many of these dark angels are in the various levels between earth, and the un-ascended realms, while still others come in human form, and continue to spread, and encourage negative energy. A better way for humans to understand what occurred with the fallen angels is to say they lost dignity before the Father, and it was their own shame that kept them from repenting. The structure of the universe involves many higher beings, not just God and Christ, and not unlike governments that run your planet. The archangels were not the level that fell. Later, some names were attached to the archangel realms, but they were not the originating pattern I am referring to. The originating archangels are quite a bit closer to the Throne Energies than those affected by the Lucifer rebellion. Lucifer was more of a system lord, and he poisoned the minds of many; even though history has given him a higher station then he actually held.

Those of us residing in heaven recognize this is a frightening subject for the human race to comprehend. When the God Source gives a gift, all must obey, but some angels chose not to. Instead, they exercised their own expression of freewill; although some felt disgraced for experiencing these feelings. Legions led by Archangel Michael bound the majority of them in the lower astral fields, and this is how the demonic plane came into existence. Without the radiance of the Father's light these angels lost their angelic presence, and their wings were severed. Many angels who have since repented still carry heavy guilt because of the separation they experienced from Source. Some who continued in a state of separation established themselves as part of the dark brotherhoods that still exist in this universe.

The Master Guide

It is worth repeating what an honor it was for me to be asked to come onto earth, and to be the representation of the Christ. I look upon each soul as chosen, and delight in your individual growth, and I shine forth immense love for all. Frequently, I hold my followers in my arms, and when they are ready I have the ability to assist them in entering the Great Stillness; you see, they must enter a void, and this is where many experience confusion because of the chaos of group consciousness. All people need protection when traversing this energy matrix field, and I will be your master guide. My beloveds, everyone has a magnetic core existing within their heart; therefore, intentions, deeds, and choices, magnetize life experiences. To rise above the energies that create chaos and confusion, ask how to erect an illustrious prism of light around the physical body; thus allowing the Oversoul of the Christ to merge and penetrate the human energy field. I also create a tonal pattern, and teach you to match that frequency. I invite everyone to hold the thought that your homes are sacred spaces, and must be protected; ask the Christ within to assist you with this.

I taught my initiates to develop their spiritual heart. It is through the Will of our Creator the descent of the Christ flame enters you. In time, you will know the frequency of this love developing within. Then the awakened spiritual seeker no longer looks upon another without seeing them as part of creation. This is the remarkable message I came with. The anger, frustration, and limitations, the majority experience creates the chaos, and the current state of earth's evolution.

There is a door everyone enters where there is a bright flame representing the purification of the soul's energy. I gave this teaching when I spoke of the descent of the Holy Spirit. Those choosing to prepare themselves for this path are being groomed to become the Christ, to receive the Seal of Abraham, and to enter the secret chamber of the Holy of Holies. Their minds will rapidly change, and they will long to be of service to God, and Christ, and in that moment God's Will acts through them. Then the disturbances in their lives will take on the resonance of my deep love.

Love is the greatest gift I receive, but again I ask, please do not worship me. I am your biggest defender, and look upon all of you as children developing in consciousness. Show me your love through good deeds, and kind acts to your brethren, for this is what I taught my disciples. Go out among the people, be of service, and deliver the message of God's love for all.

Kindness arises out of pure intentions, and is a phenomenal gift to humankind. I work with you in removing your emotional and mental blocks, and it is my special gift. Respect yourselves, and do not expect to be punished. Receive your lessons through love's gate. In ancient times, there have been many cycles when humans expected there would be harshness from our Creator. What I mean is, in previous evolutions the masses were taught to fear our Creator, and told they were unworthy of a divine relationship. This is because humankind did not always receive doctrines from the levels of the Divine Mind of Creation. Know God's perception of Its creations comes from the position of unconditional love. It is only within the limited tribal expression cultures descend in their thinking, and attribute misfortunes to an angry and punishing Creator. This askew thinking is being replaced with my offer through the Seal of Abraham, and now every single person has the opportunity to enter the threshold of a returning current of divine love.

Protection for Lost Souls

Protecting those embodied is important to me, and this is why I am part of the heavenly light structured to redeem all souls abiding on this planet. I have said, for all who call upon me, I will amplify love and sound tones to them. I open their hearts, I counsel them, and this is really what causes me to step in the position as their Redeemer.

I am also here for those who do not have direction or even know what they are seeking. My beloveds, everyone holds patterns of light, spinning currents, which cannot be understood, and this leaves many completely lost and empty. Those not oversouled by Christ or their Higher Self hold improper patterns creating hatred, and a host of destructive energies. Knots and matted masses of energy are swirling throughout the invisible realms that surround the physical body and the aura, and they block the divine light from entering. It is what keeps souls beyond the veil where I am. It is my job to spread my light around and through those who accept the Christ, and to initiate the unmasking of the fear they hold within; however, not all minds and hearts are open to receiving currents from their divine origin. To do so, there needs to be a stirring in the soul that longs to know God and self within the grand design of creation. Again, I am incapable of hating, and never judge anyone; I simply observe stages of growth within each of God's creations.

Some people have stubborn energy. They may go to church, and even partake of the sacraments, but they do not permit me to fully enter their lives. For them the spark needs to be fanned by one who has the enormity of light I carry, because even in the souls of those that seem very dark and lost there is a small remembrance of the One who created them, as there is always a seed memory within all of creation. Although, I must mention there are those who were destroyed. This means the energy patterns they created in the false image of the Godhead were destroyed, but there is still the sacrament, a blessing, and the image they originally came in with that was their blueprint that returns to Source. In time they too will learn to face the pattern of energy within, and this is another blessed principle at work within the universe.

Catherine's anecdote: Christ showed me the invisible realms where people were walking down a street. As I passed them, dark energy, like thick smoke, blew out of some of their bodies, and also out of several of the businesses.

A Wakeup Call to World Service

Responsible Procreation: Vital for Planetary Evolution

My beloveds, there is an ovoid, an egg shape, and heavenly hosts around the Source of all of creation. The Source or Great Stillness reflects parts of Itself outward through emanations of light, but each component of light holds its Immaculate Concept, and it is the divine birth we were all a part of. The story of my birth as Jesus reflects an allegory of what occurred in the beginning of time. My mother was visited many times by Archangel Gabriel, and it was through the Higher Will she conceived a divine soul; however, not all solar systems hold beings of eminent radiation. Regions are occupied by those who have not chosen to walk in their light, and many of these "rebels of consciousness" yearn to experience life on earth. That is why this planet is a home for laggards, and undeveloped forms that fancy experiencing life in the flesh. They look for opportunities to interact with humans, and they still send dark messages to anyone who calls out to them. This is a wakeup call for you: do not to listen to every voice coming from unseen regions since some of these beings do not carry any light within.

There are a multitude of future events humankind, as a species, is in the process of co-creating, and why self-worth is important.

Everyone has the ability to hold the Divine Blueprint of a Golden Age, and to formulate magnificent opportunities for higher beings preparing to experience earth at a future date. These beings are going to share in the higher conscious thought forms now incubating and the thought seeds being sown that will make contributions to each new life form. No one asks to create the soul of a murderer or a serial killer. This sometimes occurs because those "joining together" do not enter this act as a sacred union of bringing in a soul that will contribute to the advancement of earth's evolution. Drugs and alcohol lower one's frequencies, opening energy grids to lower spheres, and if ingested during procreation is how many souls of lesser development are allowed to enter earth's atmosphere.

There is a marvelous opportunity on this planet for the expression of love, and physical love on earth is unlike the love experienced in higher dimensions; this is one of the attributes that make this a desirable planet to incarnate upon. Therefore, to receive an advanced soul is a gift every potential parent should prepare and pray for, but they need to be able to hold the frequency of a higher being. If future parents coordinate through ceremony, and consciously plan for the birth of their children, there will be a marked shift, not only in intelligence, but in the light of those incarnating.

The Process of Uniting Prospective Parents with a Soul

We are some of the representatives from the Karmic Board, and we are here to tell you that without the inception of the Board, earth would have continued in a downward spiral.

We are sharing information on the conception of children to assist parents in understanding the process, and also since we are presently preparing souls to come to the planet in an awakened state. Some souls have grown quite fond of earth, and only those who identify with the human form and life on this planet would choose to return here. This is also because they have been away from their garments of light for such a long time they no longer relate to the regions of the light bodies. Often, they are so drawn to specific places, people or activities, they desire a rebirth. As an example, there are souls contracted with groups for successive embodiments to complete a certain task for the purpose of assisting earth. In some situations the soul, being part of a soul group, may already have a family it desires to remain with. Sometimes these rebirths are blessings, and other times they are not.

God speaks to each soul before it takes on a rebirth, as do those of us from the Karmic Board, sometimes directly, and other times through their Higher Self. Typically, there is a certain degree of mastery a soul desires to experience during each incarnation. In most cases, the soul seeks opportunities to learn through favorable experiences, although this is not always the case on earth because of freewill. In many instances, the incarnating soul chooses an environment that will support its choices.

The mentality of the soul before a new embodiment determines the level of intelligence it desires, and it sends a wave signal to the planet for a corresponding opportunity. The soul is then required to take a careful look at its soul records to identify the pros and cons of each embodiment before choosing its birth parents, and there are counseled meetings between the soul, and the prospective parents. Karmic patterns between parents and the incarnating soul are normally sought to strengthen the soul's experience. Before finally deciding on the parents the soul will merge with their heart flames to see if there is still a desire to choose them. Once they come to an agreement the soul prepares for a rebirth, and stays close to the chosen birth parents.

The incoming soul enters a spiral of light containing its DNA, and necessary components for birth. As the spiral comes closer to the earth plane it enters a veil of forgetfulness, and its memories from previous incarnations are placed in a chamber in the memory body in the fourth dimension. Unless the soul advances on a spiritual path it usually does not have access to these records.

Next, the incarnating soul moves quickly into a chakra alignment with the mother's system, and in some instances experiences a sensation of falling from a very high place or state of awareness, to a lower energy. The soul does not occupy the embryo during the first trimester, and spends most of its time aligning with the parents. It is during these times some contracts are broken or the fulfillment of the soul's experience did not require a complete birth. Each embryo holds its heart chakra open allowing the flow of light to maintain, and nurture the small system growing in the womb. While in the mother's womb the embryo experiences a massive light. The soul enters the embryo through the mother's crystal cord, and this is why there are corresponding karmic patterns between the incarnating soul and its mother. Once inside the embryo, the soul is able to hear faint sounds through the heart center, and begins to recognize the patterns of the earthly plane. Customarily, several archangels and angels will accompany the soul, and this is when they work with the embryo in clearing, and releasing many blockages from previous incarnations to assist the soul in its next evolution.

Most souls suffer little between lives, and many times they forget how demanding a human life is, and this is why they choose to reincarnate. Also, there are souls that have difficulty with the experience of birthing on this planet, and enter forms where the embryo is not properly developing. In some cases, advanced souls may choose these opportunities to assist parents or family members in experiencing lessons involved with providing for an infant with disabilities. Other souls entering mangled energy fields accept these incarnations as a form of service, and sometimes do not foresee how challenging their lives will be. In other cases, there are a large number of souls still fragmented when incarnating, meaning within them there are aspects of self not in proper attunement with their divine nature; these are fragmented parts of the personality where disturbing thoughts transpire, hellish images are imagined, and where too many souls lose their will to live. This explains why some personalities do not appear to be whole, and need a considerable amount of healing throughout their sojourn.

Dear beloveds, we cannot stress enough how the consciousness affects all aspects of your existence, and the planet. The advancement of humankind's consciousness, especially those considering birthing new lives, will assist earth in providing homes for more advanced souls, and not attract souls with malicious intent looking for imbalances.

Earth's Evolution and Ascension

There is a call going out in present day, just as it has in the past, to bring about change, and to work as a whole as the children of God to see the surface of this world as being one creation; from One Great Light and One Great Source. These sentiments are high now, for my name rings out as the Good Shepherd from all corners of the world. Earth is intended to move forward in accordance with the Will of God, and it is the message I brought forth, but as it goes through the process of ascension there continues to be much upheaval. It is important each of you reach a deeper understanding of your responsibilities while the earth moves into a higher attunement. Healing the planet is going to take everyone who sincerely yearns to know me to take action with the Christ, and there is seriousness in my message. Earth is on an evolutionary spin as it continues moving through gateways, and there must be global peace in order for the planet and its residents to prepare for ascension.

Earth's magnetic core holds patterns of vast light, but it also holds chaos, fear, lack, and limitation, which all cause disease. Many divine beings are working with this magnetic core to aid it in receiving more from its Divine Blueprint, and this will enable earth to hold additional radiations of light.

In the higher heavens there is deep love for humankind; yet constant fear pervades many of your minds. Earth is also seeded by those incarnating from lesser kingdoms who have called earth their home for millenniums of time cycles. In its evolution, earth became a dumping ground for a large amount of these undeveloped souls to take embodiment, but it is now going through a cleansing process. Those of us in the heavenly realms are pouring out incalculable love and joy in order to offset this imbalance, and the higher gateways are now opening for higher beings choosing to incarnate here.

As the Good Shepherd, I come as a guide to prepare you for the journey home. I am able to watch over and assist you with holding frequencies within the body of light called the Christ Oversoul, which is intended to surround you. The planet is moving through an expansion of itself to higher tones or vibratory patterns it once held as it moves into the fifth dimension and beyond. The soul wrestles between what it has termed good and evil, light and dark. These are frequencies or vibrational patterns earth must endure, which in turn creates inner turmoil and struggle.

The judgments some hold, and the lack of respect for the world is what adds to humankind's demise. To heal earth will take the combined efforts of likeminded individuals desiring to put the evolution of the planet first and foremost. The suffering that exists will carry on as long as those incarnating here continue to evolve along the consciousness that we are not one, and that energy will always create war and unrest. In addition, no matter what they are told some will still feel a dark being has a hold on this world. If only they would listen to my teachings or if they were given the proper instruction from birth they would understand that is not truth. God did not create humans to exist in a state of confusion and worry. As more and more people open the door to release belief systems holding fear, and ask to be brought to the community of light, it is there they will be given every opportunity to assist us from the heavenly realms, and the legions that come forth with us in illuminating earth; we will continue to encourage those prepared to be the bearers of light in form.

The future of earth is still undecided due to the gift of free-will; therefore, we unceasingly continue to send healings from the heavenly worlds, but planetary members within group consciousness dwell in thought forms that perpetuate the illusion humankind is not connected and part of the family of one God. This is because the soul's light, in some cases, has been extinguished; the lamp has gone out, and it did not have an opportunity to flourish within the heart of its evolving personality. This has also brought decay on earth, which was not intended. That concept came after the Lucifer and Satan rebellion, and the fall of humankind into the denser planes of matter. Lower thought forms, misguided behaviors, the intent to do harm and create unrest, are what evil is, and what humankind terms as sin or negative karma.

I mentioned earth is coming to a pivotal point in its evolution, and the patterns are spinning into a higher octave, and even time is moving faster than it did a hundred years ago. The reason for this is hearts are more open now, and many spiritual seekers are aware of earth's ascension, and preparing for it. There will continue to be group evacuations, and to avoid them choose to hold greater light. For most, uncertainty keeps them from fully embracing the knowledge and the understanding of who they are, and many are still not comfortable with the belief in reincarnation. Again, I say the physical body is temporary; it is created to allow the soul to comprehend and experience this stage of creation. The Will of God is not to destroy Its people or Its creations; blocked energy is what has caused a malfunction, and numerous dilemmas on this plane of existence. Each individual is spirit, as am I, which is not bound by earthly mass. It is desires, and for many the will to conquer, keeping humans in this containment field of reincarnation. Even though earth is such a long way from the paradise worlds where I have my home, God has still provided enjoyment here, and many blessing are available.

Think Globally

Earth is going through a dark night and some have called it *the dark night of the soul*, and we each experience it. I faced it during the forty days in the desert where I encountered the lower consciousness, which was the desire to turn away from my Divine Blueprint. Previously, I stated there was not a physical devil or any type of physical dark being there with me; however, the mind is very powerful, and it tests the soul, but I chose not to take the path away from my divine calling. Instead, I chose to honor my divine record, and be a catalyst to bring forth new thought onto this planet. Everyone has the same opportunities I was given. Every individual, in every moment, is making choices, but do not see them as good or bad, for they all bring cycles of experience. An earthly experience is a magnanimous gift; yet many may not see their life in this manner, but it is truth. In an earlier chapter, I spoke of God's many angels accessible to those choosing to experience them; so keep in mind they are always available to call upon.

Agencies of Natural Phenomena

Dominion over Earth

We all bow before the one God existing in eternity beyond the Holy of Holies. A part of God emanates within each soul, plant, mineral, and animal. Spiritually driven people will come to realize they cannot respect one part of life, and ignore another; all must be in balance. God gave humans dominion as caretakers of earth, but this does not mean the humans were intended to control any species they consider beneath them. I am speaking about the Elemental Kingdoms, and I realize this subject is somewhat subjective. If hearts are not open, people will not be able to understand my words without contemplating them, and asking me to have the energies of the Holy Spirit enter their minds, and hearts to give them the true meaning of life. The elementals that chose to come onto this planet should not be judged as a creation apart from God or lower than humankind. Just like us, they were created from the Divine Mind of what you would call the Lips of God as the Spoken Word; they are part of the Breath of Creation to bring forth beauty, and companionship onto this world, and to contribute light. Appreciation for all life will help mend bridges with the elementals.

Elementals

The elementals are nature spirits, and guardians. Their kingdom includes animals, nature, minerals, and vegetation. Parts of earth's surface were designed by the Elemental Kingdoms that birthed beauty into this creation, but now they suffer under the limitations of group consciousness created by humankind.

Earth's issues have caused inharmonious relationships between humankind, and the Elemental Kingdoms. The sun system earth is currently in was removed from a collective of the more advanced cultures existing in many universes that do not have such a degree of duality or limited thought forms. As has been said, earth, compared to other sun systems, is considered contaminated. Actually there is a dome around planet earth separating it from other realities, and this is why the solar system appears to be devoid of life. Consequently, souls must work very hard to evolve in this system of energy, and in many cases the elementals are suffering along with humankind. The degradation of the human conscience affects earth changes like a domino system, and at times causes the reaction to be violent in nature. All life is connected. If even an ant colony is in fear it affects all evolving in this system of shared thought. This is how delicate the balance between the human, and the Elemental Kingdoms are, and why earth, after many cycles, is having such weather anomalies.

It is because humankind had fallen so far it was permitted to eat the beast, fowl, and fish, of the earth. There was an earlier era when people did not need such sustenance, for they were able to drink from the fount of the spiritual light flowing within. These communities of creations have been subjected to humankind's rule for too long now, and it is time to heighten this awareness; humans must show respect toward other kingdoms that are also on an evolutionary path. While many species still contribute in service to humans, eventually they will cease to donate their bodies or be overruled. They, like humans, are developing more of a sense of companionship, and unity with the whole as the evolution of this planet continues in the process of ascension, although the plight of earth is still not clear, and those of us in the heavenly realms continue to guide, and direct humankind.

Not all animals give up their flesh bodies for food or nourishment to another life stream. Through the gift of freewill some have chosen to emanate a current of God out of respect for the whole of creation. Elementals evolving on earth are part of the co-creation with humankind. While some species have chosen to depart and evolve on different spheres or on other levels of the heavens, the majority of them feel as though they are your brothers and sisters because, like you, they have contributed much to earth.

Many souls attained an enormous amount of spiritual evolution in previous earthly incarnations, and have since left their higher domain to reincarnate in service for the good of humankind. Conversely, earth would continue to lower in density if divine creatures, both human and elemental, did not continue to incarnate here, and this is because there are still rebel forces desiring to overrun the world.

Catherine's anecdote: I would like to share a recent experience I had with God who speaks to me in a masculine voice. In a vision, I was uplifted and merged with a huge vortex of light, but God did not speak in His familiar masculine voice. Instead, He spoke telepathically. He showed me the essence of my deceased cat, Amber, and I experienced all the love she felt from me while on earth. It had only been about three weeks since Amber suddenly crossed over at seven years old, and her death really took me by surprise. A few days after she died, I was blessed with a vision of her sitting in a window as she looked outside, and she seemed very happy in her new plane of reality. During this vision, God showed me that Amber was also inside of Him. She was not separate from Him and He was experiencing her feelings of the love she received from me. Then God turned my attention toward another one of my cats, eighteen-year-old Misty, who was still alive at the time. Misty did not care to be around my other cats. As a result, for the last four years she lived in my bedroom where she felt safe and at peace. One day I discovered she had a cancerous growth on her paw. At first, the growth was small, like a pea, and in a matter of three months it was the size of a lemon. I took Misty to two veterinarians, and was told by one that at her age an operation was not recommended, but I was still struggling with what to do. I knew eventually I would have to put her down if the growth continued.

God showed me Misty did not want the surgery nor would she survive even if she did agree. Her choice was for me to shield her from that ordeal because she did not want anything to disturb the waves of peace and love she had always enjoyed, and she did not want that experience to change in her final days. During this vision, although Misty was still alive, God was showing me how loved and protected Misty felt, and at the same time she was also inside of Him, as was Amber. God felt what Misty was experiencing. While I was experiencing Misty's essence within God, she was in both places at the same time, in God; yet alive in my bedroom feeling safe, protected, and loved, and all at the same time.

This beautiful experience was a gift from God, and the peace of mind to know when Misty did crossover she would continue to experience my love, just like Amber. I thought God was only showing me this for comfort in relation to my cats. I now realize He was using this scenario to make a point, that like Amber and Misty, I still exist within Him. This taught me that each action we take toward others, even animals, is experienced by God. What a wake-up call.

Understanding the Purpose and True Meaning of Life

Surrender the Path of the Cross

For anyone thinking they were following my words when they took up the path of the cross as their purpose are sadly mistaken. Worse, it became a path of judgment toward others. This led to division among believers in my teachings. It is not the legacy I hoped to leave behind, and as you now know from this book, I did not desire to be worshiped. I gave my sermons out of a deep desire to reveal the truth to those who were hungry for spiritual knowledge. Again, I tell you my words have been misused to manipulate the masses. I spoke in a simple language so my parables would be understood, and my followers could integrate the messages to better understand the world they lived in. Those of us from the higher heavens would never choose to take away the rights of a developing consciousness, especially through any type of manipulation, control, brainwashing or dogmatic beliefs. By no means was control over others a part of my doctrine, although it already existed when I was lecturing, and at a later time it was incorporated in my teachings by others. This was also due to the improper running of the spiritual chakra system some of the clergy held at that time while receiving my teachings. They were confused due to their spiritual misalignments, and their systems were not purified enough to fully comprehend my messages. You must be able to run a full spectrum of light to wear the Christed garment, the Oversoul, and to surrender the cross, and by doing so, I, Christ, will lead you home. Then I will surround you, and expand the light within by assisting you in working with your Higher Self, and your I Am Presence, depending on where you are on your spiritual path. The most difficult task of ascended brotherhoods, sisterhoods, saints, and avatars, is to uplift humankind out of the indecision, fear, and circumstances that bind, and keep souls imprisoned on this world. I taught my disciples if they wished to understand the mysteries they needed to be determined in their walk beside me, and responsible for their choices. All of life is spiritual, and there is not one detail of life that is not part of creation. As you read my words you are in the midst of co-creation, and in each moment you are contributing to the world before you. In the higher realms we move with lightning speed, and our thoughts manifest instantly. The slower frequencies of earth created serious problems for the majority of souls, and this brought a momentum of change, and masked, beyond recognition, humankind's direct involvement with its creations. *All thoughts and every word uttered sends energy into a grid or a pattern that, at a later date, will be experienced by the person who held that thought or spoke that word; the human soul is often held within gridlock as life events move them toward what they previously created.*

As I have been saying these are serious times in earth's evolution. During some American administrations the poorer and less educated were manipulated by certain groups of politicians. They sought to suppress a class of people monetarily below themselves, and do the bidding for those behind the scenes; those who are really the ones in power, and hold the wealth of the nation. The citizens of the United States need to take back their country.

The citizens of your world must unite to put an end to modern-day slavery. Forget feeling separated by countries, and join together to prevent those who would thwart any of earth's inhabitants from prospering, and re-establish equality through currents of love, and respect for all of life. Humankind is witnessing the breakdown of the economic systems that created the current class system. Count-less souls waited a long time to be part of the creation of a new Golden Era, a new expansion of light, and an opportunity to serve our Creator. During this period of adjustment hold onto the values that honor all people, those the heart knows to be true, and benefits all living beings. You do this by taking control of your own mind, thoughts, and will. This is how you fulfill your longing to serve God, and these are the seeds that will bring about positive changes to your planet.

Your True Purpose

A fair amount of you speak to me about feeling restricted on your paths, whether it is in a job, a marriage, a relationship or difficulty communicating with your children; these are all aspects of the illu-sion. Quite a number of souls are unhappy because they do not understand the true meaning of their lives, and they are experi-encing an absence of love. Some people keep busy, and distracted. Still others are influenced by religious orders that teach followers to have blind faith. None of this occurs on other developing planets or systems where each consciousness experiences its God Presence, knows its capabilities, and is involved with the deeper understand-ing of why they chose their circumstances, and that specific real-ity. On earth, many are basically operating in darkness, and do not release the mind in independence. Plus, restrictions set up by most religions are outdated. For these reasons some of the old traditions are beginning to fall. This is why Mother Mary, many other divine beings, and I, Jesus, continue to work with those asking to under-stand the bigger picture, but each person must recognize that mas-tery begins with them. To start with, open a connection through developing intentions, and divine will, and by communicating with your I Am Presence. Often in the initial stages a wall slowly comes down, and you may even experience yourself as holding inconsis-tent emotions; as different as opposite sides of a coin. Take a good look in the mirror, and we will help you reveal your true self. When embarking on a path of spiritual unfoldment some of you may feel you are struggling to maintain the momentum. This is because the speed of light flowing through you is of a much higher frequency than you may have experienced for quite some time. To help remove stumbling blocks we recommend you accept yourselves, and release the painful, limiting thoughts, and memories; instead, focus on personal interests you excel in that create a positive stream of light to dwell in. Each time you experience the light you move to a higher vibration and frequency, but be patient, go with the flow of life, and continue to reinforce respect for self. At first the outcome may be less than desirable, but it will become easier with practice. Your Higher Self understands the Will of God, and can direct you on a positive path. Everyone incarnates with a special gift to contribute. Ask this ability be shown to you, as this will bring significant satisfaction and pleasure. Find the joy in life, even if it is quite small in the beginning. Hold your attention on the concept of experiencing happiness and being grateful, and focus on pleasurable outcomes. Allow these feelings to expand, and they will. Focus on qualifying the heart and mind energies you hold, and always know you can call on the Christ. At this level of attainment our intention is to qualify the light around you; so you are able to hold more of the light from God. Everyone is important. Those who are drawn to this type of material are already beginning to turn inward, raising serious questions about their spiritual path, and asking to understand the makeup of who they are. At our ethereal cities of light we guide you very carefully through the halls of attainment where you are taught to draw in greater light from these higher levels of self, resulting in a passion to be of service to others. As a part of their purpose many will experience an inner knowing that they came to teach the next generations to build a better world.

I am a divine being and know you to be a divine being. Look at the night sky, and pick a star. Focus on it, and know the brightness of that star exists within each of you. Allow the light and that frequency to be amplified, that code of the great I AM within you; it is a joyful experience to share, and it is part of my service. As you work with the energy signature of the Mantle of Christ your lives are more refined, and you experience less happenstance. You will be guided by divine will more often, and not resemble the salmon forcing its way against the current. What the ascended realms have that those on earth do not is *flow*, because we drift with the currents in precision with our God Presences; however, like yourselves, we, the ascended masters, are continually expanding, and we also learn from humans, and souls in all dimensions. For this reason, earth is often called a classroom, and plenty are excelling quickly. As we observe from the heavenly realms we enjoy seeing you, as spiritual seekers, unfolding like beautiful angels, and developing in to masters. I, Jesus the Christ, bless everyone, and harness infinite light for those ready to receive it. It is my honor, and duty to bring forth the Christ Oversoul, the Mantle of the Christ, to all who are prepared to receive this initiation during this lifetime. The gift of working with the Oversoul of the Christ is something I suggest you continue to pray for, especially if you are in the early stages of awakening. The majority are in, what I consider, an adolescent cycle of developing an understanding of the true meaning of unconditional love. Consequently, this is another reason why many of you do not experience enough self-worth or feel a sense of purpose. As the Redeemer, I am a shoulder to lean on, but remember, every individual has a divine purpose. Each of you is the love of our divine Father and Mother. Proceed now to fulfill your purpose by outpicturing it to the world, and doing service.

Self Mastery: Guidelines and Tools for Raising Consciousness

Vera's comment: Although this entire book is an offering of suggestions, this section contains additional guidelines to distract from the illusions of materialism on your journey for attaining, and maintaining peace in your hearts. By no means is it a complete list.

Raise Your Consciousness above the Crowd

On earth, there is a blending of consciousness resulting in group consciousness. This creates a powerful barrier because the discord within groups holds the human consciousness beneath the level of the Christ mind. It keeps people trapped, and it is hard to break free; therefore, whatever you are thinking or feeling, no matter if it is anger, limitation, hatred or racism, and to whatever degree you are experiencing it, you are sharing these energies with humankind. You need to make the decision now to raise your consciousness if you desire union with your Christ Oversoul, for that is who I represent.

Ridding Oneself of Destructive Patterns

You may want to say good-bye to certain patterns in your lives as you aspire to bring forth healthier creations; destructive patterns or old forms of limiting structure will no longer serve the spiritually awakened. These outdated creations are destroying lives as evidenced by the staggering level of abuse. Emotions can be a force of love or a force of destruction; each person must choose what they desire to experience. I remind you the Holy Spirit is always with you, and this is a gift given by our Creator eons ago. Allow this conductor of light to permanently flow through you. When I looked upon John the Baptist, I could see the Holy Spirit completely surrounding him; he was and still is a divine messenger. John had faith in the Word, and as spiritual creations everyone must live spiritually conscious lives. As I stated earlier, the future of the planet is undecided, and unless things change the outer conditions will remain the same for some time or may even worsen. You see, earth is affected by the lower astral planes, and by humans not yet ready to release the lower frequencies moving through their lives, which is creating the world around them. You are within my reach, and those who hear or read my words have a choice to experience being the chosen ones. They will be the ones who will stand apart from the masses, who will hear and understand God's wisdom speaking inside of them. Some may find they can receive messages for themselves, their families or anyone else they wish to share this gift of knowledge with. Strive to be an example of the words you live by, whether it is my teachings or the teachings of another you hold in high esteem. You truly need to bring forth more light, and know you are divine. Tell others that they, and everyone else, are divine too. If more knew this to be so they would behave as divine messengers of God, and not as if it is the duty of their minister, priest, pastor or a revered "holy" person to bring forth these truths. Feelings of worthiness and gratitude must be in all areas of expression, and this will assist God in creating healings everyone is deserving of.

We, the ascended masters, have the ability to dissolve childhood memories that create innumerable misalignments, but we need this habit of revisiting the past over and over again to stop. Step into your personal power and say: *today I create a new day, a new pattern, and I allow God's love to flow freely into my life.* See yourself experiencing the birth of a new consciousness, and those latent memories will dissolve in the flame of love.

You do not remember the deep love you have for our Creator, and the love He has for all of you, because you have dwelled in the illusion of separation for such a long period. It is time now to turn your face toward this Divine Presence in your life. Give yourself an opportunity to awaken to the divine child residing within who remembers. Try not to control this reunion. Whatever stage of growth you find yourself to be in, accept and hold the thought that if you desire this rebirth enough you will return to the system of oneness and the memory will awaken within you.

Remove the Shackles of Self-Imposed Blocks and Burdens

Many have blockages in their own energy fields, and this is another reason humans benefit from working with other ascended masters and me. Open your heart and I will guide you in receiving a blessing from your own God Presence to assist in qualifying the light flowing through you. It is why I suggest envisioning a halo above your head or imagine plucking a star out of the night sky, and placing it in the center of your heart; become that light beam, for this is how I know each soul. The blocks and hardships you encounter exist because of misguided feelings that you are alone. You usually do not remember or understand your own divinity, and the majority of religious sects do not teach this; yet you see it in me, in Mother Mary or in other divine beings, but true healing takes place when you harness the realization of this light, and see it in self. A great deal of growth occurs during this process because now the soul gains wisdom, and knows it is solely responsible. Be honest and state your intentions, but let go of any desire to control others. I do not control anyone, and there is a big difference between guiding my followers, and controlling them. Only speak in words that honor yourself, and one another. If you ask, I will awaken the heart, and encode your soul with the memory that you too are divine, and have the nature of God within. That said, all of you have chosen to experience a certain amount of discord in this life in order to grow; although there are those who take on burdens as a way to settle errors from previous lifetimes. This does not mean as a person evolves they can't release these shackles, and choose to have a more balanced experience. No one on this planet is subject to the will of another unless they allow it, in other words, unless they freely choose that experience.

Quite a large number of people have gotten used to the drama, pain, and suffering, in their lives. Remove this concept from your minds because suffering does not bring pleasure to me or our Creator. The image many hold of me is incorrect. Therefore, throughout this teaching I repeat the sentiment that my desire is to free your minds to help you to understand the true teachings I left behind. Open your eyes, and forever release this cross of burden, for I, Christ, did not give that to the human race. I walk in heaven with the Mantle of the Christ upon my brow, and this is what I wish to share. My voice is clearly heard by many; yet I am often ignored. Earlier, I explained how we continually amplify sound currents of a higher light or frequency, and then transformation comes through the energies of the Holy Spirit. Listen for my voice so you will recognize my tones; I speak softly when answering those calling to me for assistance.

Many came forth eons ago with the intentions to colonize earth, and start the *return process* or ascension. The plan was to bring about a sound current that would evolve everyone in understanding their divine parentage. As the heart flame develops through prayer and meditation, I direct this sound current to you. Some can see and hear this frequency. It is the tonal vibration of the Christed Oversoul, and it is my desire it will eventually surround everyone. It changes the tide, and awakens the human soul to higher levels of consciousness. What happens next is a stirring within, and sometimes this causes doubt about spiritual foundations that were passed down. This is not necessarily a negative thing because the majority is coming from structures of limitation. Within my light you are reconditioned to love one another as I love each of you, and this is the foundation of my teachings. The Divine Blueprint I am offering expands beyond the set parameters most were taught in childhood. Unless the mind is damaged, every individual was given a wonderful gift, which is the ability to ask questions and to reason for themselves. Some examples are: Who am I, and who or what is the Christ? What relationship should I be having with my Creator? The answers to these questions are beyond the limitations, and dogmas passed on by most established religious orders.

Let Go of the Past

Being uplifted in Christ consciousness is no small matter, and focusing on the past only stifles growth. Return to the celestial light, and ask to hold a deeper understanding of these hidden mysteries of truth I taught, and I will assist you in working within the Christ mind, for holy is the day when the spark of Divine Light awakens within the souls of all who dwell upon this planet. Every individual needs to unfold the truth for themselves, and eventually ask to understand their own personal relationship with our Creator and me.

People came before an altar in praise, and in celebration of me. This occurred because of closed minds, and limiting viewpoints that mistakenly taught I am a bridge between you, and our Creator. I say, as the Christ, the altar resides in the chapel or if you prefer, in the temple within, and you are intended to be the chalice. You are not meant to wallow in the lower tones existing in your lives. I am not saying there aren't extremely serious problems on earth, and I know there are many tears in each person's lifetime. The fall experienced on earth, and in other sectors of this universe, created chaos and confusion, and souls who still dwell in these realms are in need of a great deal of spiritual counseling. What suppresses the human race is you do not honor, and respect yourselves or each other, and this prevents you from feeling worthy of my love or of God's love, and this is one of the reasons I chose to come to earth. Be very clear, God never desires or asks for sacrifice. God does desire His creations to experience peace, love, joy, and understanding, but with such deficient levels of self-worth many people still struggle to embrace an all loving God. Balance will come to those who let go of spiritual misconceptions that are prevalent. Begin by releasing the past, and respecting and loving yourself, as this is a form of worshiping our Creator. Next, acknowledging the lessons on your path will qualify the light, and you will have a better understanding as to why you choose to place yourself in unhealthy situations, and a positive shift will often take place. When in communion with our Creator strive for perfection in your relationship with Him. Focus and be consistent, and remember the outer conditions of earth are temporary. Know God extends His mercy, although there are those who will not believe this to be the case. Communion with our Beloved God will send a piercing light through the awakened mind and heart, clarifying your existence.

God created humans to experience existence as an independent being, and still remain part of divine co-creation. During this experience souls are allowed this self-expression, and while there are times some may think God is slapping them on the hand, I assure you God does not behave in this manner. What is being experienced is a level of co-creation rebounding to the human soul based on core beliefs. From now on, expand and dwell in the nature of unconditional love, for truly this is the circuit from our Creator. God is in divine love with His creations, and does not see flaws. In fact, our Creator presents a venue of redemption to return you to a holy state of grace, and He is there for the offering.

Some may feel how they return their love to our Creator is relinquishing their independence or they are pressured to love God, but I do not see it in this manner. Each of us is a part of God, and connected as one. I chose to acknowledge I was a part of that system, and allowed It to express Itself through me. I allowed God to govern my life, and did not choose to be independent of Him. The independence I am speaking of now is the release of the negative ego, the shadow part of self, which is the prodigal child wanting it both ways. To be in redemption is to surrender, but the ego has you in a state of slumber. Most are not completely awake, and experience life through a fear-based limited understanding of spiritual truths driven by group consciousness, and supported by religious congregations. In other words, some folks give their personal power away by allowing others they respect to dictate spiritual truths; rather, than going directly to Source, as I did.

The Great I Am is a loving Presence that knows, in time, all fears will dissolve. It is only by choosing an existence in polarity you are allowing yourself to be guided by aspects created as part of a relinquishment of light, but in truth, where I reside there is only divine understanding. We, in the heavenly realms, are part of a magnetic grid that knows no boundaries of love, it is unconditional, and this is why we exist within God's favor.

Escape Emotional Imprisonment

Many are imprisoned in their emotions. I came forward as earth's Redeemer to help unlock the door, and show you the passage into the higher light that is my home, my dwelling place, and to share the gift of ascension. Look for opportunities in your lives to grow spiritually, and advance in your understanding of the Divine. Go out in nature, and listen to birds singing; look for ways to experience gladness in your hearts. In actuality, many hearts are not fully open, but if you persist there are plenty of occasions to know our Creator, other masters, and me. Do not think of only visiting with God or any of the masters during religious or spiritual services; instead, think of us as having a personal, intimate, and trusting relationship with you, and invite us home to share your heart, and your meals.

Attitude Adjustment

Your auras are crowded with images created by you. If you hope to experience significant change you need to place boundaries on your emotions, and honor self. This does not mean to limit actions of love, but strive to be in relationships, and situations that create a peaceful state of mind, and do not enter the fear of another. Create a new tapestry, a new palette of how you would like to see your life evolve. Focus on creating this reality, and accept nothing less than experiencing it in joy, and harmony. In the beginning, it will feel like an act of faith; however, you do have the power within to experience joyful creations, I assure you. A positive outlook also carries higher frequencies, and is part of your Divine Blueprint.

To bring this process in balance takes a strong will, and the desire to work on self. I am not telling anyone to be unrealistic, and sell all of their goods, and go to the mountaintop. Although, a period of time spent in the sacred sites certainly does purify the chakras; allowing them to hold more light. If you are planning to ascend in this lifetime you need to make the decision to act now, if this is your desired change. I suggest you place your attention in the center of self, in your heart, as this creates a softer journey than starting in the mind. Harness the tremendous power of the threefold flame held in the spiritual heart, and send love to unbalanced emotions. If you are uneasy, feel love for self, and try to gain an understanding of your actions and thoughts. Prayers of gratitude and appreciation will also uplift you, but notice I did not mention prayers that reinforce punishment or suggest you are a sinner. Remember, all actions can be turned around. Good feelings are actual frequencies from the God Presence, which is always in divine gratitude and appreciation for having the opportunity to experience individual consciousness outside the Godhead, and always receives you in unconditional love. If you have connected with any energy or thought that indicates you are not loved by our Creator, it is not coming from God! It is not the Father I spoke of or the One I encourage my brothers and sisters to return to.

Appreciation and Gratitude

Often, many feel overpowered by the circumstances of life. Some have lost the will to live, which is a sign they are not holding enough tones of appreciation for the gift of life God gave them. Gratitude and appreciation also affect the physical body, including the senses, and opens a light within self that allows the movement of spirit to flow through you. Some lives are difficult making it harder to appreciate blessings, but if you value life, and the people in it who love and accept you for who you are, then all of this will bring about healing on many levels. Make a sincere effort to only involve yourself with loving relationships, and their acceptance will allow you to build on that vibration.

All humans have eight memory bodies surrounding them that are invisible to the masses, and most are filled with blockages that may eventually cause disease. You see, the incarnating soul comes in with sheaths around it, and some hold patterns for medical problems; this information is what is missing from most people's understanding, and also what I meant when I told you to know thyself. If a personality allows the ego to hold undesirable traits, such as anger, jealousy, lewd behavior or bigotry, it will return to them, if not in this life then in another, and may also manifest undesirable conditions in the physical body. I am often asked why innocent children are born with disabilities and disease, and the latter are some of the reasons; however, do not judge these babies because there are many unseen circumstances. Also, judging anyone will cause negative karma to reflect back to you. You are all in perpetual co-creation; so think it through before acting. Once again, become aware of what you are focused on to avoid possibly attracting negative mental and physical circumstances, because if you are careless, most times, what you least desire will manifest.

Earth was created to be magnificent and it was once considered a garden world, and to all who came here it was a reminder of the higher heavens. It was a blueprint chosen by many I Am Presences to explore the outermost reaches of creation. It is enjoyed by the multitudes; yet not fully respected. Tones of appreciation will certainly help to bring earth back to its former glory.

Count Your Blessings, and They Will Increase

Much of life is a work of art, and there are still many places to see the true grace, and beauty of God. This is very important and it is the reason I keep reminding everyone that I would like more of you to count your blessings, and daily take time out of your busy lives to give thanks for what you do have. This sets a frequency for larger gains to be given to those of you asking for blessings. The light of God is not completely being received on earth as it is in the higher spheres because the circuits here are wobbly. Therefore, spiritually minded individuals must work a little harder to receive blessings, and knowledge of the higher heavens. I am giving you these teachings now to assist you in achieving this, and moving on to the next level.

Accountability

In time, each soul becomes accountable for all its creations. It is why you are not judged; doubting that enough souls can hold sufficient light to advance the planet would not benefit us. Negative patterns flowing out from you are considered a mis-creation, which affects your experiences in numerous ways, but you have the ability to obliterate these destructive patterns. Also, the fear grid around earth is thick, like mucus, which is a term many will understand. It takes a concentrated effort on your part to be lifted above these currents. What benefits those of us in heaven is to raise the human soul out of the darkness through the precision of the Greater Mind that holds higher intelligence, and divine love. We do this to clearly showcase situations in need of change.

As I have mentioned, presently earth is blessed with more intelligent beings than ever before, they are open-minded, and many achieve a higher education. For most souls the journey has been long, and a number of you are currently reaping rewards acquired from lifetimes where you assisted the planet in raising its currents of light. This is one of the reasons there are more benefits and advancements in healing, and humans are living longer. My beloveds, everyone has the ability to continue to bring through magnificent light from their Christ Oversoul that becomes a conductor of light; therefore, much more light is being released from the hidden chambers within as humankind develops, gaining spiritual power, and wisdom from its true heritage. Then the energies of heaven will descend once again, and more divine love will be radiated to earth. These are reasons to pray for the gift of working with the Oversoul of the Christ.

Darkness is where the energy you call Satan dwells. As I have mentioned throughout this book, Satan is no longer involved with earth, but the dark forces that abide in the lower astral planes are destructive patterns that still block the planet and the people here from receiving the light tones of our Creator, and of the Christ. Understanding no one is subjected to anyone else, only fully accountable for their own intentions, choices, and actions, is a pivotal step in the development of humankind. For too long, those who dwell on earth were liable to a ruler or a system telling them how to think and act. The majority continues to experience levels within self that limit consciousness, and this thinking must cease. Instead, think of it this way, the people committing crimes, especially murderers, affects each of you. They discharge negativity releasing blockages in group consciousness, and this prevents the light from entering earth. Each time someone is drawn to anything depicting violence, mutilation, malice, porn or perversion in its many forms or shows torment or suffering of any kind, whether it is in books or movies, recognize they are momentarily entering an ancient savage memory that is supporting and contributing, even if only temporarily, to a frequency that is part of earth's imbalanced grids of thoughts and destructive desires. They will need to ask themself why they crave this form of entertainment, and take personal responsibility to raise their consciousness, because everyone else shares in whatever type of energy they are releasing. This is due to the fact each thought holds a cell in the memory of the planet. In other words, everyone, living or dead, residing in the grids of earth and its astral worlds are contributors to what appears on the planet, and are part of creation; therefore, all of you are accountable, and responsible for one another.

If my teachings were completely understood, and fully taught in the manner I gave to my original disciples and as they are within this book, you would know in every instance you make a contribution to the consciousness shared by all who dwell upon this planet, and in its invisible regions. It is why each and every single person must act responsibly from moment to moment because; indeed, all are creating. In doing so, everyone will reap immeasurable joy and love as a reward. It is one of the reasons why appreciation is so important because it affects the magnetic core of the planet, and assists in allowing more flow from the energies of love and joy.

Your Spiritual Life, Materialism, and Balance

The goal of life is not to experience materialism to the point it consumes you; inevitably this will pull you out of alignment with spirit, and cause unhappiness. It is not to say those who have a great deal cannot dwell with me, for I sanctify all who deeply crave this depth of knowledge. You should receive satisfaction from all of your acquired creations, even if you only want to further enhance them; however, when you allow material things to own you, instead of solely enjoying ownership, imbalance is created.

This may surprise you, but not all souls come to earth desiring material gain. Yes, there are souls that chose to learn about wealth by being born rich, and do appreciate what they have. Some folks create their own abundance, and are very generous. Others are tested and fail when they step on another for material gain. Subsequently, they are actually supporting a belief in limitation and lack, which is fear-based. Your customs have brought about monumental misunderstandings, and often those people do not remember or experience the simple pleasures, and some loose a considerable amount of light in these endeavors.

Beloveds, at this present time a spiritual life is not completely understood by the majority, and it is more important than all of the material possessions on earth. The latter are only temporary conveniences, and everyone should consider using some of their leisure time to understand the true nature of their being. The indwelling spirit lives in eternity, oneness, and unity, and it is not preoccupied by any sense of status in a community. The saints experienced communion with me because they placed that as their most valued commodity, and they did not obsess very much over the outer world.

I am truly an instructor of the soul, and a doorway for you, and those who call themselves my disciples, and I love everyone. When communing we create a ripple in the fabric of this universe, and I generate wave patterns that bring knowledge, and understanding. I set this experience in motion by causing a stirring in your hearts. Most of you have dreams where you do not feel like yourselves, and somehow know you are something more. In other words, you feel there is more substance to who you are than the reflection in the mirror, and the life you are leading. This memory is given in order for the human soul to stir and hear the call I have spoken of, that knock on the door, to see if you are ready to allow me to awaken you. As you learn more of whom you are your light grows in accordance with your divine and true nature, and I will continue to work to expand your spiritual development.

As the Celestial Christ, I span many universes. When I was the embodiment of Jesus, I healed many so they would have the opportunity to love God, and to know they were loved, cherished, and perfect in God's Eyes. It is also what I do for everyone who is ready to receive me. In the early stages you hold onto me very tightly, since you do not know the way of the divine. Your hearts and minds are challenged in various circumstances as you learn the will of Christ in your life, the Will of God, and His purpose for you. You draw strength from me, and I freely share this gift as my service to humankind. The lessons are intended to be about kindness, forgiveness, love, and the sharing of God's light, for all who ask to partake of it, because everyone has a dwelling place within the Lord.

As I have been saying, each one of you, along with your planet, is on a journey of understanding, and experiencing divine love as it moves through innumerable systems of thought. During the process of initiation seals are opened, and you receive a deeper comprehension of the Allness of the Divine, and how It relates Itself to levels within creation.

To be whole and healed again requires forgiving all others and holding a just mind; this is what I taught. Not only do you need to experience a higher state of consciousness, you must remain there. The material world the masses succumb to is not evil in itself. Although, when a person is not in balance it does energetically have the power to bring forth misfortune, and misunderstandings; souls who get involved in the imbalance of materialism are sometimes called back to the center of their being through a loving act of mercy from their own God Presence.

Be of Service to Others

Service to others is a strong part of my doctrine, and largely what I taught as Jesus. My disciples, followers, and I, collected alms, and gave them freely to those who didn't have much. Saint Francis of Assisi, Mother Theresa, Paramahansa Yogananda, and numerous others are wonderful examples of what I taught, and they truthfully embraced that understanding in their consciousness. Do not limit yourselves to your immediate families. You can better your lives by looking around your community, your world, and seeing where you can be helpful to others. This call to service is especially needed right now. It will help to mend fences, and assist you in seeing each other as one family, one unit, created by one God. Call upon me, and ask how to be in service, and I will gladly come forth to open doorways, and support you in making this a better world. As you work with me, you will heal on multiple levels, and the thoughts of not being connected to our Creator will dissolve. When you open your heart to serve others you will be uplifted in the Oversoul of the Christ, and like Jesus, the crown of glory will be upon your head.

The Sacred Om

The Om many know well can be experienced, and those who use it will benefit. This symbol operates within the molecular structure, and can create optimum conditions on earth. In the higher planes it is a crystalline structure that emanates rainbow effects to the garden worlds, and holds soul memories. The Om is a frequency of love operating in this system, and it is good for manifestation, like bringing things or positive events into matter. Whole worlds were created by the Om sound, and it holds the Divine Blueprint, and the codes of the missing DNA. The Om is also a frequency of light that calls forth the Word of God, and it is the *word vibration* of the Holy of Holies that chants this Om sound in the Great Halls. Even humming the Om sound moves you into your own holy Christ vessel, while clearing earth of negative radiations; it vibrates through many systems, is related to the Holy Spirit, and calls forth the energies of the Dove to blend with the frequency of the person chanting or humming Om. The Om expands the energies into the Celestial light, and it is part of the Christ Oversoul; it operates cords of light, and can clear many astral corridors. The Om sound is similar to a heartbeat also associated with the Womb of Creation. It fills the invisible lower-bodies with a magnificent brilliant light, and it grounds through your many light bodies. It alters the crown chakra, and opens the heart, and pineal gland. While saying or chanting Om, see this symbol at the crown chakra, in the heart, and beneath the feet, and really feel it there. This will create a wave pattern that will fill the physical body with the code of the Om vibration from the realm of the Holy of Holies.

Whether you recognize it or not you are calling in the vibration of the Om sound when working with the Divine Mind, and the Divine Heart. As you step into my embrace you return to a more peaceful state of mind, and this is because, over time, you resonate with my divine heart, which also protects and clears the planet from improper radiations, much like chanting Om does.

Even wearing the Om symbol raises your vibration, and can assist in restructuring the DNA code within you. If you hold a coin, a piece of stone or metal, with the Om symbol etched in it you may actually experience the object vibrating in your hand. Many other sound currents are available to you that are operating in a similar fashion for instance, the Esh, the embers or the sacred fire, which came forth out of the Great Stillness.

Songs

Singing hymns is another way to enhance the mind and consciousness. It also opens hearts and expands the levels of love allowing your frequency to receive or experience gratitude. I hear many songs being sung in honor of me, and although I appreciate the gesture, a greater gift is to uphold the truth of my messages that we are all connected, each of you is a part of me, and I love everyone.

Stop Self-Inflicted Torture

As Jesus, I walked the earth briefly so you will know the truth of your own divine heritage, but much has taken place to suppress the deeper meanings of my mission. An excess of souls have tortured their minds, bodies, and hearts, believing they are, in some manner, pleasing me, but this is a serious misunderstanding of my teachings, and I address this error a number of times in this book. Do not settle for any belief system that endorses such nonsense or prevents you from knowing you too are intended to become Christs, and meant to have a personal relationship with our loving Creator.

Each soul is a well filled with light; therefore, always remember when you are ready a threshold of light will bring about an awakening. Every soul has the ability to replicate my essence, my heart, and my mind. When it comes to God's love, always be in expectation to receive and know His love. God did not create to punish, but to love. Our Creator is a merciful God, loving all of creation.

Peace and the Power Within

Most people do not understand the meaning or the frequency of peace because their minds are too active, and focused on concerns about their lives or the lives of their loved ones. Busy minds that do not find time for God bring about the creation of a tedious life. When this happens they lower the thresholds of light, and the frequencies of their energy, even in their physical body, and this can also cause disease. Learn to resonate to the qualified light. After practicing some of the suggestions I give in this book you may see certain people moving out of your life, your occupation could change, you will seek the meaning of harmony within, and acquire a strengthened desire to find peace.

You can always find Christ within the stillness, the breath energy, and within the light. For those who call upon me, I am in your hearts and thoughts as the Christ. It is my greatest gift to be your Christ; however, my dear ones, my beloveds, what I have been teaching for thousands of years, and now in this book, is as you deepen this experience you too hold within self the ability to walk in my sandals, and hold the light for others. How is it you raise the power within self to hold the light I hold? You do this by first understanding the staff of light I hold represents an alignment to my kingdom and my spiritual power over the lower forces. By balancing your thoughts, emotions, and intentions, you open your heart, and develop your capacity for grasping greater levels of divine love. As you deepen your ability to comprehend unconditional love you increase your spiritual power over the lower forces, the lower tendencies, and this teaches you stability. As this experience continues the light quotient you are holding expands, and you reach a deeper understanding of spiritual wisdom, which means you are gaining more qualified light. Holding greater amounts of qualified light intensifies, and causes a column of vast light to surround the aura, and the physical body. Then the human chakra system opens allowing even more light in, which becomes your seal of protection. The column of light continues to expand into columns that attune to other structures of light, including several light bodies, your I Am Presence, the Holy Spirit, and an Oversoul, which all assist in your attunement with the Christ initiation. This is how you harness light. It is what I learned as Jesus, and what I taught my disciples. The Comforter, the Holy Spirit, continues this work upon the planet. Whatever terminology is comfortable it is a time to be indwelled by the peace-filled love of divine light. This is also what the saints, and I teach when we are called upon, and oftentimes this comes forth in the form of a blessing.

Laughter

Many who are jolly and happy on earth are looked at as if they are not right in their minds; yet laughter is one of the most important tools for transmuting negative flow from the lower astral fields. Also, please be generous with your smile.

How to Balance Living Lovingly, and to Love Living

Discipline must be applied to all areas of life including your time, intentions, thoughts, emotions, and even your finances. Each part of life must be honored, and respected. You experience the freedom of choice, which is an astounding gift to humankind, do not take it lightly. You need to have discussions with your partners, family members, and those whom you interact with to make sure all your energy is being spent where it will do you, earth, and those you love, the most good. The majority is tied up in knots for most of the day, and not enough people look upon their lives as a blessing. This stifles your emotional grids, and affects your mental bodies. Not everyone, but there are those that did not learn these lessons in previous lifetimes, and are currently in such situations.

Each person is more than a physical body. Outside of the denser physical body you are a field of light, and when the Christ Over-soul combines its light with you many experiences flow toward you, while others flow away. This presents an opportunity to transmute situations you no longer desire, and creates the flow for new ones more to your enjoyment. To fully master this concept be willing to address circumstances no longer working for you, and release destructive patterns; so life can be lived as intended, harmonious and balanced. Request that your I Am Presence remove conditions from your life that do not honor you, and reflect on a prism of light focused on the mind, and emotions; this is an energy within the Christ Matrix. This step assists in releasing the false programming creating limitations, lack, and the illusions, many were taught. Within each soul there is the ability to dwell in higher consciousness containing clearer thought forms and more balanced emotions, and this is the Will of God for His beloved creations.

The Christ is a replica of whom each one of you truly is. For most of you, the next step is to recognize there is a divine being within you that has a divine calling. You can mentally go to the River Jordan to be baptized, and bathed in the light of the Higher Mind, and ask to receive the Higher Will. On a daily basis ask to know self, to know God, to know the dwelling place of the Most High is inside you.

Evolve in to Christs

The way and the light I represent are a frequency above earth; where my kingdom resides in the heavenly realms, and where the residents exist in divine love. All earthly souls have the opportunity to evolve in to a Christed being, like Christ Jesus, and this was always the intention, and the message I shared.

The Office of the Christ equally radiates immense love to all who call upon us. As a representative of this office, I came in as an intermediary between heaven, and earth. If you are a spiritual seeker, a disciple, then after your death I will stand with you when you have your life review. (For an indepth discussion on this topic, please refer to the chapter, Resurrecting the Christ Within, page 103.)

Patience

Have patience, and unwavering faith, as this assists in developing the qualities discussed in this book. Patience is an attribute contained within your Higher Self, and your Oversoul. Focus your intention on knowing, and understanding God's love for you, and you will grow in wisdom; this is what Mother Mary teaches, and she represents a reminder of God's love. Mother Mary comes in the feminine form because most people are more open to allowing themselves to receive *a pure mother's* love, and she will occupy that space for them. If this is a current of energy you need to fill or is comfortable for you, then turn your face to the Mother Mary, and utilize the tools I brought forth to assist you in understanding the teachings I left behind.

Final Thoughts from Master Jesus

Observations from my life as Jesus

Some did not choose to come through enlightened parents who could assist them in awakening, as I did. As a matter of fact, there are those who were actually taught to close down. Everyone has the opportunity to go within the depths of self to open this door again, and be enveloped in divine love. Chastising yourself and others causes the blocks and limitations creating chaos in the world. This also prevents humankind from entering the Divine Mind where health, happiness, and joy, exist for all. *Humankind is part of a higher circuit of energy where we all were birthed from the Divine Mind of God, and exist as an I Am Presence, a divine being, created by the Will of God.* I came forth to birth a new consciousness, a new awakening, an expansion of love, and light that will cause many to experience an enlightened part of their soul, and receive advanced spiritual wisdom, and knowledge. This enlightened part of soul, of self, is a member of the higher realities, and with your permission, I will qualify the light, and speak to your heart of the memory of when you dwelled in the most high place with me.

There is a seed concept stored within each of you. It opens the possibility for the human soul to know the meaning of my mission on earth, and it was never meant to estrange one from another or create wars. Mass murders or wars were never part of my teachings or my thinking. I was a man who wanted peace and to bring people together, not divide them. I taught my disciples, and those who listened, to see each other as brothers and sisters, united as one family. I also taught them to love one another as I love each one. In every person, I see the Immaculate Concept. I do not see the human population as a fallen state, and yes, I do have the full record of everything that has occurred on earth. Too large a number of people are still without mercy for one another. Yes, you are protective of your own, whether it is your family, your friends or your affiliations; nonetheless, there is not the full understanding that everyone is connected, and all I Am Presences dwell in heaven as a whole. (For more information on the Immaculate Concept, please refer to the glossary.)

Make big changes by allowing your consciousness to resonate to the frequency of the Christ mind, and to the Mantle of the Christ, which is the robe of Christ as in receiving the *coat of many colors,* and the traditional robe of light energy from the Office of the Christ. Those seeking true knowledge must have a deliberate intention to heal the soul so light may enter, and when this healing takes place the body's afflictions are affected by this master light. This is another example of why many on the planet do not seem to be aging at the same rate they did two hundred or even a hundred years ago. Another contributing factor is the structure on the planet is now able to support this change because more people are experiencing an increase in thought forms of higher consciousness; thus supplying earth with possibilities previously not available. Also, there are more socially and spiritually advanced systems existing beyond earth, and they assist humankind by directing prayers, and opening thresholds of light, creating numerous waves of awakening. For this to continue and excel, fear needs to be reduced, and eventually eliminated. It is highly beneficial to planetary peace, and spiritual understanding to no longer see temptation as the devil anymore, knowing Lucifer and Satan were eliminated from this universe long ago.

Sometimes it is necessary to remove oneself from daily concerns to create the opening to meet our Creator to learn of your divine nature, and that of all living things, to stand in the truth of who you are to receive that divine image, and pattern back in your heart, mind, and soul; I accomplished this by seeking the wisdom within me. I was truly a merciful man of deep counsel with God. I also studied with many masters, and listened to those who taught the ancient scriptures, but I chose not to accept only the outer meanings given by my teachers; I sought within myself the true meanings, the hidden meanings. It is what every individual must do.

Inspirational Insights

Many look up to me as a pillar of strength; yet I am but a reflection of the One residing in all souls. I explained in earlier chapters, I did not hold the karmic patterns most do; so I radiated more light. I had a greater thrust from the Holy Spirit because it was developed over time through many experiences, and I was aware of myself, of my true calling as a teacher, mentor, and healer. As I have said, I was also greatly chastised in my day. Not all came to listen to me speak or to take upon themselves the higher wisdom. Some came just to criticize, and mock me. They were not there to learn how to deepen their knowledge of who they were, and to gain an understanding of their true relationship with a loving God. Some came with closed hearts and minds, but I spoke freely to all, sharing my words, and wisdom to better the world, and to be of service, although I recognized earth was not my home. Dearly beloveds, I patiently watched this planet develop through numerous time cycles, and yearned for the day the seeds I sowed would grow in humankind's hearts and minds; that God's love, and light would be the beacon shining upon every soul, and this world. I was, and still am a messenger of hope.

Throughout this book, I spoke about the sacred heart within the soul, and made clear it is not the heart of the physical body, but the heart of your God Presence. It is the heart each one aches to experience, and the Presence of God loving His creations. This magnanimous light is what I came to share. I come toward you when you say my name out of love, respect, and honor, not solely out of worship, for I desire to move you away from that thought system, and have your minds and hearts embrace me as your elder brother guiding you home from this journey. It is important to say here that reverence, which is not the same as worship, is what you should direct toward me, for I have traveled beyond your present spiritual experience. With your permission, I will occupy a place in your soul, and together we will unravel the issues that plague your life. I only leave your side when asked. I am a consciousness of magnificent love with a desire to work with you, to light your path, and to welcome you home. I honor our friendship, and it is sealed in a brilliant light. Make no mistake, I intend to remain as your shepherd for as long as I am needed. When I wore a human body I believed my life would reflect the love of God, and that knowledge was to be shared.

As the Celestial Christ, which is more than the one personality of the man Jesus who demonstrated this office, I continue to remain with earth through its many cycles, and I have many disciples. Conflict is within human minds and hearts, and there is sadness where there should be joy. Poverty and sickness is where abundance and health could be. You need to put down the weapons of hatred, the fight over boundaries of land, and the ills expressed toward each other; these are destructive forces for all of creation. Be the creations of light you were meant to be. Your divine souls are intended to merge with the human soul, and in its purity it knows only oneness.

Earth is missing an orientation to the Will of God. Most live the will of man, which is unfortunate, and it is because of this you continue to suffer. Do not restrict me or your spiritual path with the limited understanding that was handed down. *If any of you want to know the man who was Jesus, ask to resonate to the true messages of my life then, and of my heart and soul.* Do this, and the memories of your own divine nature will return. Each person has a divine call, just as I had a mission, a purpose, to teach you to love one another. Work out your differences, and have patience with one another. Strive to be the best you can be in all you do. Recognize your accomplishments, give compliments to others, and acknowledge their self-worth. Be independent thinkers. Pray for deeper understanding, and the wisdom to look at each situation to find the solution that is the Will of God, and then more hearts will open to my messages, and my voice.

The Christ is an overtone on earth. It resonates to those who are listening with an open and loving heart. I have messages for many, if only they would just make themselves available by being still, and listening for my voice. The door to my heart is forever open. I long to give the Mantle of the Christ to all of you, but in order to do this you must completely forgive everyone for everything; totally surrender all parts of self not resonating to unconditional love, and then you will reverberate with Christ's love for all of creation. Many do not feel worthy of this gift of love, but I tell you this inheritance is your birthright. Do not continue to be imprisoned in a belief system that does not contribute to your humanity. When you are speaking to another remember what I suggested, and see my face over theirs, and ask yourself these questions: Would I speak to Jesus in this manner? Would I curse at him? Would I raise a hand to Jesus? For as the Christ, I live in all beings, and this is made possible through the Immaculate Concept.

God has the ability to elevate anyone, male or female, to the position I hold for earth. Certainly, this should be the goal all of you hold in your hearts. Nearly everyone is told I only come to very few. That is not true. God created the level of the Christ to welcome all of you home, and made it possible for Christ to abide in each individual so they may fully and completely awaken, and attain this stature. Many times I appear holding the staff that empowered me, and it is symbolic of someone guiding people to a safe haven. The initiates of the brotherhood and sisterhood of Christ also walk with a rod of power that holds the currents of light they have achieved for themselves. What is missing from the levels of earthly consciousness are ways to empower yourselves without crushing another. Too often one achieves prominence, power, and wealth, on the back of another. If you did not dwell in fear, and insecurity you too would hold that rod of power while standing shoulder to shoulder with your brothers and sisters, as they hold their rods of power. Before the Lucifer and Satan rebellion, this was so. The nature of God is to expand love, and this cannot be done through war. Compassion is within reach of everyone. You need to decide to choose peace. When you call out to me it is important you know I hear you, especially when you are in despair. Give me your consent to show you a path that will bring forth blessings in your lives. Once you raise your consciousness you are immediately welcomed back to the heavenly fold.

The Second Coming

In this book, I already expressed that my energies have never left nor will they ever, but the expectation I will come to earth again in a body of flesh as Jesus, is misunderstood. *The second coming is intended to be the development within of the human soul to the Christ plane, allowing Christ to embody every soul; the coming of the Christ happens within the hearts and minds of my disciples.* So no, I, Jesus, will not return born of woman again; however, there are many masters now holding the Mantle of the Christ that may also choose to visit earth, and every soul will have an opportunity to evolve in to a Christ. When I, Jesus, do return, I will come as the Celestial Christ with a spiritual hierarchy of those who stood with me, and are filled with the light of the Holy Spirit, and my return will occur in accordance with the Will of our Creator. I don't expect this to transpire until earth enters a higher alignment, and no longer is separated from the more advanced planets. Nonetheless, I already "return" many times to earth, and walk among you, but few see me because I am still cloaked from their vision. I continue to come this way to raise the consciousness of those who follow my words, and ask for my teachings. You, as spiritual seekers, will climb various vistas with

Christ as we travel this ascent together, and you learn to trust me. Eventually, you will know when I am present by recognizing my sound tones, even if you are unable to hear my exact words. We will discuss an array of matters, and I will assist you in developing the divine aspects of self. This is so you will function in a more highly developed consciousness, able to think and perceive more clearly.

A frequency or the outcome of a situation can be altered by focusing God's love, and light on the circumstance, and asking the energies of the Holy Spirit to go before you, and make your way straight. It does not mean there will not be bumps, and hurdles along the way, but certainly there will be fewer of them, and you will feel more protected, and loved. You will also notice certain scenarios that continue to occur in your life no longer affect you in the same way. In other words, turning your life over to your own Holy Christ Self and your I Am Presence is truly what the Will of God is; to know thyself as a divine creation.

A Closing Message from Christ Jesus

For quite some time earth has been preparing for a Golden Age and Christ is very pleased with the spiritual progress on the planet. This is the work of the Body of Christ, and it is elevating those who are ready to move into a deeper, expanded personality known to be the true self, and not limited by this planet's structure. Many among you are my disciples, and walk with open hearts to receiving me, but I cannot come to all of you in the manner I come to Catherine, because each soul is being groomed to know me within the structure most beneficial to them. The way you are familiar to receiving me is how I will approach you, and from that point I will instill within you the celebrated love of our Creator.

The structure of the church and ministries were erected because many needed congregations to support their beliefs, and faith. However, as your yearning deepens, your understanding will too, and you will acknowledge what I said earlier to be true; *the chapel* (or if you prefer, the temple) *has always resided within you.* Throughout this teaching, I have been planting seeds telling those whose hearts remain open to think for themselves. If a teaching promotes fear, separation, and drives a wedge between people, it is not from the highest heaven.

Some time ago I made a pledge to my followers to remain with them, and to expand their understanding of their true home. Within these pages, and those to come, I will continue with that commitment. Go in peace, and love one another. Grow in the expression of my teachings. I remain at the apex of the Golden Ray, and the kindness I bring forth is always nurturing.

My love is without measure, I am the Christ.

Christ Answers Frequently Asked Questions

1. Why pray to Jesus, and ask for his forgiveness if he is not God?

This is a wonderful question. Serious prayer should be directed to our Creator, and I recommend deep consultation with Him. I am one who has demonstrated the wearing of the Mantle of the Christ. Allow me to step forward, and present you with *your* Mantle of the Christ. I work with the multitudes on earth, and love them as the Father loves them, and in this act I show mercy, but many humans fear me because they have been incorrectly instructed by religions.

When you pray *with* me, I come before you as the bridegroom; for this is the promise I left behind. In this alignment, with me as the bridegroom, you receive the blessing of an outpouring of golden light that holds the Christ mind. As you enter this pattern of light energy you become wed to the Christ, which is an Oversoul. You do not actually marry the personality of the man Jesus, although I have allowed myself to be portrayed in this manner during this earth cycle, because the full doctrine of how one receives the Mantle of the Christ was not passed on to humankind. This is all part of the redemption I offer as an awakening to my brothers and sisters. I have the full power of the Godhead to instruct on earth, and be the representative of the Father's love, and forgiveness. I am proud to say, I am not the only representative of the Father that has visited the human race, and even though other agents of God have come to earth many times, they are not always recognized.

I repeat, you should not worship me; rather, honor, and respect me. If you ask for my forgiveness, know I will uplift you, and carry your burdens. I will hold you until you learn to hold yourself in the light of Christ. I am somewhat like the arm of grace surrounding you with love, and mercy. I am not far from you, I am within your heart, and can be within your mind and emotions if you allow me to be. I came forth out of the Spoken Word of creation. I hold a pattern of understanding the majority in human form have long since forgotten. I "marry" you in your higher light body, which holds a pristine cloth of immaculate beauty, and there I counsel you. I am one whom you can always trust, and will always remain with those who call upon me, and I honor my word to each of you.

2. I am nearly twenty years of age. Will you be returning in my lifetime?

I have returned many times because I am able to move through the ethers and visit, but not in the form you are talking of. Often, I stand next to world leaders, speaking to them while trying to teach them to hold a global view. No one should be afraid of the Christ. The Christ walks on earth, still not in human form, but I have not left this planet. Even now, I speak to you through this lovely disciple Catherine, whose heart has remained open to me throughout several of her lifetimes. (Please see the section on The Second Coming, for a deeper explanation, page 262.)

3. Jesus, I would like to know if there is value in carrying guilt over something you did years ago?

There is a time of repentance, but I would rather see God's creations involved in community service to wash away their "sins," than carry guilt. Mirroring the negative aspects of life contributes to a misalignment with earth's grids, and does not support a filter of light intended to surround you from your God Presence. It also destroys the God image you hold toward self.

Everyone is able to come before the Throne Energies and ask for forgiveness. If your action was severe, then look for ways to remedy the violence you set forth. Prior to incarnating, everyone who chose to embody clearly understood they were going to experience a consciousness, and emotions based on duality, to one degree or another. Forgiveness is part of the energy of mercy coming from the heart, and the Will of God, and should always be understood as being available. If you choose to align with the goodness residing within, you are forgiven. If you continue to create suffering with intentions to bring harm to yourself or others, then it is not God who does not forgive you; rather, it is your level of understanding the truth of the Will of the Father that is misaligned, and you will merge with the pattern of suffering you are choosing to create. Also, levels of mind and emotion will remain in separation from truly knowing your relationship with me, the Christ, and our Creator.

4. Is it a sin not to trust in God's forgiveness?

God is in love with Its creations. The Great Silence actually created for companionship. God did not create to punish, but to love. When you do not trust in Christ or God's forgiveness, what you are actually saying is you are refusing to accept the Mantle of the Christ, which is the Christ Oversoul I speak of in this book. If you choose fear, you will not remedy this or any situation.

This brings me to the topic of dogmas based on a punishing God. This is a foolish concept, and it does not teach accountability for your intentions, your speech or your actions. When I was placed on the cross, and looked down at my disciples, I told them not to be afraid. I spoke those words because it was important they understood this was not a punishment from our Father, it was my choice. I was permitting this experience, and using the opportunity to bring forth conditions that would structure, and harness the light of the Christ to many. Not trusting in God's forgiveness causes you to remain in separation. As long as you are in separation the light beneath your feet will not open, you will not receive the tributaries of light, and the Holy Spirit will not be able to descend upon you.

5. Where does fear come from? Does it come from God? What is my purpose?

Fear comes from the shame you carry, which is stored in many levels of your thoughts and emotions, not balanced in the light. Again, I say you chose the experience of a feeling world, and the consciousness you hold is complex. It takes courage to look at your lives, and analyze where your thoughts, and emotions originate. Humankind has difficulty maintaining the pure coding without having the additional strands of DNA that were removed quite some time ago.

There are levels of instability within the chakras that are receiving sound, and light currents. This is because not all chakras are open or in the correct positions; often they are misaligned, and hold denser energy. These create impure thoughts, desires, and actions, and many of you do not allow spirit to guide you to offset these impurities. You succumb to a level of action, and reaction based on imbalances where you experience discord, and then ask for mercy, and to be forgiven. Precious souls, how can God and I not forgive you? Ask us to pass the I

Am Flame through you, and you will learn to harness this frequency. This will draw you to the Oversoul of light, and to the gateway of my kingdom, and your personal I Am Flame will expand in to the heart of God.

Fear did not come from the Mind of God, He adores His creations. The missing key to understanding your lives is in maintaining balance on all levels, and to turn your consciousness, and emotions over to our Creator; *that is your mission, and purpose.* Many lift their eyes to God in sorrow and in pain, but many more do not realize all aspects of self will eventually align with the Christ mind, and the Christ flame.

6. Are we to fear God, and also love Him?

Please do not fear God or any of us in the higher realms. When you align with spirit you receive a blessing. Understand our love for you is everlasting, and unconditional, as is the love our Creator gives. Strive for a heart-to-heart connection, and allow me to bring peace in your hearts, and souls.

Fragmentation from the Will of God is where the thoughts of separation and fear of an Abiding Light come from. This light is an all-encompassing flame, and knows no judgment. The love you have for our Creator is returned through your I Am Presence, and it does not relate angry, hateful or dark thoughts toward God back to the Godhead. That originated from the level of the human personality because darkness is not an energy signature that would ever return to the level of God. You dishonor yourself and your Presence by despising our Creator, but it is not a frequency that will enter the region of God. That level of negative thought, spawned from the ego, actually spins in the lower consciousness, and stays attached to you, preventing you from experiencing, and merging with the fire of creation. Instead, you diminish your light, and understanding of our Creator and of me, the Christ. This is yet another form of separation.

7. To have fear, and anxiety be a part of everyday, and the feeling of doom hanging overhead, can this be from God?

No, this is not from God, and it stems from not reaching the higher realms. Many times this occurs when your spiral of light has insufficient energy patterns, and you do not hold enough love of self. Then the human mind, through the ego, puts blame on our Creator, and you prevent yourself from receiving an attunement to a Christ realm, and the gift of the Holy Spirit's blessing.

There is absolutely no dark force in this universe able to prevent the light from blessing you. Only you can prevent God's Light from blessing you through your thoughts, actions, and emotions. The root cause of all problems lies within, and how you perceive yourself within this universe. Begin by creating opportunities that bring respect, and love back in your lives. Introspect every day, look in the mirror, and accept God's love. This will align your chakras with the light, and assist you in understanding your multi-level intentions.

8. Is there a way, through God, to overcome the trials of life without turning to drugs?

Absolutely! Many turn to drugs because they are absorbed in fear, and again for the reason they have limited access to the higher light patterns. Also, many allow others to control their emotions, and their thinking. They need to accept there is justice in the region of the heavens, and recognize where their fears are stemming from. I suggest they dig deep to look at their core beliefs toward themselves and others, even if it means examining shortcomings without judgment, exploring ways to hold a new thought or seek services available to overcome repetitive situations. Some of this occurs because the light around them is not complete, and they do not have a filter for their emotional protection. They can find strength in God, and draw in light through their Presence, which is the ultimate healing. If they allow, I will also emit an energy frequency to their emotional bodies to assist them with receiving the light from the level of the Christ mind; so they can deal with their pain without drugs. If this is something they would like to do, they can continue to call upon the Celestial Christ, and their own Christ Oversoul.

9. Many teachings say God is Love, but my church also teaches fire, and brimstone. Are we to live in fear and guilt?

I have said throughout this book my teachings are not based on fire, brimstone, lack or limitation. My teachings are about peace, harmony, love, and attunement, with the Holy Spirit. It is very unfortunate my teachings were changed, and taught as sacrifice. I walked the path as a master to teach you to harness the energies of the magnificent light called the Christos, and I taught how to embody that light. The sacrifices many are experiencing are part of the dogmas that came about through a mis-understanding because the dwelling place within them is not holding a pure shaft of light. Many souls who are now embod-ied have serious problems in their lives, as do their extended families; all are heavily burdened. Call on me and ask for my assistance, I will help carry your load and teach you to har-ness these frequencies, but not all of your burdens will be taken away in our first encounter, and for some they will remain with you throughout this life. This is because there are souls who have come to experience these conditions that can be part of an earthly life, but I can assist you in the way you move through these events by lessening their effects.

Beloveds, I did not come so you would continue to sacrifice to measure up to me; rather, I came to show you a graduated path of accessing the eternal light amplified within the image of my sacred heart, and I enfold you in that light. Your suffering over my incarnation as Jesus is not what I desire for you to hold onto. There was a series of talks I gave that were not recorded, and held the blueprint of anchoring to your own Christ Over-soul. After my death, my mother and Mary Magdalene continued to teach that doctrine, but during that period their voices were not heard as the authority. That was a softer path because people's minds were stained, and could not accept God's love, and blessings. Instead, they sought a teaching of sacrifice, and hardship that eventually came through the priesthood. The tones I held were very loving. If you study the scriptures on my deeds, and focus on how I shared my essence with all, you will come to know the man I truly was, and you will learn to harness this frequency, regardless of what is being taught to you.

10. Why wasn't Jesus clear when he spoke?

I chose parables as a way to ensure my teachings would be handed down, generation after generation, through the art of storytelling. This was a means of teaching then, as many did not have access to manuscripts nor had the ability to read. In addition, the parables were less likely to be tampered with than formatted teachings, and people could ponder the stories to find the hidden meanings; however, there were some clear teachings given, but not all were recorded. Also, several of my disciples went among the people, and did speak in everyday language, without using parables.

For me to give a deeper teaching to the masses there needed to be a higher level of surrender to the frequencies of divine love, and in those days there was very little mercy shown toward others. The rigid belief systems also prevented many from comprehending a teaching such as mine. Understand beloveds, I was tearing down very old doctrines, and teaching the law of one; that we all are one community of light, and there is only one Loving and Merciful God. I showed many the way that were hungry for knowledge, and they truly developed a deeper understanding of my works, and words.

11. We often hear everything happens for a reason. Is that true or are there accidents in this dimension?

We, of the ascended realms and archangels see accidents do occur, and there are degrees of incidents; therefore, I will say because many align to the frequencies of suffering, you are not totally free of accidents. Other heavenly hosts and I provide a certain amount of protection for the human race, but some have chosen these experiences, while others have tendencies toward mishaps. This should not be held in judgment for the reason when accidents do happen they occur on deep levels of subconscious thoughts. This is why a peaceful state of consciousness should always be your goal. In your world, I see many rushing around, and not focused on their surroundings, this often brings misfortune onto the path.

12. What about sacrifices and the benefits of our intentions?

Beloveds, the benefits are for you. With highly conscious intentions you are reaping the rewards of learning to work with, and control the tributaries of light; consequently, you are experiencing a more joyful expression of life. The only one suffering from impure intentions is you, and those you interact with. Do not view suffering as a reward or a punishment system. This is a major step toward healing. For a moment, let's put aside the thought God is punishing you or not favoring you. I assure you, the heavenly realms are *just* toward all of creation. Now give yourself permission to accept the opportunity to look at what brings you joy, and acceptance of self. If you enjoy gardening, writing, painting, singing, music, crafts, children, animals, being of service or whatever it is that brings forth pleasure, feel what these emotions are like, and choose to remember them, and then bring the energy of these feelings in all your situations. Are you not doing the same thing with fear when you readily accept negativity?

Some believe God is an action behind all that is occurring in their lives, and He feeds the negative as well as the positive. This is not in accordance with the Will of Creation. If you choose love and joy, then accept God is blessing all conditions. In the higher universes there is not an experience of duality. The Mind of God is not out of balance because of the experiences *you have chosen* on earth. You are in a human body that holds limited opportunities for expansion of your spiritual nature, unless you truly desire to take on this path of enlightenment.

13. Why is there reincarnation, and is there a point to it?

Reincarnation began on this world and several others because of the distance the soul is from the higher, purer realities known as the heaven worlds. For the soul to experience balance there are many nuances and this is why the human soul, in its desire to understand itself, reincarnates.

Reincarnation should be understood as an opportunity for soul to take on additional lessons; so it can release judgments it holds from one incarnation to another. It is used as a way to teach the incarnating part of soul to be skilled in carrying enough light to expand beyond the seal surrounding this cosmic experience called your earthly life.

Your current personality goes with you in death. Most souls decide to continue with their likes, dislikes, and attitudes in their next experience. Some choose to deepen their understanding, and the meaning of the life they just left by attending schools on the spiritual planes to develop their soul qualities. This gives them additional choices, while others are still consumed with the distractions of what earth held for them.

My beloveds, there are many other experiences for souls who can journey beyond earth. This is why you need to live your life introspectively, and bring every aspect in balance, such as how you speak, what you feel, your intentions, deeds, and even what you expect back from another while giving or donating. For example, do you crave gratitude from others, and is this the reason you are generous? Are you gracious with spending on others; yet at the same time you cannot give a compliment? Or is it you are able to give love and support, but cannot give away money or goods because your soul fears lack, and you cannot part with money? If that is correct you may be moving toward the frequency of being miserly, and you may not be conscious of it. Soul may even mask these fears with judgments toward others. In the latter case, I will say at the root of your soul's convictions it does not truly believe in abundance, and your life is out of balance. These same applications apply toward anger, jealousy, bigotry, control, accountability, and all other imbalances. Mastery is learning to be in balance, and this is what soul discovers from experiences lifetime after lifetime. As you bring all you are under the control of your spirit, and allow your God Presence to remain with you, and act through you, only then will the wheel of rebirth come to an end. Until soul becomes self-realized, and balances sufficient levels of love toward self and others, it will not attain an understanding of unconditional love, and earn its Christhood. As you learn to harness your Divine Blueprint you will become quite spiritually powerful, and a leader to many, as I did.

14. Do we come back as insects or animals?

No, because the human consciousness is intended to hold a separate DNA structure than the Elemental Kingdoms. Few would return to this planet in the form of an insect or an animal. Some that do are very low in nature, and still others are from the lower alien races that do not abide in the light. They come in that way when they want a body here and can no longer carry human DNA coding. Do not let that statement frighten you; however, if this occurs it is because they did not hold enough of a Divine Blueprint from their Divine Monad or none at all. In rare cases, they have moved into an elemental alignment. Some vile creatures did descend to a much lower consciousness for a period of time. However, not all insects or animals are part of the lower aspects, and most animals come from divine creations. Insects that carry disease were created by the darker brotherhoods. If you treat animals, and vegetation with respect, you will prevent the lower forces from attempting to occupy them.

The Elemental Kingdom's plants and animals are under the protection of the bearers of light. Actually, a very ancient sun system in a celestial corridor created the animal kingdoms you have. It was Adam that requested earth be given companionship in the form of animals because he had experienced elemental creations when he encountered other planets and other forms of creation, and in that pure state they were not used for food. A huge amount of the Elemental Kingdoms were delighted upon his request, and many of these creations continue on their own evolutionary journey of understanding, and contributing more to the service of co-creation. Some of these creations are experiencing fear, like many of you, which was not part of their Divine Blueprint. They occupy the same planet as you, and because of this they are also contributing to the misalignments, and pressures currently placed on earth.

The Elemental Kingdoms are also developing, but along a completely different spiral of energy. *They are not less divine, and this is the reason some alien races utilize elemental spirals in a way to gain light, and advance in consciousness.* The heart centers of domesticated animals are learning from their notable teachers how to be more in tune, and helpful to the human race. Choosing to be of service to humans does not make them beneath you, and you may be aware of animals serving by learning to sense illnesses in humans. The animal kingdoms also have their own chakra systems they align to, and like humans they can experience being out of balance with the Divine Force of Light, and this imbalance causes many earthly species to suffer.

15. What is ascension? Is it possible for me to achieve ascension in this lifetime even though I am almost fifty?

Ascension is always accessible at any age. This is actually the teaching I left behind, which is to allow the Holy Spirit to descend upon you. The Holy Spirit is a tributary of light that will draw you into the Christ mind, and from there you will learn to work with your God Presence. That process will give you ascension from the earth plane.

16. Why does there seem to be so much good surrounding some self-centered people, while some very kind, and conscious souls seem to suffer?

Unconditional love, and acceptance of self is essential; yet many good people find themselves in a victim consciousness that misaligns them with the co-creation of a loving, and abundant universe. This is why I taught your rewards are in heaven. I understood there are those who are selfish, and eager to advance without regard to the conditions of others, and able to create with that pattern on earth.

It is not a negative spiral, but many institutions have hammered in to the consciousness of their followers that those who are pure of heart should be without worldly goods, and only desire spiritual merit, and then rewards will come through their suffering, and lack. This has actually created enormous pressure on the Christ Oversoul to bring forth the blessings of creation. It would be best if you understood your being an intricate part of the teachings interacting with co-creation; somewhat like electricity or water running through a pipe. The electricity and the water flow to all the buildings whether or not the people in them hold criminal intent or are praying for God's Will; they can still turn on the light switch and faucet.

This is actually an abundant universe, but do not look down on yourself for not having abundance. Some chose lessons of trial, and tribulation from previous lifetimes when they held fast to a belief system taking on that pattern. There have been wonderfully advanced saints, and teachers of the light that did not choose to be the demonstration of outer abundance. This is not held in judgment. The reason this came about was by desiring outer rewards many were not able to hold enough light to balance their karmic patterns. Instead, they delve deeply in the importance of accumulating the outer master, and not developing a relationship with the inner master who can perform many miracles, and bring much into manifestation.

We would first recommend you release judgment, and see it is merely a circuit, and recognize how you maneuver in this energy field of abundance. See if you are in a frequency of acceptance and to what point. Do you feel discord when you desire something? Do you feel shameful or deserving? One way to overcome a negative feeling toward receiving is to hold the excitement you had as a child when you did not judge yourself for wanting a toy or a day of recreation. Try to work with that image of self. Learn to release the judgments you have been taught about having such things; however, excessiveness is never good in a world so out of balance with materialism, and it has pulled many potential masters from the path. Balance unconditional love with all you are creating. Know God is a Creative Force, and you are intended to be a part of that. Allow that circuit to work through you by learning how you value yourself, and what hidden meanings are a part of your intentions. This is going to take you on an inner journey of your deepest feelings and thoughts held within subliminal levels where some have been told, lifetime after lifetime, they are unworthy.

Don't punish yourself for not having what another has, and shed those ancient beliefs of lack. Do not permit the more recent teachings of abundance to limit you or allow another to say, *you must be doing something wrong if you cannot create what you want.* This is a misunderstanding of the law of attraction, and those suggesting this may find if they do make a judgment they will soon be walking in your shoes, for this is how the universe, which is conscious, works. *Realize you cannot judge without experiencing your own judgments.* This does not mean God or your I Am Presence will take anything away from you, but your energy patterns will create a bridge to that circuit the soul is judging, and set up a lesson for you based on that judgment. This occurs on levels below the conscious mind and your conscious feeling world, but this is not done to disgrace you. It is to teach that all of you are a part of experience in the realms of duality.

You have accumulated good in the spiraling rings around your I Am Presence. This is where your miraculous gifts come from, and why small indiscretions you perform fizzle out easily in comparison to the good you accrue. Our Creator is truly a God of Reason. Allow Him to come to you in this manner, be a just person, and you will reap a rewarding afterlife.

17. Is there life on other planets?

There are many expansions of co-creation from the Mind of our Creator. Your universe is only one small part, less than a fraction of what has been created, and there is much more for you to discover once you elevate your consciousness, but you must first complete your journey here. Tap in to this All-Powerful Being, and allow Him to electrify your life, and create the spinning action needed to move through the pillar of light, creating your ascension into the celestial realms. This is where my kingdom is, and I taught this advancement of spirit.

18. This question is on the religious life. What is the benefit of seeking you in solitude, and why did you pray in the desert?

When you seek me in solitude you have more of an opportunity to enter the tributaries of light, and experience the unconditional love I have for you. You each have an opportunity, without ritual or stance from any structure, to be drawn into the Abiding Light of your own God Presence, and to allow truth to be given directly from me. *When you separate yourself from the religious life, and enter a spiritual life, you gain wisdom.* As Jesus, my intention was never to bring forth another religious structure given as a doctrine of limitation that would bring about separation from our Creator.

You abide in a sun system separated from the higher gateways of the Godhead. This is what is creating duality within your experience, and what is operating within your mind and heart. Most religious sects of your world are well intended, and some have contributed to the evolution on this planet; however, there are souls ready to stand apart, such as I did. I learned enough in my solitude, and in my direct communication with our Father and my Christ Oversoul, to stand apart by speaking without judgment, and to speak the truth I was directly given. I communicated divine love without limitation to my disciples, and to those who chose to listen. In my lifetime, I pierced the veils, elevated my consciousness and soared quite high.

The religious life has communicated much of my teachings to earth, but it has also taught a great deal of fear and separation, and for this my heart is heavy. I would prefer you seek me in solitude, but you do not have to go into the desert for forty days, and nights. In my day, the concept of fasting was a standard method of purification to develop the mind, and to withdraw from the needs of the outer world. In the desert, I stood within my pillar of light, and communicated with my God Presence, and our Creator. Here I go again speaking about what I mentioned earlier, that what you have been taught about the devil being with me, trying to tempt me, was actually my own fears and demons endeavoring to bring me back into the structure of life. I had the opportunity to bring many riches on my path as one who prophesized the future or I could choose to bring forth pure teachings, and the light of the Christos onto the planet, which was my decision.

19. How may faithful Christians challenge the church to become the spirit reflecting the Father's Will?

My messenger would tell you she hears me laughing because unfortunately this will not occur in your lifetime; for the reason that churches have become institutions. I am not saying the churches have not benefited anyone, because they have, especially in third world countries by bringing nourishment, much needed medical care, and education; however, the majority teach a doctrine of fear and limitation. It is not my job to judge them or anyone, for they believe in the structure they are working within, and I continue to strengthen the orders seeking me for the purest of reasons. I pray with many of the monks, nuns, priests, and preachers, and there are several I have had heart-to-heart communication with. If you are a church member then take the best parts your religion has to offer, but still seek the truth within. Ask God and Christ for the divinity residing within you to be your personal teacher. I would also like all the churches of the world to teach every individual a doctrine of attunement with their God Presence; so the seed atom that carries divine nature can be awakened within the heart flame, and develop many more Christs walking upon planet earth.

Vera's comment: A seed atom is the feminine ray from Source, and anchors the energy of spirit in matter at the lower spinal chakra. This is commonly referred to as the sacred fire or the Kundalini.

20. With millions praying why does it seem prayers have little effect?

Prayers have a positive influence; however, some of the prayers received are holding judgments. Allow the truth of God to flow freely through each living being, and each living organism, but without judgment. Earth would have already had World War III if it were not for all the prayers, and unconditional love pouring out of the many that put their hands together in deep concern for the conditions on the planet. Please continue to pray, whether you are part of a structured religion or not. Amplify the light released in prayer to all upon this world; so each person can benefit from coming to know the purity of the Mind, the Heart, and the unity of God.

21. How did you plan to help the Jewish faith?

It was my plan to speed up the frequency of the Jewish consciousness. As I saw it then and now, the Jewish teachings are in a bottleneck. Many of the hidden Jewish mysteries would help the whole of humankind, and be beneficial to the mainstream if the Tree of Life were understood, especially how the human soul must ascend through it. To understand the ebb and flow of life there are many good teachings in both the Kabbalah and the Torah, which refers to the five books of Moses; however, these teachings also need to be brought into the reasoning of the modern world. Many, many, times, the depiction of God in the Old Testament is not the actual reflection of the love of God.

22. Can I offer my suffering up to you, and will my suffering benefit another?

You are truly the ruler of your own kingdom, and out of deep love I will teach you another way to behave because suffering causes damage to your spiritual circuitry. This way of thinking came about due to the amount of negative karma piled on some human beings, and it was a way of assisting them in feeling more love by surrendering their suffering. Truly, God only wants to bless you. He wants your consciousness to be pure, and for you to love one another.

We, who are governed by the Great Light, would never destroy the image of God in an individual. This is actually the difference between speaking directly to Christ, and speaking through a religious class system, such as priests and ministers, who preach that they know what I would say to you. If you have a serious illness or problem you can ask me to come, and share this burden. I will attune your frequency with mine, and in this way I can subdue the pain, and suffering. What will happen is you walk into my heart, which is like a chapel or a temple of light, and I hold you within my arms as I teach you to surrender to God. I came to support God's beloved creations, and my messages now are much like they were when I walked the earth as Jesus. If you desire happiness in its fullest measure then align with peace, and you will find your God Presence brings many opportunities to experience satisfaction in your lives.

The energy produced by a wanting heart contributes to an unbalanced state of mind where people no longer feel deserving, and this is because as children the level of expectancy was drawn out of them. These are patterns of light that need to be explained. In many wealthy countries children are encouraged to feel deserving of receiving, and this is taught to them by their loving parents who receive pleasure in being able to give them what they ask for. In this example the parents also experience joy by satisfying their children, and this is not unlike what is occurring between you, and the operating energy of your God Presence. Our Creator does not get joy in bringing punishment, shame, lack or fear. For ten minutes a day practice recalling your consciousness as an innocent child, I mean this in the sense of expectation. For instance, relive the joy you felt as a child when you knew the gift you asked for would arrive on a special occasion like your birthday, Hanukah or under the Christmas tree. This will teach you the magnificence of who you are; however, I would not overindulge an adult asking to be a pure vessel for the Christ mind. If you want to become a Christ be reasonable with your requests, and work with intentions to do world service, focusing more on conditions that will benefit humankind, and not personal desires. To me, while I want to see you benefit from the whole of creation the model of your car, and your bank balance are not the fullness of my work with you. My mission is to bring forth peace and goodwill to each member of the Body of Christ; consequently, the benefits will far outweigh the materialism. Each person deserves to receive the bounty to benefit their life, and the lives of their children, and loved ones. Each child should live with the expectations of hopes and dreams, experiencing the satisfaction of loving God, and knowing a loving God returns their love. They should do this without fear of this Divine Being, our loving Creator. In these times, one of my messages is to teach you not to desire to carry my cross, for I lived quite happily until those last days. I drew forth from the Universal Mind, I manifested, and created. I felt completely deserving of my gifts, and the abundance I received, and you should too.

23. Should we pray for the souls in purgatory?

Prayers are still needed for those beings, but the prayers should go toward heaven. Do not attempt communication with those who reside in these regions. You can pray to their I Am Presence to awaken them, and call them out of darkness.

These are the regions with dark life forms, and they exist in the lower astral plane, which is not part of the fourth dimension. Purgatory is beneath the fourth dimension, but it is not the fourth dimension. It would benefit humankind if they will assist in clearing these planes, but do not give energy to souls who dwell there because some of these beings, even in death, still look to destroy the human soul, and those who play with the black arts align with them. Some are weakened masters that need your power, having no light of their own. Many try to communicate with humans, and they have managed to destroy souls, and this is why you need a strong filter of light around you. The forms residing in purgatory were actually the beasts spoken about in the Bible. As this book explains, Lucifer has been gone from this circuit for quite some time; however, there are still many rebels around, but they are nothing compared to the masters of the light. Those dark beings do not dwell in the light or hold celestial consciousness, nor do they have Oversouls of divine light. Divine messages can only come through someone who is able to carry the frequency of the Christ. As previously mentioned, our selection of messengers on earth is quite limited, for they have to hold a certain range of mastery previously developed within them, and their hearts have to be extremely pure. Allow the master within you to recognize the mastery within another.

We end by saying the purgatory worlds are nothing more than an energy alignment of the lower astral plane where those who choose to continue to feed upon another are grouped together. They are separated by a veil of light because they have destroyed their original inner light. When they choose to be of the light again they will be shown another experience.

24. Will there be a transformation?

Those of you aspiring to be like Jesus should be expecting transformation, for you are not yet able to release the illustrious light necessary to move through you as a sound frequency from the regions of the Christ Oversoul. When this occurs, many diamonds are placed within the etheric sheaths holding additional DNA patterns that develop your level of thoughts. A way to accelerate the transformation is by earnestly working with the threefold flame, and releasing yourselves from judgments on earth, and from those who reside here. You may not agree with the actions of another, but you cannot control anyone; instead, use wisdom. I am not speaking of hardened criminals because they also have a choice. Separate yourselves from those who choose to fall, for they have little or no light or substance, and many times they create burdens on society.

In time, you will receive your Divine Blueprint, and within it are compartments of the awakened soul. As you occupy this level of mastery you will gain peace and know your I Am Presence, and the Will of our Creator. I, Jesus, am rooting for you, and have always been in your corner. I will continue to be your defender, and light your path.

25. Can you speak of the Elohim?

Not all of your questions will be thoroughly answered now because they are not of the level this book is intended. I will start by saying your story of Genesis actually unfolds over several generations. Throughout the God realms is where eternity is, and it is quite pure. A resounding silence, the Nucleus, spins in the center of the omniverse we call the Great Silence or Stillness. A beautiful star is emanating from the circle around the Great Silence that experienced, and was involved with levels of God's Mind energies rippling out in patterns of creation. That thought created the Elohim. They are the guardians of the light force energy used in the formation of many universes, including earth, but the Great Silence is where we all place our origins. The first ring outside of the Great Silence is where those known as the Elohim maintain the created regions. Even at the first ring, where the Elohim govern over many creations, they exist at quite a distance outside of the Great Silence. We, in the ascended realms, occupy a space between those rings, and the Great Silence.

As I approach this subject it is essential to remember the Father Himself created our souls, our divine nature, and our God Presence, and this is where the Elohim, you, and I, all originated from. Again, there is only One Supreme God or Great Silence. The Elohim are also called the architects, and are mentioned many times in the Bible, and they are also the "eyes" of God. They are co-creator gods existing at a very high level, and assist God with the created worlds. Once again, the Elohim did not create your Presence; they were very involved in the design of the physical body, and a place for it to inhabit.

Glossary

Akashic Records

This Sanskrit term stands for the etheric records. Every single impression that has ever taken place in the universe is recorded in the akashic records. Some describe this as a universal or cosmic library where every detail is registered through sound, vision, and thought. Those with developed souls can read these records. *Vera's comment:* Consider living life as if every act is being videoed, because in a sense, it truly is.

Antakharana

Within the Universal Mind is a structure used for creation. It is a bridge of light called the **A**ntakharana, which your consciousness uses to transcend. It is also called *the rainbow bridge* or the *web of life*. It is a net of light, spinning spirit and matter, connecting, and sensitizing the whole of creation within itself, and to the heart of God.

Ark of the Covenant

A long time ago a circuit of bright light called the Ark of the Covenant was established on earth, and it was intended to be in your heart to hold the DNA code of the Immaculate Concept. It would bring through the ability to emanate the attributes of our Creator while you are embodied, and enable you to bless all of earth. Few were enlightened enough to partake of this gift; consequently, it was moved into a higher octave. The ascended masters continue to develop our initiates to pass through that system to retrieve their original DNA codes. Moses was also aligned to this grid, and it is where he received his initiations.

Ascended master

See avatar.

Astral Bodies and Astral Worlds

Earth is surrounded by rings of light, and these are the sub-planes for the astral worlds. When most souls leave earth they enter the mid to higher astral worlds where everything has a synonymous astral counterpart. In these worlds you even have an astral body that appears to be as physical as your earth body is, although in some of the finer dimensions you can choose to appear young. However, this is not the region of the I Am Presence or even the area of Christ consciousness that I discuss in this book. These are levels of transcendence for soul to relinquish the lower denser existence it was familiar with on earth. The astral planes give soul a chance, if it desires, to become accustom to finer dimensions, and opportunities to continue in its evolution, according to merit. Also, there are systems of thought where the mind has the possibility for expansion.

Astral world residents can experience more satisfaction here than during their life on earth. Areas exist in these regions you would think of as a reward for having lived a high quality of life when your intentions toward others were of peace and love. If they choose to, residents can spend a good deal of their time visiting with relatives, and old friends from various lives, and there is more time for relaxation than most had on earth. Nevertheless, even on these planes there are still a series of lessons you will need to learn, and your Higher Self contributes to your life in these regions as well. While preparing for rebirth in a more awakened state, some souls pass through their astral plane experiences very quickly before returning to earth or continuing to another destination. At the time of physical death from earth each person should remember how much God loves them, and expect to enter the purest of these regions.

The lower astral realms are the worlds still polluted, and residing here are those whose emotions, and minds are diseased with thoughts of hatred, and anger. As you refine your energy, and move through these dimensions you experience purer energies closer to the realities of spirit. These regions have a great deal of activity, and empires exist here that were once on earth, but have not yet made their full ascension.

Avatar or Avatara, and Ascended master

This is Sanskrit meaning, *down, pass or descent.* It refers to the descent of an ascended master or a Christ returning to earth as a teacher in support of humankind. I, Jesus, walked earth at the level of an avatar, an ascended master. I did not partake of the lower mind consciousness. I entered earth from an advanced system where I held the position of Christ, and because I was self-disciplined during my lifetime, I was able to reconnect with my Christ mind.

Body of Christ and the Holy Order of the Body of Christ

The Body of Christ is a Celestial Order of Divine Beings showing the inhabitants of earth, through the messages of Jesus the Christ, their divine heritage. The Holy Order of the Body of Christ represents the Divine Blueprint each of you will one day hold, and will return you to the Trinity when the flame bodies start to align through a progression of attunements to the central flame, and you expand the light merging with the Christ Oversoul.

Capstone

The capstone is a point of light descending and mirroring the image of the I Am. The accumulated good you hold in your treasury of light descends through a prism of light called a capstone, which holds the Divine Blueprint, and an attunement to the I Am Presence. During the process of initiation the capstone is lowered through an octave of light; it is part of the work of the Golden Ray. The capstone creates a force field of light around the initiate. Unfortunately, those who open dimensional portals before the capstone is completely anchored enter a region called the fourth dimension, which is another field of light, but you are not as protected there as you would be in an ascended octave. As you hold the tonal frequencies of the Golden Ray the capstone aligns with you. The capstone is within the celestial corridors known as the heavens. It holds a sound frequency for ascension, and the beginning of the Golden Age, which is part of the root race in its final expansion, and it attunes to a community of ascended light realms.

*The capstone Moses brought forth was from the Arc of the Convent, which was a path for ascension, and actually held the commandments Moses received. The Old Testament tells us Moses was aligned to this grid, and this is where he received his initiations. He also held the Golden Ray.

Causal World

This is the world of thought, beyond the physical, astral, and mental worlds. In the casual world whatever you think will instantly manifest. This is why preparation in the matter and energy worlds is necessary. These are the regions where souls go after ascension, and understood as the heavens. It is an advanced universe, and many ancient sun systems sprang from these regions.

Celestial Christ

The Celestial Christ is the divine nature of the spirit that pervades all living consciousness, and is the Oversoul of those who now exist in lower states of awareness; it holds the Mantle of the Christ for all beings. I, the Celestial Christ, am the way and the light to the pattern of energy known as the Christos, the Diamond Mind, and to the purity of the Spoken Word that brought consciousness in to the form of flesh. As the Celestial Christ, which is more than the one personality of the man Jesus who demonstrated this office, I continue to remain with earth through its many cycles, and I have many disciples. As the Celestial Christ, I oversee all who dwell on earth, and I have the ability to dissolve your karmic patterns through the form of blessings, and dispensations. The name Emmanuel is how those on earth will recognize the tones of the Celestial Christ.

Chakras

This is a Sanskrit word meaning wheel or disc and everyone has many chakras. In your physical body they are located along the spinal column, and in other parts of the body, but you also have invisible chakras extending beyond your physical body. Essentially, these energy centers are sound currents holding waves of light within the physical form, and they vibrate to a sound current the Christ Oversoul utilizes in the higher heavens.

Chakras need to be in balance and cleared. If they are not in the correct positions they will be misaligned and hold denser energy; subsequently, causing you to succumb to levels of action, and reaction based on imbalances where you experience discord. Allow spirit to guide you to offset these impurities. This will draw you to the Oversoul of light, and to the gateway of Jesus' kingdom, and your personal I Am Flame will expand in the heart of God. Ask the masters to pass the I Am Flame through you and you will learn to harness this frequency, which is the Mantle of the Christ. Staying focused on pure intentions keeps karmic patterns balanced, and helps maintain your chakra alignment. Spending time in meditation and in sacred sites does purify the chakras; allowing them to hold more light. Introspect daily, accept God's love, and this will also align your chakras with the light, and assist you in understanding your multi-level intentions.

Christ Consciousness

This is pure, all-knowing, Cosmic or Celestial Intelligence, ever present and universal, directly from God. The anointed title of Christ is given to those who are one with this consciousness.

Christ Matrix

This is a living energy grid from the Body of Christ that supports, and assists souls on their personal journey, utilizing and developing the Christ energies. The Christ Matrix originates from the Breath of Creation, and is part of the Trinity. It holds the sound code for those who are able to work within the Divine Blueprint of the Holy Christ Oversoul.

It is a complementary energy to the works of Jesus the Christ, and it is also a domain operating under a magistrate of those who come from the order of the Office of the Christ. The Christ Matrix creates a cosmic alignment with that office.

The Christ Matrix came into the patterns of this earth under the symbol of the Star of David, and later the cross represented that frequency. We, the ascended masters, gave our messenger Catherine Julian Dove the Christ Matrix® name to use for our work through her and this is also given to our daughter, Vera Lauren.

Christ Self

The Christ Self serves as the communicator, and master counsel for soul to raise consciousness for the purpose of ending compulsory reincarnation, and becoming self-realized Christed beings.

Column/Tube/Pillar of Light

This is the qualified light, the pure energy we receive from our I Am Presence, and our God Source, as a protective shield for soul evolution and for man's four lower bodies. According to Jesus, within this column, tube or pillar, are many descending columns of light.

Corridors of light

There are many corridors of light that are my true kingdoms. This refers to dimensional layers in the higher octaves each soul eventually needs to transcend, and this is one of the reasons initiations are necessary.

Crystal or Silver Cord

The cord is actually a stream of God consciousness. Its light feeds, and sustains the soul, and the four lower bodies.

Divine Monad

The Monad is the spark of God within each person, and is a collection of experiences of an All Pervading Consciousness experiencing. In other words, the Divine Monad is a concept to understand the expansion of the God Presence. It can be taught as a tree expanding, as wheels of light, as a spiral staircase or even as a ladder, as in Jacob's ladder. A simple explanation of the Divine Monad is how consciousness began the illusion of separation from an All Abiding Light.

Etheric Duplicate

This is your mirror image in the invisible realms where you are still connected to an ego.

Eternal Self

This is the divine personality of the God Presence. It is in constant reflection of its God image.

Faith

Being in faith means to know something within your heart, and to claim it as your own before you actually experience it.

God and His many names

To define God, Christ explains, is a concept beyond comprehension for most people. Throughout this book, Jesus chose to familiarize the reader with the many names of God: Almighty, Creator, Father, Source, Great Stillness, and the Great Silence. Each title holds various levels of energy, for example: Father or Mother God references positions involved in diverse levels of creation, and holds different frequencies within the Mind of God. Many teachings, including this one, also reverently apply the word "It" when referencing God, not choosing to place a gender. Christ said the Nucleus of God is referred to as the Great Silence or Great Stillness, but God also has a divine personality and a voice. Christ suggests the reader use the salutation they are most comfortable with, and resonates to the highest form of love.

Catherine's anecdote: God spoke to me three times. Twice He identified Himself as God, once as the Almighty. The first time I heard Him speak He said He was God. The second time He said He was the Almighty. Both times He had a gentle, masculine voice, and I felt such deep love from Him and He felt familiar to me. The third time God communicated with me it was telepathically, as I was raised into a loving vortex of light. In future books, we address the names of God, and how they interact with earth.

God Essence

This is your divine image.

God Presence

Your God Presence is an incredible being of immeasurable light and joy. It is a reflection of the prism of the light of God. At the point of the God Presence, Christ explains, it is best understood as a sound within God. Your I Am Presence is a step down from the frequency of your God Presence, meaning it became more individualized. (For more on this topic please refer to the chapter, Templates of Creation, page 88.)

Golden Ray

This is the ray of Christ consciousness, and the Celestial Christ remains at the apex of the Golden Ray.

Grounding Cords

These cords support you in keeping fully present, and focused in this reality. They steady the light flowing through you, and balance the chakras. When not grounded you are off balance, out of sync, and this can cause mood shifts.

Higher Self and I Am Presence

The Higher Self is a tool of your I Am Presence that holds the Christ mind. It is through the Higher Self the image of the Christ is reflected to you, and the door to the Heart of God is opened through it. Your Higher Self has the ability to reveal expanded understanding, and indepth wisdom on your path. It also has a heightened consciousness; able to provide solutions to everyday situations an ego-based personality may not be able to process. Your Higher Self can be thought of as a spiritual bridge to greater wisdom, and you can ask the ascended masters to intercede, and assist you in removing any negative blocks to crossing it. The Higher Self is also the energy grid the saints held to communicate with the heavenly kingdoms, with God, and with Christ.

The Higher Self is a perfect radiating light incapable of imperfection; however, it is aware of the limitations that surround the physical body and its experiences during its sojourn away from Source, but it will not allow imperfection to penetrate itself. As you learn to call upon and merge with your Higher Self it works with you to do everything possible to restore your awareness to your origin, which is your I Am Presence or your divine nature. The I Am Presence is a more individualized component of your God Presence, but a step down. It also originates from the Divine Unlimited Mind of God, and holds the vision of its perfected self and there the Higher Self thrusts forward from the I Am Presence at a much lesser frequency. The I Am Presence focuses the Immaculate Concept image through the Higher Self to those embodied on earth or in another realm that are not fully purified or sanctioned by the Father's Will, and restores the Divine Blueprint. If all you do as a race is to always keep your focus on your I Am Presence in every thought, word, and deed, united you will raise world consciousness to a level familiar to your Higher Selves, and forever be transformed back to your true divine nature.

Holy Christ Self

The Holy Christ Self is a vessel everyone will delight in, but it also purges your energy fields to create a bridge between your emotions, and thoughts. You, as a spiritual seeker, tend to think your thoughts, and emotions operate separately, but in time they will work together, and you will exist in balance. I, Christ, guide your way until you are able to guide yourself. Release the suffering, and embrace the God qualities within, which is the indwelling master each of you desires to know. Consciousness is born in the heart. As you reinforce the light from within your Divine Blueprint an embryo of consciousness develops in you. As it expands you experience a soul merge when the columns of light pierce the veil of your four lower bodies, and balances your physical chakra system.

The Immaculate Concept

God sought to create of Itself an expression of immense love, and then all of creation was brought forth as particles of divine light called the Immaculate Concept. At this stage, do not occupy your minds with any form of limitation of the Immaculate Concept. For now, I, Christ, tell you the Immaculate Concept is understood as your origins beyond this time cycle. It is how I experienced the Godhead, and it holds the original complement of DNA. It is when God individualized you, and it filters through your many Oversouls. We are all sons and daughters created from the Mind of God. *At the instant each and every one of you was birthed you were in a state of purity as part of the Immaculate Concept, just as I was birthed with you in that second, and during the same process.* The Immaculate Concept holds your original blueprint, and in due time it brought forth the Oversouls. This whole idea will be troubling for some to understand, but it is in fact the divine birth we were all a part of. The energy of the Immaculate Concept is both masculine and feminine. The Seal of Abraham is part of the Immaculate Concept each soul received on the day of conception out of the deep love of God that brought forth all life, and respects all life.

Light

This refers to the all-powerful, loving, and healing energy, of God's spiritual light.

Light Bodies

These are the garments of light of the I Am Presence, and the Higher Self. These light bodies connect your soul to the Christ mind, and in more advanced stages to your I Am Presence. They are graduating points of consciousness that are part of the Higher Self, and the I Am Presence. Light bodies are part of a matrix of light that contributes greater wisdom, awareness, and understanding, to the developing consciousness on earth. They can also be understood as holding a bandwidth. Imagine a fiber optic cable with filaments of light frequencies that need to be grounded to the earth plane. They spin in a clockwise rotation elevating the consciousness and merging with the Father systems, spinning a web of light in the physical aura displacing and clearing the lower tones, preparing the human to receive expanded bandwidths of light pulsations. They first benefit the etheric duplicate, and then begin to merge with the personality on earth.

The light bodies contain many more chakra systems than I am discussing at this time, and they are coded within the DNA originating from your I Am Presence. Your I Am Presence then steps down levels of consciousness that are sealed, and not part of your earth personality, until a level of initiation, and spiritual attainment is reached. At this point, initiates have the ability to expand into the columns of light connecting to the regions of light bodies, and levels of Oversouls. This level of spiritual attainment is a soul merge or soul fusion, and occurs on the seventh ray, which is the violet ray, when you unite with the higher components of your soul's light. The divine soul is part of a component of light that exists in levels of the Oversoul. The human soul has several initiations it must pass through before it awakens to the consciousness of its divine origins, which is its divine soul. The human soul moves through many opportunities of learning, and some of these circumstances can be understood as experiencing limited light, and limited spiritual understanding toward itself. This is a rudimentary explanation.It is unfortunate most religions have lost a great deal of information about the energies of the greater light bodies you all hold, and how to serve others, as well as self, by raising the frequencies, and merging with your light bodies, and the divine soul. What is left is an abstract understanding of allowing the Holy Spirit to merge with you.

Light Rays

Rays are light emanations from our Creator, and they are beams of light or other radiant energies of light from the Godhead. The rays are a concentration of energy taking on enormous God qualities, such as love, truth, wisdom, healing, and transmutation. When invoked in the name of God or Christ they are projected into universal consciousness. They burst forth as a flame in the world as an individual ray, and may be projected by God consciousness through the chakra system, spiritual heart, physical body, third eye or in situations in need of balance. The energy of these rays must never be misused.

Many studying spiritual teachings are familiar with the seven rays of the white light, which you merge with through the prism of the Christ consciousness; however, there are many more rays than the seven or twelve planetary rays many speak of, and actually there are an infinite number of rays. Each person's I Am Presence has a primary ray, and the qualities of this ray are how it became individualized from its God Presence. The human develops on its I Am Presence's ray as well as mastering additional rays. Your I Am Presence, along with the developing soul's agenda, determine what ray it will advance on. All rays represent the qualities of God to enhance life experiences. This is what makes us all different. Many rays are connecting to you, but a larger amount of one specific ray predominates, and penetrates the column of light, and is intended to surround you. This is because, along with God, you chose a particular pattern that would amplify light to you through a specific ray. As you spiritually develop you work more consciously with the rays, and are taught to harness, and ground these frequencies through the physical body, the aura, the nervous system, and the organs of the body. Even those who do not understand the concept of the rays will unconsciously work with them through color, since all rays hold a predominant shade that carries a specific frequency they are automatically receiving God's graces through. For example, people will find themselves attracted to a certain color, and it becomes their favorite, and everything has to be that color, including their car, and clothes.

Mental Bodies

The mental bodies are the vehicles manifested by the Higher Self as solid intelligence, and this is where the powers of the mind are developed, such as your imagination, thoughts, and memory. As you evolve this provides a separate, and distinctive instrument of consciousness where you can exist, and function apart from both your physical, and astral bodies. Some people are very kind, conscious souls, and others seem as though they have no conscience at all, but the truth is they do not feel remorse for their pernicious acts because their minds are at a very low level. This is another reason why I chose to speak in parables, for most people could not yet hold enough light to develop spiritual consciousness. The mental bodies are extremely active, and they are fierce at times. This is additional motivation as to why it is essential to discipline the mind, as it affects all of the lower bodies.

There are eight mental bodies you will transcend. The higher mental body opens the doorway to levels of light that are the Oversoul's octaves. You pass through these energy grids or fields when you incarnate on earth. As your consciousness is lowered through the eight mental bodies you take on the pattern of forgetfulness, and this is for your own protection because the memories held within these layers are from previous lives, and could cause insanity. When these lower grids are cleared the quality of thoughts and emotions improve greatly, and the energy held around the human aura expands in universal light, and love. This is the work of Mother Mary, and other ascended masters; they support the planet in harnessing divine love through soul levels to the levels within the human heart.

Octave

An octave is the next level of consciousness that exists in the subsequent upward spiral of light, awareness or higher levels of insight. Octaves are like tributaries to states of awakening where you experience more clarity or as some would say a light goes off in your mind causing you to review an event from a higher perspective. In future books of this series, I will dive more deeply in to this material.

Office of the Christ

The Office of the Christ is part of the Trinity energies, and responsible for assisting the residents of earth in receiving their Divine Blueprint.

Omniverse, omni universe, multi-universes

In this book the word omniverse is used; however, omniverse, omni universe, and multi-universe are all similar in meaning. They are set in motion by the Mind of God, and in each universe God is an All-Pervading consciousness. Omniverses are part of the Breath of God spiraling out in descending patterns of light, and radiations. Around each universe is a ring of light that is the Universal Mind for that universe.

There are many universes God gave us to co-create in that span the central universe. Several of these universes are currently in a lower part of creation, like the universe earth resides in. This universe you exist in is quite a distance from the central universe, the Thought or Word of God made manifest. It is hard for the human to understand the Divine Mind or how the Divine Personality operates within omniverses. Most of your universe has experienced a fallen state of consciousness in comparison to other universes, but it is beginning to cycle upward. Your universe can be depicted as spiraling up or ascending into regions of the Universal Mind. Other universes are closer to the ancient central suns positioned nearer to the All Abiding Light. Some of these energy realms are where spirit energies only exist, which means there are no cycles of birth there, and they are as they have always been.

Oversoul

The Oversoul is a shaft of light, a structure, which holds several luminous bodies of varying degrees to assist in experiencing the Mind and Heart of God. This shaft runs through your Higher Self. The Oversoul represents the combining of light frequencies, a blending of the energy fields, "as above so below," that create an arc in alignment with the Celestial Christ who begins to overshadow those who are ready. The process of being overshadowed by Christ prepares you, the spiritual seeker, to receive the Mantle of the Christ, which is a part of your Divine Blueprint, and incrementally your divine nature is returned to you. Hence, the ascended realms have termed this expansion of light the Higher Self.

Qualified light

This is pure, positive energy we receive from our I Am Presence, and our God Source, and it holds pure thought. The impressions received from Source are always of the highest form, but you have the freewill to mis-qualify this pure light resulting in holes in your aura; thus allowing negative emotions, thoughts, and actions through.

Reincarnation

Reincarnation is the return of the memory patterns, and the soul's energy as it incarnates, once again, to a plane of experience. In the majority of cases the soul is educated before a rebirth; therefore, it has a greater opportunity to expand its awareness of the nature of its divine heritage or a particular issue from a past life that it had difficulty understanding, such as forgiveness, unconditional love, power, greed, selfishness, beauty, illness, abuse, violence

or compassion. In addition, reincarnation offers an opportunity to be of service to an evolving system of thought. A soul can also reincarnate because
of strong desires of unfulfilled emotions, and feelings originating in the
desire body, and become part of the lower frequencies of co-creation. Believe
you always have a choice in these matters to ensure you are not drawn to a
new birth by a whirlwind of emotions.

Jesus the Christ was my last incarnation on this planet. Some who read
this book will not be comfortable with these non-traditional beliefs that speak
about reincarnation, but truly, when I walked the earth as Jesus many of the
people, besides me, understood, and knew this to be true. The physical body
is not the form I hold any longer. The body is temporary, and was created to
assist the human soul in understanding this level of creation.

Vera's comment: Initially the early Christian church believed in, and taught
the doctrine of reincarnation. This was supported by the pillars of the church,
and it is also mentioned in Jewish text. (Reincarnation as part of Jewish tradition may shock some people; yet they only need peruse Jewish mysticism to
see it is mentioned in numerous places throughout these classics.) In a.d. 553,
the doctrine of reincarnation was proclaimed heretical at the Second Council of Constantinople, and this is when the decision was made to remove all
Biblical references to this belief. Their thinking was the idea of reincarnation
would distract man from God, and he would not wisely use his time on the
planet; however, their attempts were not fully realized as there are many references to this principle still found in Christian Bibles. It is easy to research
these Biblical references to reincarnation, and a reliable source is the Second
Coming of Christ, The Resurrection of the Christ Within You, by Paramahansa Yogananda, where it is footnoted: "That the concept of reincarnation
was known to the Jews is evidenced in several New Testament passages, as
when the "priests and Levites" ask John the Baptist, "Art thou Elijah? (John
1:21m /Discourse 6); and when Jesus' disciples tell him, "Some say that thou art
John the Baptist; some, Elijah; and others, Jeremiah or one of the prophets."
(Matthew 16:14; see Discourse 45)." In the Autobiography of a Yogi, according to Yogananda, "When John denied that he was Elias (Elijah), he meant
that in the humble garb of John he came no longer in the outward elevation
of Elijah the great guru. In his former incarnation he had given the "mantle"

of his glory and his spiritual wealth to his disciple Elisha." "And Elisha said, I pray thee, let a double portion of thy spirit be upon me. And he said, "Thou hast asked a hard thing: nevertheless, if thou see me when I am taken from thee, it shall be so unto thee.... And he took the *mantle* of Elijah that fell from him." Yogananda explains, "The roles became reversed, because Elijah-John was no longer needed to be the ostensible guru of Elisha-Jesus, now perfected in divine realization."

Root Race

Everyone incarnated in a root race, which is an evolving consciousness called group consciousness. What is missing from your history are the facts regarding earth's previous root races because there have been many that have come, and gone from the planet. During the Golden Age, they had additional strands of DNA not readily available to all of you during this time cycle. In those bodies the blood held properties humans do not currently have. The blood of an incarnated ascended being on earth holds crystalline structures that appear as small pyramids in the blood, and has properties the majority do not currently have. (Proof of this is Saint Bernadette, and the avatar, Paramahansa Yogananda. Saint Bernadette died in 1879 in Lourdes, France, and was buried for approximately 122 years before her grave was discovered. When church officials decided to examine her remains they found her body never decomposed! When visiting the church in Lourdes, France, visitors can still view Saint Bernadette's body. And at least three weeks after his death Paramahansa Yogananda's body was in "immutable" condition, without having decomposed, and his remains showed signs of incorruptibility.)

Seal of Abraham

This is an activation of a level of initiation used by the light bodies, and the release of the Holy Spirit's light.

Self-Realization

There are many steps to spiritually awaken, but you first enter self-realization where you become aware you are part of a Higher Self. This step is called a soul initiation, when the spiritually advancing adept is taught to dwell in its divine soul body that now surrounds them. At this stage of the soul initiation you, formerly the spiritual seeker, now the initiate, are spiritually advanced compared to most human beings; you, as the initiate, will start encountering visitations from the heavenly realms, and are now able to communicate, often by carrying on conversations, with those in the higher levels of the heavens. You are preparing to become the master by working closely under the tutorship of one or several other ascended masters or with me, Jesus, and further demonstrating the process I came to teach; however, there are many steps you must take before you are self-realized, and from self-realization to God-realization.

Secret Chamber of the Heart

The secret chamber of the heart we are referring to is a sanctuary that can be accessed during meditation. This is the place to which the soul withdraws. It is the nucleus of life where the individual stands face-to-face with the inner teacher, the beloved Holy Christ Self, receiving soul instructions and guidance for all it needs to proceed to obtain higher consciousness. This is the alchemical union with the Holy Christ Self.

Seven Sacraments

The seven sacraments consist of baptism, confirmation, Holy Communion, confession, marriage, holy orders, and extreme unction or the anointing of the sick.

Vera's comment: The seven sacraments are ecclesial efficacious symbols of grace, and they are an integral rite of the Catholic Church; however, they will not be further discussed in this glossary since there are many other sources of reference.

Soul merge

A soul merge or soul fusion is when you unite with the higher components of your divine soul's light.

Spiritual Heart Center

It is located behind the physical heart, where the part of self remains in grace. The spiritual heart center is not your physical heart and refers to your inner chapel, temple, mosque or kingdom. It is a threshold of light behind the physical human heart where you gain entry to a system of energy and can directly experience God or your own God Presence.

Spiritual planes

These are dimensions of consciousness on other planes of reality.

Star of David

This is a six-pointed star representing a state of being self-realized, "as above so below," a human becoming a Christ, which I came as Jesus to demonstrate. This symbol is not meant to be associated with any religion.

Threefold flame

Within each developing soul there is the threefold flame. It is the flame of the Christ, that spark of life, which resides in your light bodies, and burns within the secret chamber of your spiritual heart. You can best know yourself through an awakening of the heart energies, and by holding the intention to expand the threefold flame. It is where you, as the spiritual seeker, come to understand the nature of God, and the nature of creation. The threefold flame is made of three intertwining plumes of sacred fire. The center plume is golden yellow representing God's wisdom. To one side is a pink plume signifying God's love, and the other side is a blue plume to signify God's power. The balance of this triple plume is also held in the pattern of the fleur-de-lis. (For more information on the threefold flame please refer to the chapter, Templates of Creation, page 84.)

Ten Commandments or the Decalogue

Religious conservatives believe the commandments were revealed to Moses on Mount Sinai in the form of two tablets.

Vera's comment: The Hebrew teachings list over six hundred moral imperatives; rather, than just the ten commonly known Christian precepts. Hebrew leaders regard the Ten Commandments as foundational, implying they are not Jewish laws. The Ten Commandments were recorded in Exodus 20:2–17 and Deuteronomy 5:6–21.

Tetrahedron

The tetrahedron is a pyramid structure also known as a triangular pyramid with four triangular faces. It is part of the blueprint of creation, and comes under sacred geometry, which attempts to describe it. The tetrahedron is considered one of the building blocks of our unique identities.

Thresholds of Light

When we, the ascended masters, speak of the thresholds of light we are speaking of the realms of heavens, and regions where those residing there experience qualified light, and are pure of heart, thought, and deed.

Violet Flame

This is the seventh ray aspect of the Holy Spirit, and it is also referred to as the flame of freedom, forgiveness, and transmutation. Its flame transmutes negativity, including karma or the memory of wrongful deeds.

*Since this is a channeled book we want to be clear, although many terms and definitions are from Jesus this glossary was primarily written, and researched by Vera.

Biographies

Catherine Julian Dove
Messenger for the Christ

At a childhood birthday party, I was running across the lawn playing when I ran into an invisible force that spoke to me. It said, "I have to leave you here now. You will know me again." Then it separated from me. I felt alone, and at that moment I knew if I said something about this to anyone at the party they would never understand.

Years passed, and in 1983, I married my husband, John. Six months later, I saw an uncle who had passed away when I was about fourteen. That in itself was not strange because I had seen him and my grandmother several times since they had both passed on. At first, I would tell my mother these things, but she thought the spirits were trying to take me away. She told me not to speak to them anymore; consequently, I stopped telling her about my visions. However, in 1983, when I saw my uncle three nights in a row, it was different. On the third night I went to kiss him good-bye, and he turned and handed me a light. It was so bright that even in my dream state I had to turn away. I knew something was about to happen.

I began going to Metaphysical lectures and met new friends. This is when I met my sister friend and spiritual partner, Vera. New acquaintances told us about a woman, Orpheus Phylos, who was an unconscious channel for Archangel Michael, and was scheduled to speak at a local community college. We went to hear her, and at first, I felt Michael was speaking directly to me, but I found out later many of us felt the same way.

I took more classes and had a wonderful opportunity to have several private sessions with Archangel Michael. Before my first session, I was sitting in my condo when a big, blue ball of light came floating toward me and stopped in front of me, then floated around the room. For some unexplained reason, I felt it had something to do with my reading the next day. During the reading I was informed Archangel Michael is the blue ray and the light I had seen was indeed him. He told me by making an appointment I had given him permission to visit me and to see how he could help. I went to the reading with questions, but during the session I did not feel the need to ask any, for Archangel Michael already knew all that was in my heart. I did not understand much since I was a novice in this new world. He told me things would take time to unfold, and I clung to his words. I took many more classes, and had several more fascinating private sessions with Archangel Michael, channeled by Orpheus.

After a while, Mother Mary appeared to me with Saint Theresa, and it was a wonderful experience. I worked with them for a number of years, and it was around this time Mother Mary asked if Jesus could come and talk to me too. Mother Mary also took me many other places, and once we went on the spiritual planes to see Saint Bernadette and I was able to speak to her. In the beginning, I did not understand many things, like initiations or receiving gifts from Mother Mary and from other teachers.

Life became very busy for me, and I must have fallen out of the vibration of being able to consciously do much with Mother Mary. My husband had various unsettling changes in his career, and eventually my parents came to live with us for a while. I would hear or see Jesus from time to time, but I thought that part of my life was over and it had just been a short-lived gift, although I remained devotional.

We moved to San Antonio, Texas, and with many of the family issues behind me, I moved to a new level of communication with my beloved teachers. In San Antonio there is a replica of Our Lady of Lourdes where Mother Mary appeared to Saint Bernadette. It is known as the Grotto of the Southwest. I began to attend Mass there, and would feel the same way I usually felt when I spoke daily with Mother Mary. It was easy for me to once again open myself up to her and to Jesus, but this experience was different. She began giving me messages for friends and allowing them to ask her questions. This never happened before. (Occasionally in the past a family member would ask me to pray for them. As I started praying, Mary would come in and I would tell them what she said.) It started out with one friend, then another, and it kept growing. Almost immediately, Jesus and Mary were having conversations with my friends, assisting them with their paths and life purposes. Soon, other masters asked to speak to the group. Other than a very early experience involving Vera, this is how it all began.

Originally, I thought my relationship with Mother Mary, Jesus, and the many ascended masters were only for my group of students and me, but since then I have numerous initiates. I am now told to share my experiences, for the time of ascension is here.

Catherine graduated with honors from Heald College in San Jose, California, in computer programming. Catherine is an animal lover and has had dogs and numerous cats at any given time. She is also an animal communicator, and every so often will anonymously contact the "parent" of a missing animal to offer some tips to find their beloved pet. Catherine never accepts a financial reward, because she feels the peace of mind of reuniting loved ones is payment enough.

Vera Lauren

Besides channeling the masters, Ms. Lauren is a writer, editor, speaker, spiritual teacher & consultant, life coach, and emotional healer. Although she considers herself more of a conduit for healing, believing "Spirit is the only true healer," she takes none of the credit and asserts, "Your body is your mind in action because your mind controls your emotions." She goes on to say, "Even science has proved everything is energy and nothing dies; it only changes form." Vera has formal spiritual training and numerous certifications in various modalities of healing, Feng Shui, and Chinese medicine, having continued studies in Hong Kong, Singapore, and Bali. Intuition and experiential opportunities through actual events, and meditation all inform her personal philosophies.

Earth's tough classroom and the people agreeing to show up in her life are her greatest teachers. Her earliest memories are of being on her sainted mother's lap, and endlessly talking about God, the saints, and an inner knowing she had lived before. Vera, the youngest of eleven, fondly remembers her mother reading the Bible during dinner, and being fascinated, but many of the stories did not always settle right with her. At age six, she was already questioning religious teachings not resonating to a loving God. She was always passionate about spirituality, and was chosen to teach Catechism at the early age of twelve, but after about a year was dismissed for teaching *free thought*, a term she did not understand at the time. She affirms, "With a balanced mind, and an open heart you will come to understand that there is no conflict between science and spirituality. The pure fundamental nature of spiritual teachings is scientific as are the techniques, such as meditation and prayer. Often what we think we already know is what will stifle growth."

Vera has had visions of Jesus the Christ, Mother Mary, and other ascended masters and saints. She also remains close to Archangel Michael, who years ago appeared before her and continues his loving guidance and support. Through her dear friend Catherine, Jesus and the Office of the Christ asked Vera to collaborate on this valuable work.

> "Partnering with the Christ and Catherine was a gift and an honor I was unknowingly preparing for all of my life; however, I was not completely ready for the incredible life-altering, and sometimes profound spiritual experiences, and lessons that took place during the process."

Vera believes she was called upon to do this work, which explains why she had to go through a great deal to get to this level of consciousness. She wishes to share the spiritual techniques and philosophies she has cultivated to assist others in achieving a similar frequency of peaceful awareness, while balancing everyday trials. "My intentions are to empower people to be independent not dependent on anyone or anything outside of themselves, believing God is within each and everyone—albeit this Consciousness is dormant in some. Only be satisfied when you have a direct personal experience with God."

Vera Lauren graduated summa cum laude from the University of New Haven, Connecticut. The Lee Strasberg Theatre Institute granted her a "scholarship" in both New York, and Los Angeles. She has credits in theatre, film, radio, and television. She especially enjoyed her experiences as a producer, and as a talk show host in several metaphysical films, and as co-host for the radio show, Dialogues with the Ascended Masters. She was affiliated with Kaiser Permanente Hospital in Redwood City, California, as their first and only non-denominational minister where she also served, along with her therapy dogs, for nearly a decade as a volunteer hospice caregiver, and grievance counselor. She is the Christ Matrix® President and Spokesperson, an initiate of the Healing Order of the Blue Rose, a disciple of Christ, and a member of Self Realization Fellowship. Vera is a vegetarian and an animal lover, having rescued many, and pleads: "Please neuter your pets and contribute to animal rescue services in support. What a difference this will make." Vera is a lifelong activist for many causes besides animals, writing and publically speaking against genocide, modern day slavery, and the plight of Darfur, and is available for lectures.

Bible References

"Greetings, you who are highly favored! The Lord is with you."

Luke 1:27–28

"But I tell you, do not resist an evil person. If someone strikes you on the right cheek, turn to him the other also."

Matthew 5:39

As referenced in your bible: for as he thinks within himself, / so he is; or for as he puts on a feast, / so he is.

Proverbs 23:7a

"Let there be light," and there was light.

Genesis 1:3

"I tell you the truth, it is hard for a rich man to enter the kingdom of heaven. Again I tell you, it is easier for a camel to go through the eye of a needle than for a rich man to enter the kingdom of God."

Matthew 19:23–24

"Do not let your hearts be troubled. Trust in God, trust also in me. In my Father's house are many rooms; if it were not so, I would have told you. I am going there to prepare a place for you. And if I go and prepare a place for you, I will come back and take you to be with me that you also may be where I am. You know the way to the place where I am going."

John 14:1–4

"I am the way and the truth and the life. No one comes to the Father except through me."

John 14:6

"Do not be deceived: God cannot be mocked. A man reaps what he sows."

Galatians 6:7

"Listen and understand. What goes into a man's mouth does not make him unclean, but what comes out of his mouth, that is what makes him unclean."

Matthew 15:10

"I am the gate; whoever enters through me will be saved. He will come in and go out, and find pasture."

John 10:9

Illustrations

The symbols are illustrated by artist, Vera Lauren. http://www.christmatrix.com

Visionary Artist Suzy Addicks illustrated the three-fold flame. http://www.eysoflight.com